Photograph courtesy Washington University-St. Louis,
Missouri, Photographic Services

HOWARD NEMEROV

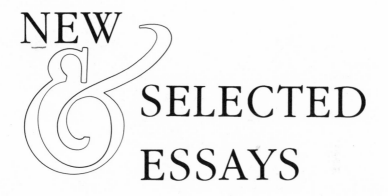

NEW & SELECTED ESSAYS

By Howard Nemerov

With an Introduction by Kenneth Burke

Southern Illinois University Press
CARBONDALE AND EDWARDSVILLE

Copyright © 1985 by the Board of Trustees,
Southern Illinois University

Printed in the United State of America
Edited by Dan Seiters
Production supervised by Kathleen Giencke
Designed by Design for Publishing
87 86 85 84   4 3 2 1

Library of Congress Cataloging in Publication Data
Nemerov, Howard.
    New and Selected essays.
    1. Literature—History and criticism—Addresses,
essays, lectures.   I. Title.
PN511.N38   1985   809   84-1411
ISBN 0-8093-1182-8

Contents

Introduction: Burke on Nemerov

The Basic Design is this:

Howard Nemerov is, first of all, a professional poet whose splendid work in his field is handsomely recognized. This collection of his prose criticism clearly reflects the exacting judgments of his verse. And there is a third strand in his literary make-up, major as regards the matter of livelihood; also of great importance to the very substance of both his verse and prose. He himself coined the name for it: "teacherly." For many decades he has had the privilege, the luxury, of academic sermonizing in and about the humanistic field of great poetry, which was always in the background even when the job involved much serious attention to students' papers that could be almost obscenely far from great. He had a word for that, too, the administrative clutter accumulating in the course of a term and to be disposed of at the end: "teachersht."

The three strands of motivation—those of the poet, the critic, and the teacher—are in a harmonious relationship that does well for his psychic economy as a whole. For as he tells us, there are long stretches when the poetic springs run dry—and at those times he does much reading. Many of the essays in these pages testify to the great widening of Nemerov's intellectual horizon that resulted from this way of turning periods of drought to advantage. In the interview included in these pages he says, "I'm afraid most of my access to the world is from reading," but he doesn't do himself justice in putting the case that way. Every "fact" in every science is such because it's in some text. Geology is *words* about the earth. Our geological "access to the world" has been recently widened by our *reading* the theory of "plate tectonics."

The interview, by the way, is a lively job. And I cheered when things went thus:

I. Do you think your poetry is getting simpler; I don't mean to say simpleminded.
N. I would accept simpleminded.

And he develops the thought. He had already exclaimed enviously, "Imagine inventing a cliché, inventing your own platitude." It's not the whole story, but you can always depend upon him to keep limber in his attitudinizings. He derives mobility from his lyric aptitude, per Emerson's oracle: "Our moods do not believe in each other." Thus "The Pond," which Nemerov says a "nice review" in the *TLS* called "a teacher's poem," has one of the slipperiest oracles ever uncorked: "immortality/Is ours until we have no use for it."

In an earlier draft of these avowals, before I had hit upon this obvious triadic design of Nemerov's psychic economy, I first thought of taking up each item one by one in the order of their appearance and saying something about it. That policy would have saved me a lot of time, but within the limits proper to this introduction it would have amounted to little better than a more specific expansion of each title.

No, I'd have to select one particular text that seemed to offer the best opportunity for use as a point of departure. I could use references to that as a handy device for giving an overall view of the teacherly-writerly resourcefulness embodied in these accounts of the speculations, contestations, confessions, professions, and protestations that turn up in passing, along with constant evidence of his spontaneous responsiveness to whatever text or context is being touched upon.

Having read and "creatively" remembered many books which are worth while reading for one reason or another, sometimes even for stupidities which he can cherish and tell about, come the appropriate moment, Nemerov schemes much in his reader's behalf—and thus he is alertly on the lookout for relevant details with which to enlighten or entertain us. And when I was casting about for a piece that might be a handy place to start commenting from (on), I realized how well that "occasional" item, "Some Minute Particulars," would serve this purpose. For once you call attention to the constant eventfulness in this letter on the "occasion of the *Post-Dispatch*'s making its century," any reader can note what a variety of considerations turn up in that first paragraph, followed by the many twists and turns of the second paragraph in its role as introductory sequel, the various points also involving many shifts of attitude.

Though I am sure that any reader will note, in the third paragraph, Nemerov's ingenious maneuvers when launching his answer to the editor's questions, they are easier to spot than to label. But the second sentence is well worth our trying to quiz for its eventfulness, particularly since it is surprisingly long. (A mathematical colleague in whom I have implicit confidence tells me that it is composed of 81 words, or 82 by one way of counting.) First, it has a touch of what President F. D. Roosevelt would have called the "iffy" questionable. The assertion in the quotation that the sentence builds around is formally attributed to a hypothetical single voice in an individual broom closet—and it might say that, as compared with the many hardships that have beset the Western world since the Middle Ages, "I'd say we weren't getting on badly, no, not badly at all." Nemerov responds that a man "would surely lay himself open to accusations of ... hardheartedness"—and that partial disclaimer prepares the way for Nemerov, as Nemerov himself, to give samples of a "list that could be endless" of vexations that plague us now, and many that, he knows from reading, assailed our ancestors between the year 1300 and now. But hold! He says it eventfully: "since, say, Easter week of 1300, which Dante spent in hell, purgatory and heaven"—and we'll see later why that is not just a date he has read *of*, but one he has read *into*.

Just watch how many hithers and thithers he takes us through. Before the paragraph is over, for instance, he has introduced the thought "that our lives, those of ordinary citizens," are more comfortable than in the past, but he does so not in a way that would justify the attitude of satisfaction implied in the tonality of the judgment, "I'd say we weren't getting on badly," etc. And at the end, our "sins," "remedies," and "virtues" are all of one piece, as in Coleridge's "Religious Musings".

> So Property began, twy-streaming fount,
> Whence Vice and Virtue flow, honey and gall.

and

> From Avarice thus, from Luxury and War
> Sprang heavenly Science; and from Science Freedom.

—except that Nemerov wouldn't let it all look like as much of a happy ending as that. Then comes a whole series of swoops from one angle and another, ranging from Blake's *Jerusalem* (whenever Nemerov quotes from that text he is in dead earnest) to Eisenhower, whose botch with the language was an exhibit to treasure. But we should all be piously grateful for the line he bequeathed us in his farewell address, helping us never to forget the existence among us of a "military industrial complex."

That word "complex" introduces a development in my attempt to characterize the personality implicit in these texts that I would praise. Regardless of what Nemerov may say in behalf of simplemindedness, I would contend that he has an acute Complexity Complex. For you couldn't read a single essay by Nemerov without being struck by its constant shiftings in its approach to any subject. The talks that his *Figures of Thought* end on, "What Was Modern Poetry?", are an almost poignant example of his ways.* For the almost sloganlike settling on (as though "folding up with") the theme of "The Great Change" never rests.

I at first identified it, in connection with Yeats, with the First World War, though even at first I allowed the War to be a peculiarly dramatic and apocalyptic revelation of it, and not it itself. But as I studied my examples, I was led on to say that quite apart from any historical attachment The Great Change existed always and in every individual's life; in effect it is only for that reason, of a metaphysical and psychological priority, that the Great Change can get into history at all. Also, though for the present age science and technology appear as the great agents of that change, I am persuaded that before science and technology were, at least in anything like their modern forms, The Great Change was.

And then he adds:

Perhaps after all it is nothing but growing up, a peculiar form of growing up, or else the sudden after-realization of what growing-up has entailed.

But that won't rest. For elsewhere in the book he admonishes,

to say even to yourself, "I have finally grown up, I am a mature human being," is perilous, it generally means you are about to commit some drastically magnificent folly, such as running away with a sixteen-year-old chick or giving all your savings to an Arthur Murray dance studio or an obscure sect of snake worshippers.

The exquisite poignancy of the issue comes to a focus in the fact that the "simple-minded" aspect of the poetic act can get along quite well with

*To illustrate my thesis I will go beyond the boundaries of this volume.

the complexities of theoretic discriminations. For each lyric attitude is in itself an Absolute within the confines of its duration, even if its theme is one of discord. Nemerov quotes a poem of his own which "is part of the theme, one more variation on the sense of a Great Change." Look what happens in the long paragraph of prose comment that follows. And when Nemerov brings the whole subject to a culmination in comments on the poetry of Randall Jarrell, I incline to surmise that, in the light of Jarrell's tragic self-inflicted destiny, his "variations on a sense of a Great Change" would involve prose discriminations quite different from Nemerov's ways of tempering ("temperamentalizing"?) the theme. Nemerov says:

Jarrell sees it particularly in respect to children who suddenly penetrate behind the story books, the fairy tales, and see death in its lonesomeness, its decisive and destructive effect on all that is loved, especially the self.

One thing is certain: Whatever its twists and turns, Nemerov's "self" is minded to survive, as Jarrell was not.

At least by that time everything had fallen into place. Well, not quite. For in the attempt to play up the great variety of approaches Nemerov brought to his subject, I played down the resourcefulness of the transitions from one point to the next—and that kind of summarizing quite misrepresented the quality of his pages. But to track the nature of the whole development would cause me to use up more space in my account of the making than he used for what he made. But by stressing the design I believe I can economize on details if I contrive to select the most representative ones.

As my convictions about Nemerov's obviously tripartite psychic economy shaped up, there would be a rough approximation of a grand design; namely: his poetizing would equal "power"; his prose theorizing would equal "wisdom"; and for the analogue of "spirit" there would be the communicative bond between them. Whereat it became clear what pieces of his collection would best serve as an o'er-all trilogy to build around.

Putting his wish and actuality together, the first choice should be "Thirteen Ways of Looking at a Skylark," a title which, besides permitting us to think of titles by Shelley and Wallace Stevens if we want to, begins: "It has been suggested that I discuss what it is like to be a poet these days . . . or, if that is immodest, what it is like to write poetry, what one thinks about the art, what its relation is to the life we supposedly live these days, and so on." Next (to show the whole design at the start), would come "Poetry and Meaning," which begins: "What I have to say to you is very simple; so simple that I find it hard to say. It is that poetry is getting something right in language, that this idea of rightness in language is in the first place a feeling, which does not in the least prevent it from existing." And the third is "The Dream of Dante," which begins: "The dream nowhere says it's about Dante, it doesn't even mention his name, nevertheless I woke up knowing it was."

All told, the successive subjects of our trilogy are: (1) What it is to be a poet these days (and in particular what it is to be a Nemerovian poet); (2) What it is to be poetry these days (while they last); (3) What it is to be so great a poem that, though one might not believe literally at all in the theological rationale in which its "huge design" is grounded, Dante's "kind of divine chutzpah" is redeemed by the sheer "power of the poetry." Proclaiming in advance his great admiration for the poet's ability to hang on, "a true life task lasting so many years," Nemerov says it is "as if he had said to the Muse—dared to say to Polyhymnia, Muse of Sacred Song—'Lady, you show up at nine every morning for a decade and more, and I'll let you know when we're finished.'"

Let's go back now and sample enough of his literary "ploys" in these three essays to illustrate the delightful resourcefulness, the varied inventiveness, even to the extent of contradictoriness, in the range and quality of the approaches he brings to the "rendering" of his subject; for he would move us to "feel" it. Wordsworth's ode, "Intimations of Immortality from Recollections of Early Childhood," which came "trailing clouds of glory," attests that this state survives somewhat in adolescence, the age of "the growing boy," the "Youth" who on his way is still "attended" by this "vision splendid," until "At length the Man perceives it die away,/and fade into the light of common day."

Decimotertiary View of the Poet as High-Flying Song-Bird has the best of connotations, yet in that scheme the subject is not at all on parade as it is in the ode's version of the growing boy's descent from the Supernaturally inspired remembrances of Childhood. Rather, "poetry, like acne . . . may belong to adolescence. . . . If that is so, the inference is inescapable that a poet is a person who in some sense never got beyond adolescence, or who somehow repeated his adolescence several times during his life. Empirically, there is a good deal of evidence to support that assertion; poets do tend to be a touch Peter Panic"—a "touch" that in itself is a good illustration of how agreeably often even his way of saying something adds something. Wordsworth's ways with the "egotistical sublime" required a tough comment from without (by Arthur Hugh Clough?) to the effect that he "had one eye on a daffodil and the other on his canal stocks." Nemerov says as a matter of course, "you cannot make a living by writing verses," though some poets, Frost for instance, have fared quite well by going on the academic circuit as readers of their own verse, plus comment. And Nemerov himself has found it a profitable enterprise.

My purpose in discussing this matter at some length is that it does help characterize the quality of his critical prose. For he "naturally" considers the likelihood that a gift for poetry in one's maturity may augur a state of arrested adolescence in this regard, yet feel no need to "defend" it. In effect his attitude says, "So what"?, but without the slightest accents of defiance. If one wants to be a poet as much as Nemerov does and is, any psychic way of getting there is all to the good. My own conviction is that adolescence is the stage of life at which the individual, emerging from the "autistic" incunabula of childhood and coming to realize the communicative obligations and opportunities of words, may in effect, implicitly and to some extent explicitly, "take the vow" to become a poet—and the vague memory of the vague possibilities that were somehow both near and beyond the horizon can keep one goaded to keep searching somehow for the "right" words to transform the wordless realm of experience into a verbal counterpart.

As I interpret Wallace Stevens, the impulse is grounded in the attempt to experience "things" as the infant experienced them before it began to think of things as namable (the infant bringing with it from the womb the kind of experience our primal ancestors had before they had acquired the ability to go from sensation to words for sensation). But as I take it, with that ultimate "neo-infantile" goad at the roots of Wordsworth's glorified "clouds," the poet at adolescence wholly confronts the symbolic problems (and problematics) to which poets in later, mature, years "regress" insofar as the goad towards poetizing in essense is at the roots of one's exercisings in the way of new verbal discriminations.

I wouldn't do valiant battle for my secular psychologizing of Wordsworth's borrowings from Plato's Heaven, but I do think this: As a rule Nemerov is right in his notion that the poet must never wholly outgrow the kind of attitudinizings and corresponding limpidity characteristic of adolescent waverings, be they waverings such that the emergent bard can now and then swoop down upon an avowal with certainty while the mood is on.

Poetic action in particular is a subdivision of symbolic action ("verbal behavior") in general, but they are not identical. The distinction is somewhat analogous to Coleridge's distinction between "primary" and "secondary" imagination, the first applying to us all, the second to the poet.

The next step in this discussion requires me to observe that the con-

cept of the "Complexity Complex" includes two aspects sufficiently de-
marcated in themselves to merit specific designations: "Duplicity" and
"Perplexity." I shall discuss "Perplexity" later. A variation on the theme of
"doubleness" (Nemerov's term) is in reference to Yeats. The theme, but
not the word, discusses how a poem belongs to "two worlds outside itself." "One is the world of the poet's work entire. . . . The other is the
world we believe." In matters of ethics a common instance of Duplicity
figures in cases where a diplomat does his best (worst?) to speak in behalf
of a governmental policy that he personally despises, or a lawyer does all
in his power to defend a person or a corporation that he takes to be at
fault.

But Nemerov's complicated account of the many varied stories and
attitudes he found necessary to suggest in prose the unitary essence of the
poet *qua* poet gives us a quite mellow kind of Duplicity. Not only are
poets "excentric oddities," on a closer inspection they "turn out to be
excentric oddities like everyone else," but "like the weak criminal whose
confession implicates the others." At this point he propounds it as a law:
"In any discussion of what it is that poets do, you will not be surprised if
you keep coming across that curious phenomenon we have just noticed,
of the odd turning into the even." Accordingly, on the notion that the
poet's language "should be 'poetic,'" he forthwith evens the oddity by observing that "almost all language . . . has in addition to its practical purpose
a poetical purpose."

Then he takes a true oddity if there ever was one, a headline, DOLLAR
BILLS GUSH FROM SEWER. He doesn't "at all remember, or want to remember, the perfectly rational explanation that no doubt followed." Rather, he
will even its oddity by showing that the headline had "a certain universality
behind it," since it "repeats the connection, so well-established in folklore
and psychoanalysis, between money and shit, betwen all man's idealizing
symbol systems and his physical reality, as it is asserted in the medieval
saying, *Super cloacam, ecclesia*."

That leads to "the chief device of poetry, metaphor," via a transition
from odd-even to "the assertion of a likeness between different things,"
and thence to an anecdote (with corresponding asides) about an occasion
when he "was nearly run over by an ambulance racing along on its errand
of mercy." The design brought out what, borrowing from Coleridge, I
would call the "twy-streaming fount" aspect of the odd-even Duplicity,
since "'being run over by an ambulance' was a very fair definition of the
paradoxical nature of civilization itself, which comes at you with a gun in
one hand and a healing hypodermic in the other." (Of a sudden it occurs
to me: What an amusing match with the daffodil–canal stocks pair.)

But since he felt required to say that the near-calamity happened on a road in Austria, he got into the matter of the poetical "mysteriousness" of proper names (having to do with their uniqueness), a concern that leads to the notion that "in its highest range the theory of poetry would be the theory of the Incarnation," as explained to Dante by Beatrice in Canto VII of the *Paradiso.*

He now sums up what he has said so far, incidentally in a sturdy paragraph that uses the Duplicity principle to great advantage. The poet can express "no thought so secret or so unique, so wicked or shameful or sublime, that the same has not quietly occurred to many others." But since poetry is not in the practical realm, "its subversive character is highly civilized and civilizing." We're here more directly in the field of poetry than of the poetizing poet, but we'll be back soon in a big way; in the meantime, "poetry may be thought of as both pedagogic and therapeutic, because of all it may imagine, without settling for one among a million fables as the truth." And the poet's "childlike, or even childish" delight in language is actually "sophisticated and very grown-up" because "He says to himself: 'Everything we think we know is a figure of speech,' and 'Every word in the language was beautiful once.'" But though "poets have only rarely been interested in killing people because they say Sibboleth instead of Shibboleth," surely "career-wise" many poets or teachers of poetry would gladly kill others' reputations.

With the statement, "Sooner or later someone always says, But what is poetry?", there begins the new start. After a muster of charmingly varied selections from the Complicity Complex (beginning with the shrewd observation that definitions can have a way of putting a stop to things), Nemerov gets launched on some most ingenious exercising, by taking as his texts two poems about poetry which he will poetize about, along with comments from outside all three.

(1) "You could say, after Marianne Moore, that the poet presents for inspection 'imaginary gardens with real toads in them.'" (2) "A celebrated attempt at definition is given by Archibald MacLeish, in a poem which . . . ends by saying that a poem 'should not mean/But be.'" Then look what happens. Nemerov shows for sure why MacLeish's oracle doesn't make sense. Then he ironically defends it on the grounds that when he was editor of a literary magazine every mail brought to his desk "a large number of poems which perfectly fitted the definition: they meant nothing, and there they were."

But Nemerov hasn't yet put us through our paces with that. To do so, he takes MacLeish's "famous definition," puts it together with Marianne Moore's "famous definition," and turns out some lines that poetically botch

them both. Then, having said that he still likes MacLeish's poem though
he had contradicted it, he quotes from Blake's *Jerusalem* (always an authority with him) a quatrain allowing for poetry as "a place where Con-
trarieties are equally true."

But I wonder whether MacLeish's oracle might involve an implicit Duplicity of this sort: Take, for instance, a shopping list. Call its meaning its
"substance." And one might conceivably use it in a poem, worded exactly
as if one were using it for the purely practical purpose of serving as a
reminder for the next time one went shopping. But in the poem its "substance" would have a different "stance." It might, for instance, serve as a
sly bit of self-portraiture, showing what some character in the poem (perhaps the poet's own poetic self) "had on its mind."

As I now size things up, the step from being a poet to being poetry
began to emerge when Nemerov did a Nemerovian trick with two poems
about poetry—and to the rest of the chapter we're in that exquisitely "Du-
plicitous" (we need that word) realm between "stance" and "sub-stance."
In the same paragraph where he thinks of "defining poetry as an activity
resistant to definition," he says "there is something rather poetical in a
definition." (It is a sentiment that gladdens my heart. For I have admitted,
"I see in a definition the critic's equivalent of a lyric, or of an aria in
opera.") Then he goes on to say that there is "something rather heroical
in the *attitude of definition toward the world*, if only we are able to realize
at the same time, *with respect to the subject matter of poetry, that the substance of what is defined does not remain the same*." The italicizing is
mine, done in the hopes that it will help accentuate my point. The attitude
of definition equals the poetic stance. The poet is writing a poem in particular, not just using language in general. The sub-stance, or meaning, the
subject-matter of the poem ever changes. But the cult of definition, like
the cult of poetizing, embodies a principle, it just is.

For the remainder of the chapter Nemerov will be at his most sensitive
and ingenious in working with this "now-you-see-me/now-you don't" wav-
ering study of the poet's Duplicity, using language in two overlapping
ways, with regard to the shiftings between *poetic imitation* and the "doc-
umentary."

But I propose a compromise. I'm sure that many readers will ask whether
Nemerov's account of what it is to be a poet tells us rather what it is to be
a Nemerovian poet, with a Complexity Complex like no one else's, and so
exceptionally expansive that the prose correlative of its poetic stance bus-
ies all these pages. And the concept of a "bad Nemerovian poet" would be
a "contradiction in terms." But there are kinds of contradiction which an

observer of the verbal situation who has Nemerov's responsiveness to the Duplicity of the odd/even design is "naturally at home with"—and the chapter will continue along that line.

There is the tension in terms that subsume tendencies, since a *doing* is not the same as a *tendency* to do (which is also a tendency not to). Nemerov develops variations on that theme in his discussion of Shakespeare's sonnet 129, "Th' expence of spirit in a waste of shame." Then comes a splendid poem, "A Spell Before Winter," the author (Nemerov) not named. It leads a section entitled "Emblems," and is surely of Vermont in October, telling of how the very conditions of the weather are foretelling winter (which, if you want, can be emblematic of a further, deeper sleep).

Then Nemerov employs his teacherly rhetoric at its most persuasively eloquent to analyze the imagery in a passage from *Measure For Measure*, the Duplicity being in terms of Angelo's likening his lusting after the virtuous Isabella to dead meat rotting in the sun beside a violet. (Where Shakespearean dramaturgy is concerned one might also sample the work for another brand of Duplicity, as the situation may be so developed that it titillates the audience's pruriency while in effect blaming it on Angelo.)

Also, to keep things moving with maximum suggestiveness, he has tossed in now and then, *passim*, such formulary moments as these: "Poetry is a species of thought with which nothing else can be done"; "Poetry seems to be a unique mode of language in demanding an intransitive attention, an attention to itself, other than and more vital than the transitive attention you give, through it, to what it talks about"; and, "Poetry perceives the world as a miracle transcending its doctrine, or any doctrine."

I had to sum up with comments in general on the ingenious way whereby Nemerov's variety of approaches has given us a good feeling for the poetic Stance as he experiences it. And these remarks would come after his culminating wind-up, with some pages on Yeats. But see the footnote, "Alas! (1975)."

Croce uses figuratively the word "palimpsest." Just as in the days when scrolls were written on parchment, a scribe might impose a new text atop a different one, so history in itself can become such a "palimpsest" by obscuring from us the exact knowledge of the situation in which the work was written and to the "challenge" of which it was, in effect, a response.

The historical palimpsest in this case has to do with a poem by Yeats which, Nemerov says, sums up what he takes to be "the attitude of poetry toward the world." And it builds about the term "gay," which does not here have the connotations it has come to take on since Yeats wrote on

Shakespeare's images of "tragic play" and "poets that are always gay," of figures that "Do not break up their lines to weep," for "They know that Hamlet and Lear are gay." Using the term "gay" in a more general sense, Nemerov ended his chapter on this most complete Duplicity,

And it is possible, drawing on Yeats, to add one more characteristic to our description of poems: we recognize poems because, among other things, "they do not break up their lines to weep." They weep, but they do not break up their lines to weep.

The next piece, "Poetry and Meaning," in focusing upon what it is to be poetry, fits the design to perfection. But the poet's stance and the poem's so readily overlap that the shiftings between the two become quite complicated. Thus Nemerov starts things with quite a twist. His opening salvo is clearly in the Stance groove: "poetry is getting something right in language." But via a reference to "one more variant of the common cry of middle-aged poets, 'I had talent once, where did it go'," he goes through a quick series of steps that have gone from the superannuation of the poetic impulse in Wordsworth's Growing Boy on growing up; and now here's Nemerov's growing conviction that poetry itself is on the way out, superannuated because the world will have lost the concern with "getting something right in language" as the poet means it. He has considered the possibility that Wells's misgivings might be a matter of being "mortally ill," the likelihood that people won't later find it absurd to think of machines as thinking (Hannah Arendt had added the particular hermeneutic detail there)—then the authoritative swoop:

And Owen Barfield, possibly the clearest and most searching thinker of the present time, says—though he calls it a provocative heterodoxy—"I have been coming to feel for some time that imagination, *as an end in itself*, is a vein that has been, or very soon will be, worked out. I am in doubt whether much more that is really significant can be done with it" (*The Rediscovery of Meaning*).

Then this Poet so competently at home with his Complexity Complex turns to the question of the "teacherly response" that engages his verbalizing genius midway between strict poem and strict theorizing for its own sake.

But I must admonish me to remember: My self-assigned job here, when I undertook the obligation and corresponding opportunity to say things in celebration of this volume, is primarily to ask that the reader pause to realize what a variety of perceptions we can enjoy by going along with his ways of confronting "this business of poetry as getting things right in language." Quite a range! "A primary pleasure in poetry is surely something low enough to be beneath the notice of teacher or critic—the pleasure of saying something over for its own sweet sake and because it sounds just right." A "riddling song" that "has the refrain" "Sing ninety-nine and ninety" charmed him enough with that "to say it over and over" to himself for days, without his "ever having a single thought about its meaning except for a certain bemused wonder about how different it was from singing "a hundred and eighty-nine." Some lines in the *Inferno* refer to a conversation between Dante and Virgil where Dante "is talking in effect about what he is not going to talk about." "A joke" (like poetry) "is a way of getting something right in language." "It is part of the power of a poem to generate meanings from what may originally be meaningless." "I want the idea of rightness to be as open, contentless, empty if you like, as may be." "If silence is the appropriate response to rightness, it may be that the real use of talk is about wrongness." "This poetry is intense, indeed, with the grim intensity of someone trying to masturbate too soon after having masturbated." "Imagine someone living through the fall of the Roman Empire in a provincial town, in Marseille say, or London; he would live his life day by day, as we all do, and never know that he had lived through the fall of the Roman Empire." What he called "the slow collapse in the idea of meaning" gets tied in with a turn from questions about the meaning of a poem to questions about meaning in general. "Anthropology, too, with its close relations, folklore and comparative religion and mythology, gets into the act." "A vast increase in knowledge . . . simultaneous with a slow collapse in the idea of meaning." Even if he is right that "the great period of art may now be over . . . it may not be altogether a disaster," for "the end of a particular form of experience does not mean the end of experience." Whereat doubtless the realization of his own resourceful agility in the consideration of these matters. For he's certainly talking from his own way of seeing when he says "forms are there to be transformed and of all this something kind and good may come one day."

Incidentally, the very statement reminds me that I certainly should have listed his stirrings about how the terms "subjective" and "objective" got turned around over the centuries. But we might note a further twist in that development. A key Greek word for "sub-stance" is "hypostasis," the *hypo* corresponding to our preposition "sub." Christian theology applied the term to the most fundamental of all usages, to signify the "persons" of the Trinity. The Greek *hyper* (which corresponds to our preposition for "over," "above," "upper") generally gravitates toward connotations of "excess." But the Marxists' contrast between "superstructure" as "ideological" and "substructure" as "objective," the materially real, adds another slant to the "sub-side" of such terms.

Before moving on, I believe we should think a bit more about Nemerov's form-transformation formula. His essay "On the Resemblance Between Science and Religion" begins that "poetic exercise" with this theorizing profession: "When two things are said to be opposites, it becomes a duty of the intelligence to look for their similarities." "When two things are said to have nothing in common, it becomes a pleasure of the intelligence to find out what they have in common."

Having such a slant in mind, he is ideally equipped to oblige at the last minute when a colleague who had contracted to speak on biology was incapacitated, and Nemerov helped out by hurrying up with that limber and mellow and graceful performance, "Lewis Thomas, Montaigne, and Human Happiness." To come up with that, and in a hurry yet, is a major achievement. Not only does he swing in from many angles; every point he makes has niceties of its own—and his variations on the theme of "Happiness" are good civilized fun in every sentence. Moreover, he has a good "homemade Jewish joke" to end on. Again and again, in going over these things (many of which, such as this one, I never saw before) I realize how easy he makes it for me to be honest in my praise. Yet at the same time I feel punished, for I can't stop and say just how many "rightnesses" he keeps turning up (in his prose style; for damn it, it's not just poetry that loves the *mot juste*). Even the tiniest of such, as you go from sentence to sentence, helps as they add up. For instance, when he says, "And yet happiness is what it's about," he didn't say, "is what it's all about," in keeping with the norms of current stylistic automatism. But we must hurry on.

Before closing, I want to show how a Complexity Complex also allows for a Complicity Complex. I dare hope that, by then, you'll be enough at home with Nemerov's pliancy of critical and teacherly resourcefulness to welcome the obviously reasonable possibility that there can even be sheerly "playful" kinds of complicity. Recall that we have already been asked to consider "Shakespeare's images of 'tragic play'."

In the meantime, before turning to "The Dream of Dante," I should say a few words about another aspect of Complexity; namely, Perplexity. It also, as I interpret it, allows for a wide range of dispositions, particularly at the hands of a confirmed Transformationist such as Nemerov. (For instance, I would class under that head his sophisticated approval of MacLeish's "not mean, but be" oracle). But there's one place where he confronts it head on. I refer to his quotations from an article by Paul Riesman (in a volume *Sign Image Symbol*, edited by Gyorgy Kepes): "When we ask of science the question 'Why are we here?' or 'What is our place in the universe?' ... we feel somehow that the question has not been answered. ... What we want to know is something quite definite: 'Where are we?' ... Science tells us that our place in the universe is nowhere in particular ... or anywhere. I think that this is the best that science will do for us. For it is true. ... Yet in all times and places human beings have resisted the idea that they are nowhere for no particular reason and for no particular purpose." The quotations—there are considerably more—Nemerov gives us in their unrelieved despondency.

But his essay, "The Dream of Dante," is built about the appreciation of a great poem whose author gave an astoundingly assertive and comprehensive answer to the question that, Riesman says, science wholly fails to answer. Nemerov's pages on *The Divine Comedy* are an exceptionally admirable accomplishment, its poetic stance being substantially, doctrinally, grounded in a theology, that is, a "science of God." Se we have seen enough of Nemerov's skill at "transformations" to expect some "critical" moments in this chapter.

We have considered what it is to be a poet in general and/or a Nemerovian poet in particular. We have considered what it is to be a poem and/ or poetry. Now we are going to consider what it is to be one particular great epic poem (and the author of same) as appreciated by a connoisseur of poetry whose keen admiration for it as a poem must greatly tax his "willing suspension of disbelief" with regard to the doctrinal substance about which its poetic stance is built. (I take it that "willing suspension," etc., is a notable variation on the theme of Duplicity).

But his enterprise does start with a twist: "The dream nowhere says it's about Dante, it doesn't even mention his name, nevertheless I woke up knowing it was." As if he were on a Freudian couch, he freely associates his ideas for us until it works out that the *dramatis personae* of the dream are Dante Alighieri, Scholarship, and Scholarly Apparatus. I take it that they represent, respectively: Nemerov's primary affiliation with matters of poetic stance and its corresponding substantiation; his prose theorizing in general; and his classroom homiletics (the pronounced overlap in offices two and three accounting for the overlap in their designations).

The reference to Dante's "kind of divine chutzpah" reminds me of our earlier reference to the "homemade Jewish joke" he offers at the end of his essay, "Lewis Thomas, Montaigne, and Human Happiness." For as I see it, the principle of Duplicity figures here in this way: Nemerov's primal homage to the power of a specifically poetic stance is such that he pays brilliantly, even contagiously, urgent tribute to Dante's epic; yet I could not for one moment conceive of him as becoming in actual life a convert to the theological doctrines (in the ecclesiastical sense) on which the poem's *substance* is based. His ways with Complexity don't, as I see him, encompass a Duplicity of that sort.

I make this point because my whole view of Nemerov (as "Poeticizer," "Prosifier," and "Teacher") finds no place for it. And for that very reason, to help make clear the nature of his tripartite psychic economy as I see it, I must so state my case. Otherwise I could not accurately characterize, as I conceive it, the nature of the overall personal equipment he brings to the job and professionally performs it with.

The principle of Duplicity figures from many angles. He does not begin with *theological* aspects of the headquarters in which, according to the eschatology that Dante believed in, all the good guys and bad guys that ever lived on this earth will be eternally domiciled, even after the universe we experience has gone. Rather he deals with such purely physical concepts as "Dante's neat Ptolemaic universe . . . the elegant Copernican universe that replaced it . . . the vast universe more recently offered us by Harlow Shapley and others," and now with "the effects of the scientific and technological civilization" that, at the time when Nemerov was writing, had made it impossible for him "to see any Milky Way at all."

"Duplicitously," he observes that "Dante has a small universe, but a full one, and he knows it thoroughly," whereas Nemerov has "a vast universe, but it is empty and dark, and compared with what is to be known" he does "not know it at all."

That is "poetically the point." "Away from the *Comedy*," he may have his "doubts." But while he is reading it, "the illusion of plenitude is complete." There he hits it: the "illusion of plenitude [is] . . . the supreme illusion possible to poetry," and it makes him "think of the *Comedy* as a kind of holography, in which everything is always present at every point." On this subject he refers to "a famous remark of Whitehead's, that 'In a certain sense, everything is everywhere at all times, for every location involves an aspect of itself in every other location. Thus every spatio-temporal standpoint mirrors the world.'" Yes, there he hit it. From now on, from out of the Duplicity of his situation, he will muster his critical and teacherly remarks to the end of showing how the design of Dante's poem converts the complexity of the substance into a unity of poetically imitative stance.

The problematic "doubleness" (one variant of Duplicity) is viewed as felicitously resolved in the resultant "illusion of plenitude." And I take it that from now on he will be admiring the poem for both its internal organization and its external confrontations, in accordance with Emerson's early Transcendentalist essay, "Nature," with its notion of the Poet so divining the divine origin of nature that its implicit moral discipline becomes "transparent" and the "axis of vision" becomes "coincident with the axis of things."

The next paragraph outlines the poem's "purely arithmetical or numerological disposition." Then he gives the feel of the astounding ethical rationale behind the arrangements whereby scenes in the supernatural realm of eternity are provided to fit by way of rewards and punishments the worldly acts of human beings when in the realm of time. One gets the feeling that even the poem's mere ability to survive as a poem after so much bookkeeping adds to the sense of its "plenitude."

Nemerov next introduces lines from his poetically infallible Authority, Blake's *Jerusalem*. And he follows that with a reference to the section in the *Purgatorio* in which Dante gives the Church's opposition to theories of astrological predestination. (There was also a compromise; the stars could not cause our destiny, but they could foretell it.)

Then comes a startling twist. It looks as though Duplicity has suddenly relapsed into a wholly unsympathetic attitude: "Against the background of the circles of Hell, the terraces of purgation, the starry wheels of Heaven—all that insane arithmetical regularity as circular as a Kandinsky, which in my moods of disaffection with the poem make me think of it as *The Rube Goldberg Variations*"—but no, even before the sentence is finished all is as was, and more so: against all this "is placed the wild richness and unpredictable particularity of people in their ways through the dark wood or their moving over the great sea of being." Here perhaps is where the illusion of plenitude is not convincing (or is it totally convincing). Per the French proverbial formula, *reculer pour mieux sauter*, Nemerov was but drawing back, the better to leap forward.

At this point I had a dream that Nemerov had here introduced the New Testament word, *pleroma*. But no, he stayed with "plenitude." Looking it up in my lexicon, I found: fullness; plenitude; the full number; the fulfillment; the fullness of time; the fullness of Christ, i.e., the Church; the fullness of the Godhead, all divine attributes. Speaking of Duplicity in this connection: Once I had a kind of mystic-experience-in-reverse. Having been much engrossed in the dialectics of "negative theology," and living alone in a rented room, I returned to that room, poured myself a single drink, and suddenly woke up to find that I had fallen asleep. Not only was my glass empty; the room was empty. But it wasn't just empty, it was full of emptiness. And I had to do quite a bit of psychic maneuvering (mainly by way of socializing gossip-wise) to get rid of the feeling that that room was so damned positively empty. Maybe it all touched upon the last words of my early book, *Permanence and Change* (published 1935): "men build their cultures by huddling together, nervously loquacious, at the edge of an abyss." (Feminists, please forgive the "men.")

Nemerov makes convincingly clear the plenitude of resources that Dante has to offer here, by knowing so many people, knowing so many stories, and being able to fit all that lore from so many angles into the grand design of his poem as a whole. He sums this up by saying, "It is in this poetic power of com-position, literally of putting together, that he is supreme."

"Com-position" as "putting together"? Near the beginning of the essay, referring to quotations from Bishop Burnet and George Santayana, Nemerov had said, "though written three centuries apart . . . I'd had them about for some years, and here seemed to be an excuse for putting them together." There's a variant of the Duplicity we saw as early as his paragraphs on being a poet. "Com-position" is not just a "poetic" power. Nemerov's prose is, again and again, studded with such puttings-together as the result of things he learned when the Pierian spring of his poetizing had temporarily run dry, and he had so profited by these intervals that his prose is a com-position studded with a great variety of such parcels, each bringing with it a somewhat different "axis of vision," and his way of fitting that in helps keep things on the move. He's good at "retrieval."

He further says here that Dante, being "the most learned of poets," thus "relies the most upon learning and allusion," but he also refers to Dante's "magnificent attentiveness to the visual," at which point the reader should duplicitously recall a prior qualification in the same article: "The poem . . . is to be read with the mind's eye, not the body's eyes, which are the necessary but not sufficient receivers of its words or of its visions." That poetic charmer, William Carlos Williams's would-be poetic stance, "no ideas but in things," didn't make sense even in Williams—and Nemerov rightly points out how much farther Dante is from such "imagist" or "objectivist" ideals of poetic purity. (Yet I'm far from being content with my Duplicity here, and am scheming to set matters right by some things I'm planning to say elsewhere about Williams's "contact" in his *Paterson* epic.)

Complexity, Complicity, Duplicity, Perplexity—I am adopting and adapting the form of Bentham's nomenclature in non-Benthamite way when

I use them all indiscriminately as "neutral, eulogistic, or dyslogistic appel-
latives." As Riesman presents it, in modern science the universe is greatly
"perplexing"; by contrast, Dante's geocentric universe, in which the virtuous will have a happy afterlife forever, is not at all perplexing. But Nemerov does have a word for perplexity in a quite felicitous sense. It turns
up in his discussion of the poem's "riddling diction." In contrast with the
"power of putting before us with the utmost plainness what he is seeing,
so that we see it too, there is this other power of riddling diction, that is
constantly making us supply more information than the words themselves
convey, and infer whole stories from an image or a line. . . . The passage
about Rome is thick with famous names to which the reader's memory
must supply the stories, and includes even the destruction of the Temple
under Titus, given in a sentence so riddling that its full elucidation by
Beatrice takes up the whole of the next Canto." But it seems to me that
the grandest piece of riddling is in Canto XXIX of the *Paradiso*, where
Dante sings his way through the dialectical Perplexities involved in the
derivation of temporal sequence from a background of timelessness. The
"beginning of the fall" (*Principio del cader*) was in a realm where there
was no *was*, only an *is* and *will be*, as an *eternal now*. Among what Beatrice
calls the "equivocations" of discourse there is the ambiguity whereby there
can be two quite different kinds of "firsts" (temporal, as with "yesterday-
today-tomorrow," and purely logical, as with "first premise, second premise, conclusion" of a syllogism).

A bit of Duplicity was added to the riddling, when Dante leaves it for
Beatrice, along with her talk of "equivocations," to dodge the six successive "days" of Creation, followed by the Sabbath, in the book of Genesis.
She builds up a kind of simultaneity as perplexing as the Big Bang that
modern science would begin with. In any case, Nemerov announces "one
last illustration of what I have been calling the illusion of plenitude . . .
that idea of the presence of everything in something, which is of the essence of poetry."

In the next several pages he develops the thought that "The scheme of
the poem is in a certain sense anecdotal and picaresque." Its "anecdotal"
aspect introduces "a temptation to read each episode as entirely separate
from all the others." However, per the *reculer pour mieux sauter* principle, his very reference to such a "temptation" sets the stylistic conditions
for him to drive home his "plenitude" theme: "But there is, owing to Dante's
power of composition, a further dimension, of resonance, of symbol, or
mysteriously allusive interconnection, between this example and that, between the examples and Dante himself, and so on." He could have in-

cluded, as he does elsewhere, Dante's "typological" inclinations, a hermeneutic tendency strongly shaped by Christian theologians' zealous search for "types of Christ" in the Old Testament.

I was puzzled by the adjective "picaresque." Life as a sea voyage is an adventure, particularly in those days: and some adventurers are rogues. But the term "picaresque" suggests to me that Nemerov is concerned with a Duplicity of this sort: The "rogues" were engaged in strenuous undertakings which they performed with as much thoroughness and energy as Dante brought to the construction of his *Comedy*; but they were in such different grooves that the quality of their experience, or knowledge, requires a wider orbit than the characteristic ethical and theological emphasis that the epic encompasses for its "plenitude." Nemerov even brings up the knowledge-power equation, though that would not be explicitly formulated until approximately three centuries later, in the works of Francis Bacon. But the idea was clearly forming in the work of Roger Bacon, contemporary of Dante. If one ever cares to glance over a record of the middle ages' strivings toward a rival vision of "plenitude," by all means sample *A History of Magic and Experimental Science: During the First Thirteen Centuries of our Era*, by Lynn Thorndike. I take it that Dante's awareness of this movement was implicit in Nemerov's term "picaresque."

Time is nearly up. Yet one thing still seems called for. How about him and me? What's the excuse that the introduction celebrating him should be by me? I would say some words about the twists of Complicity that seasoned our Duplicity.

The Duplicity with its twists and turns is this way: Having much in common, each of us has had much to tell the other, in our roles as concerned citizens of a great nation riddled with advanced technological pollution. By my being older, we met through his reviewing (and with the competence an author's grateful for) some books of mine, whereby *our* dialogue began with *my* having said some things to him first. But fortunately I need talk about *us* only insofar as my comments might help portray the ingenious busynesses of *him*.

First, there's a matter of Duplicity that took on the dimensions of a Complicity. It began this way. I wrote a bit of nonsense verse, total nonsense, which I mailed to Nemerov in an envelope without another word. In answer I received a Sizzler. For he had "cracked the code," and he had no intention of dismissing it likewateroffaduck'sback. Presumably I was "in good fun" sending him one of those mean "whom the shoe fits" valentines—and he had at me in kind. I released my "Sphinx" along with another one, with an explanation that they were both nonsense, and my

solemn wisecrack: "Contemporary criticism has attained such competence, it can crack any code, if only the enigma is in verse." But I'd not be
surprised if my pal and sparring partner of many years shed his line likewateroffaduck'sback.

But this volume's essay "The Winter Addresses of Kenneth Burke" begins with a "movement," the Complicity of which is a sheer delight, to
analyze my office and residence addresses during a term at the University
of Pittsburgh as though they were a poem. How entitle it in the light of its
prowess as a kind of hermeneutic shadowboxing? Relish its great virtuosity as a display of exegetic diegesis. He e'en goes so far as to mock-seriously
introduce disciplined recognition of the problems involved when prob-
lem-solving in such an enterprise, until, like some of the New World literary critics at Yale, his gestures of critical interpretation are themselves a
kind of free verse, with its rare variety of Stance.

Yet he moves, and develops developments until he ends in and on a
poem of his own. But what an essay, to emerge out of sheer tomfoolery!
We go through things like Steven's riddling oracle, "The poem must resist
the intelligence/Almost successfully"; a paraphrasing of Levi-Strauss about
"a view of the mind imitating itself as object"; his final decision that "Mr.
MacLeish's celebrated slogan to the contrary, a poem must be and mean
at once"; an "exchange" between Robert Frost and himself that "took place
only in dream"; many other stages; then a truly *central* paragraph telling
when he came to know Frost personally, the whole performance culminating in a poem, "For Robert Frost, in the Autumn, in Vermont." It's a
handsome tribute, full of old New England and when about, as in the
autumn it gorgeously and gorgonizingly is. The bustling article has much
more that I haven't mentioned, including "a translation, or imitation," by
Ezra Pound, of an "oriental" poem of "imagist" cast—and I guess it will
strike the readers as more in the way of "riddling" (though not so desig-
nated) than the venturesomely perplexing operations under that name he
refers to.

There is a further item to be considered in the him-and-me groove. A
fellow-thinker, Mildred Ligda, whose husband, a printer, had seasons when
trade was slack, suggested that they might reprint some of my O. P. books
when he had the spare time. Nemerov worked up a lively way of building
his essay, "Everything, Preferably All at Once," around the resonant complicity of the term, Hermes Publications. I gave the project the Hermes
angle, having particularly in mind the god's link with the theme of communication. Also I worked up a logo around the songful duplicity, *her-
meneutica hermeticaque.* Since the last sentence of Nemerov's Dante piece

refers to "a riddling hint of a oneness in the world that for a moment shines through the manifold appearances," I could (if I wanted to) feel happy that I was at least in the vicinity of *bona fide* "plenitude." And along that line, I could call attention to his triumphant masterpiece of retrieval, his article "On Metaphor," with its notion that metaphor condenses a manifold of associations whereas a simile ties things down.

True, he does a Duplicity on me in this summarizing sentence which, after the third comma, does a bit of a switcheroo: "Everything is always being used for all it's worth, and sometimes maybe more." However, there is the Complicity of this Complexity. The article ends by associating me with a riddle, than which nothing could be more honorific but to end on quotation from Blake's *Jerusalem*. Yet alas! a Duplicity figures here as well, for he twice calls it not a riddle but an emblem. At least, hermeneutics-minded, we can profit by the indication that in Nemerov's nomenclature riddle can = emblem.

One parting observation, and we can hurry to our wind-up (or wind-down). Nemerov, referring to his already mentioned essay on my work, says: "Burke said to a young man of eighteen . . . 'Everything is a language.'" Burke should have been more specific in what he said to that bright lad. This introduction began with a quote from Nemerov: "Imagine inventing a cliché, inventing your own platitude." My corrective platitude is to this effect: "Within the infinite word-less Universe, there developed human 'bodies that learn language.' And they can't talk about anything without talking about it, which = language."

If, in conclusion, we were allowed but one overall formula from which to derive all the Complexities, Complicities, and Duplicities we have hurried about among, beyond question I would choose one from the last paragraph of his somewhat eschatological summary, "Poetry and Meaning." Here Nemerov calls "the period that is over," which "lasted from the middle of the last century to the middle of this one," "The Age of Art, or The Aesthetic Age." In keeping with the outlaw thought that Dante profits by being approached in terms of the "Aesthetic Age," Nemerov says: "Forms are there to be transformed."

Turn from that to his devout testimonial, "The Miraculous Transformations of Maurits Cornelius Escher." For our purposes all comes to a focus when he refers to a picture where "the artist gives hints of a situation in nature possessing these illusionist properties: the situation of water, which you simultaneously see and see through and see reflections from." Having already said that he was "charmed" by what he would later call the "endless problem of true illusions," he said that he was using the word in "its older and magical senses: bemused, enthralled, hypnotized, or be-witched." Before he ended, he "freely" extended his *visual* experience to such texts as Proust and, on the same page, Shakespeare's "riddling."

At this point, before hurrying to a close, I would insert a footnote that takes off from the first paragraph of this focal essay with its reference to "the fact that what it defines is simultaneously a part of and apart from the surrounding territories."

The Duplicity of Nemerov's usage here bears down hard upon a sheerly morbid simplicity of a terminological investment by the present author. In Ego's book, *A Grammar of Motives* (1945, pp. 53–54), with regard to standard dialectical finaglings, the text says, "to adopt a very suggestive usage in Charles M. Perry's *Toward a Dimensional Realism*, the notion of nature as *a part of* God could be converted into the notion of nature as *apart from* God." Later, the sheer design as such, with reference to the theological usage, refers to the "transformation of something which is 'a part of' a larger context into something which is 'apart from' this context" (p. 107).

It's not the terms I am referring to. They are in use everywhere. It's their use in pointed contrast.

If you knew me as morbidly well as I do, you'd know how much it hurt Ego to acknowledge that that particular verbal twist was not mine own. Then, lo! having occasion to go back over my *Permanence and Change* in connection with plans for the current new edition, I found in it, a book published several years *before* the volume that had so grievously taxed Ego to give it credit, this passage: "Are the microscopic creatures in our blood stream *separate from* us or a *part of* us? They are members of a 'civic corporation' which we call *the* organism. Who knows?—perhaps they were originally invaders which the body, in learning to tolerate, eventually naturalized as an integral part of its economy" (p. 233; italics added). To a later edition (1953) I added: "We were merely 'improvising' when we wrote those sentences. But we could now cite the biologists' statement that a termite digests wood by the aid of certain micro-organisms which enter its body from without."

And though I don't quite go along with "such an amusing sally" as Richard Dawkin's *The Selfish Gene* (p. 298), I do believe that we haven't completed our step out of geocentricity until we realize in all its fullness the fact that we as persons don't own our bodies, with their biologic ways, but happen to be their tenants, while their genes are somehow scheming to survive, just "naturally" using the likes of us to help them on their way.

Our main and most human Duplicity is this: On the beginning end of our line, Nemerov spoke up on my side. Now, towards the ending end of the line (doubtless, at least as belated on his end then as he'll be on our way out), I cherish this opportunity to say hello-goodbye.

We are celebrating texts that have this advantage: They are "privileged" by their devotion to a field of speculation such that all readers can feel human and humane with, in a mood of relaxation. His concerns are the fruits of matters to do with cultural fruition, even at times (not often!) when the yield is sparse. His sense of an audience, in the best sense of the term, shows in his efforts always to write in his readers' behalf.

There is constant evidence of the felicitous fact that his psychic economy led him, in periods of poetic sloth, instead of temporarily falling apart, to tide himself over by the prosaic discipline of study. Thus in his memory bank he has had much interesting data for retrieval when the time came.

To the store of information he had collected by study, he added the learning one derives from teaching, reinforced with the kind of incentives implicit in his rule of thumb, "forms are there to be transformed." Whenever he settles on a subject, he surrounds it with a varied population of stories, ideas, images, and sentiments that, given the added qualities of interaction natural to terms, help him to keep bearing down from many angles, or perspectives. Under these conditions, combine his knowledge of the cultural situation in general with his special experience to do with the realm of literature, and things add up to considerable evenfulness.

All told, shopping about in the pages of this book, readers can profit by a quite pleasant way of keeping in intellectual trim.

KENNETH BURKE

Acknowledgments

"The Swaying Form: A Problem in Poetry" is reprinted with permission from the *Michigan Alumnus Quarterly Review* (Winter 1959).

"The Poet and the Copy-Writer: A Dialogue" is reprinted with permission from *The Nation*, November 10, 1956. Copyright 1956 by The Nation Associates, Inc.

"The Dream of Reason" is reprinted with permission from the alumnae bulletin of Bennington College, where the author was a member of the literature faculty from 1948–1966.

"The Poetry of Wallace Stevens" was first published in the *Sewanee Review* 65, 1 (Winter 1957). Copyright 1957 by the University of the South. Reprinted with permission of the editor.

"Everything, Preferably All at Once: Coming to Terms with Kenneth Burke" was first published in the *Sewanee Review* 79, 2 (Spring 1971). Copyright 1971 by the University of the South. Reprinted with permission of the editor.

"Figures of Thought" was first published in the *Sewanee Review* 83, 1 (Winter 1975). Copyright 1975 by the University of the South. Reprinted with permission of the editor.

"Randall Jarrell (A Myth about Poetry)" is reprinted with permission from the *Kenyon Review* (Fall 1969).

"Bottom's Dream: The Likeness of Poetry and Jokes" is reprinted with permission from the *Virginia Quarterly Review* (Autumn 1966).

"On Metaphor" is reprinted with permission from the *Virginia Quarterly Review* (Autumn 1969).

"Composition and Fate in the Short Novel" is reprinted from the *Graduate Journal* (Fall 1963).

"Themes and Methods in the Early Stories of Thomas Mann" is reprinted from the *Carleton Miscellany* 2 (Winter 1961).

"Thomas Mann's Faust Novel" is reprinted from the *Graduate Journal* (Fall 1960).

"Two Ways of the Imagination: Blake & Wordsworth" is reprinted from the *Graduate Journal* (Spring 1967).

"The Dream of Dante" is reprinted from *Prose*.

"The Winter Addresses of Kenneth Burke" is reprinted with permission from *CCTE Proceedings* 39 (September 1974), 8–17. Conference of College Teachers of English of Texas.

"Some Minute Particulars" is reprinted with permission from the St. Louis *Post-Dispatch* Centennial Edition.

"Lewis Thomas, Montaigne, and Human Happiness" is reprinted with permission from *Washington University Magazine* (1981).

"On the Measure of Poetry" is reprinted with permission from *Critical Inquiry* 6 (Winter 1979), University of Chicago Press.

"It (Commencement Address at Bennington College)" is reprinted with permission from the *Bennington Review* (Summer 1966).

"The Other Vision" is reprinted from the *American Scholar*.

"Rainer Maria Rilke" is reprinted from the German Library series, Vol. 70, *Rainer Maria Rilke: Prose and Poetry* edited by Egon Schwarz. Reprinted with permission from the Continuum Publishing Corporation.

"An Interview with Howard Nemerov" is reprinted with permission from the *Massachusetts Review* (Spring 81).

The Swaying Form: A Problem in Poetry

The present essay is not an attempt to solve a problem so much as an attempt to make certain that a problem of some sort exists, and, if it does, to put it clearly before you. No matter how many problems really exist—and now, as at all times, there must be plenty of them—the world is always full of people inventing problems simply as make-works for their prefabricated solutions. As a friend of mine wrote in a prize-winning poem at college, "We know the answers, but shall we be asked the questions?" He has since become a novelist.

The problem I want to try to elucidate is most often discussed as one of belief, or of value, which is prior to poetry, and the great instance of Dante's *Comedy* stands at the gate of the discussion. It is usually argued on this basis that an explicit and systematized belief is (a) intrinsically of value to the poet in his composition and (b) a means for improving his communication with the mass of mankind.

Now I shall be taking up this theme by what many people will consider to be the wrong end, and talking from the point of view of the poet. My reflections are very far from being impartial and objective, and positively invite objections, or even cries of protest. I shall be suggesting, roughly, that the poet, if he has not attained to a belief in the existence of God, has at any rate got so far as to believe in the existence of the world; and that this, sadly but truly, puts him, in the art of believing, well out in front of many of his fellow-citizens, who sometimes look as if they believed the existence of the world to be pretty well encompassed in the sensations they experience when they read a copy of *Time*. (These, by the way, are the people who, adapting a metaphor of Aristotle's, think of poetry as a gentle laxative for the emotions.)

So when I hear discussions, or see symptoms, of some *rapprochement* between religion and the arts—A has written a passion play in modern dress, B has composed an atonal oratorio, C has done murals for the little church in the hometown which he left thirty years ago to become a not quite first-rate cubist with a world reputation—my response is not one of unmixed happiness, and I incline to see, in the characteristic imagery of this period, religion and the arts as two great corporations, each composed of many subsidiary companies but both in roughly the same line of business, circling each other warily in the contemplation of a merger, wondering meanwhile where the ultimate advantage will lie, and utterly unable to find out. To unfold a little this metaphor, I should say that in my view the persons seated around the conference table on this occasion are not the inventors of the product—not the prophets, saints, teachers, and great masters of art—but the usual vice-presidents, accountants, and lawyers on either side; the bishops and grand inquisitors, the critics and Epimethean pedagogues who arbitrate these matters.

In other words, between ourselves and any clear view of the problematic area lies the Plain of Shinar, where the usual construction work is going forward vigorously, and the serious planners exchange their watchwords: *culture, responsibility, values,* and *communication.* In this Babel, the word *religion* may mean "weekly attendance at the church of your choice," or it may mean the sort of thing that happened to Job—impossible to say. Similarly, the word *art* may be applied equally to the forty-eight preludes and fugues and to advertisements for whisky. That these things are so says nothing against either whisky or church attendance, but may be seriously damaging to art and religion.

Somewhere toward the beginning of things the two have a connection; as our somewhat frequently employed word *creative* will suggest. "Non merita il nome di creatore," said Tasso, "si non Iddio od il poeta." Clear enough: God and the poet alone deserve to be called creative, because they both create things. The recent history of this word is revealing: one reads, e.g., of "creative advertising," "creative packaging," and the possibility of becoming "a creative consumer." A dialect usage may be equally revealing: the mother says of her infant, "he is creating again," meaning either that the child is kicking up an awful fuss, or that he has soiled his diaper.

The relation of religion to more wordly activities is frequently characterized by extreme positions. To show what I hope I am not talking about,
I shall give an example of each. Here is the extreme whereby religion, in
seeking a connection with the world, becomes worldly itself:

SEES BOOM IN RELIGION, TOO

Atlantic City, June 23 (1957) AP —President Eisenhower's pastor said tonight
that Americans are living in a period of "unprecedented religious activity" caused
partially by paid vacations, the eight-hour day, and modern conveniences.

"These fruits of material progress," said the Rev. Edward L. R. Elson of the
National Presbyterian Church, Washington, "have provided the leisure, the energy,
and the means for a level of human and spiritual values never before reached."

Despite an air of farcical silliness which will accompany any display of
hubris which is at the same time unheroic, this statement—a kind of car-
toonist's exaggeration of what one suspects is the real belief of many right-
thinking persons—does fix the attention on a real question: whether it is
possible for a religious attitude to exist in the acceptance of prosperity,
and with its face set against suffering; a question near the heart of Christianity, and a question asked over and over, always to be answered negatively, in the Old Testament, where any statement that "the land had rest
for so and so many years" is certain to be followed by the refrain, "And
the children of Israel did evil *again* in the sight of the Lord, and served
Baalim and Ashtaroth. . . ."

The opposed extreme, wherein religion purifies itself quite out of the
world, may likewise be identified by anecdote. At a conference on Eliza-
bethan and seventeenth-century poetry, where a number of college students presented papers for discussion, the first three or four essays dealt
with the lyrics of such poets as Campion and Herrick; after which a most
serious young man arose, frowning, to say that his topic was George Herbert. He completed his impromptu introduction by saying, "We have heard
a good deal this morning on the subject of *Love*; well, now we must turn
our attention to an entirely different and more serious topic: *Religion*."
This inadvertence, I am sorry to say, seemed to me the revelation of something sad and true in attitudes bearing the official institutional name of
religious attitudes. We might compare a remark of Yeats, that only two
subjects are of interest to a serious intelligence: sex and the dead.

But our problem may be as easily obscured from the other side, the
side which professes to be that of art, as from the side of religion. If we

look to that great arena of the war of words where there are no poems but only Poetry, no paintings but only Art, we find statements of similar monolithic simplicity, which affect to find nothing problematic in the matter at all.

In that arena, for example, a well-known literary journalist has written (*New York Times book review*, May 3, 1959): "What the arts, literature included, need more than anything else just now, is a declaration of faith—faith in man's potentialities, faith in God, however you may conceive Him."

As a citizen, I may incline to accept the vague benevolence of all this. But as a practitioner of the art of writing, I am bored and disturbed by this sort of loose talk; just as I should probably be, were I a member of some religious community, by the pseudo-liberality of that casual rider to the idea of God—"however you may conceive Him." Again we might compare the view of an artist, in the saying of Joseph Conrad that it is the object of art to render the highest kind of justice to the *visible world*: "It is above all, in the first place, to make you see."

By such exclusions I come to some definition of my theme: the elucidation of what things may be called religious in poetical works and in the professional attitude of the artist to the making of such works.

Even in this somewhat narrower definition, the problem is not easy to focus. I shall be trying to say that the artist's relation to spiritual and eternal things is comprised rather in the form of his work than in its message or its content; but that form is itself somewhat elusive, as I have indicated in titling these reflections "The Swaying Form" after the following passage in Florio's translation of Montaigne: "There is no man (if he listen to himselfe) that doth not discover in himselfe a peculiar forme of his, a swaying forme, which wrestleth against the art * and the institution, and against the tempest of passions, which are contrary unto him."

Florio's somewhat dreamlike English duplicates nicely the possibilities of Montaigne's phrase, "une forme maistresse." The form, that is, is simultaneously ruling and very variable, or fickle; shifting and protean as the form of water in a stream, where it is difficult or impossible to divide what remains from what runs away. The passage, read in this way speaks of something in us which is double in nature, on both sides of things at once or by turns. And I would identify this "forme" with the impulse to art, the energy or libido which makes works of art. It is no paradox to say that the artistic impulse fights against "the art," for anyone who persists in this

---

*The phrase about "the art" is not included in all editions.

business knows that a part of his struggle is precisely against "the art," that is, against the accepted and settled standards of art in his time.

So this "forme" has the following characteristics. It is (1) allied with religion, for it is against "the tempest of passions" and thus in favor of control, discipline, *askesis*, renunciation. But it is (2) opposed to religion, for it is also against "the institution," that is, against church, state, dogma, or any fixed habit of the mind. Finally, it is (3) against something in its own nature, called "the art," against, perhaps, the idea of form itself.

For a curious tension exists between poetry and belief, idea, principle, or reason. That is, while we hear a good deal about poetry's need to be based upon an explicit view of the meaning of existence, we are very often bored and exasperated by the poetry which testifies to such a view, and incline to say that it is bad poetry precisely in the degree that the poet has insisted on referring the natural world to prior religious or philosophic valuations.

Perhaps it will be illuminating now if I try to sum up the swaying form, this complicated condition of the mind, by imagining a poet at his table in the morning. He faces the blank page, the page faces his mind—which, if it is not also a blank, is a palimpsest on which fractions of world, which he receives chiefly through language, are continually being recorded and erased and coming into strange, dissolving relations to one another; these are, for the most part, not the consequential relations of thought, but rather insanely atomic instead.

To be piously in keeping with the values of the age, I imagine this poet as asking himself, "What can I afford this morning?" And going on to consider the possibilities, or impossibilities: A little *saeva indignatio*? Something smart and severe in a toga? A romantic pathos, or pathology, with wild glances *de chez* Hölderlin? The dewy freshness of an early lyricism, say about the period of Skelton and really, after all, noncommittal? And so on, since the alternatives are very numerous.

There is only one, however, which now arises to give him trouble: "How about me? Shall I be me? And who is that?" He looks doubtfully at his tweeds, his grey flannels, stares at his alert (but modern, but rootless) face in the mirror, and tries to view that crew-cut in quick succession as a Franciscan tonsure, an Augustan wig, a Romantic disorder. No good. He would like to be himself, but acknowledges that himself is poetically not what most interests him, nor what is likely to interest others very much. Sighing, he wonders if poetry, if all great effort in the world, does not involve a necessary hypocrisy (even if one calls it, more politely, not hypocrisy but drama or metaphor, a necessary approach by analogy), and now he gratefully recalls having read somewhere (it was in Castiglione, but he likes the elegant indolence of "somewhere") that Julius Caesar wore a laurel crown to disguise the fact that he was bald. Encouraged a little, he jots down a note reducing to iambic pentameter mighty Caesar— "Who hid his baldness in a laurel crown"—and adds, in prose: "Poets do this, too." Comforted, he occupies the rest of the morning contemplating the publication of a small volume of epigrams on this theme. But come lunchtime, his wife having uncanned a can of alphabet soup which seems to him the image of his condition, the problem remains: Hypocrisy. Seeming, Angelo, seeming. The truest poetry is the most feigning. But is it, really? And how shall we edify the common reader this afternoon? By being Plato? Moody and Sankey? The Pope? Alexander Pope? How shall we solve the problems of society? Affirm the eternal verities? Become rich and famous and sought-after for our opinions (the filing cabinet is full of them) on all sorts of important themes?

No, this will never do. Hypocrisy merges with cynicism. Where is that portrait of Keats?

And so the weary circle begins again. Only once in a while it opens, as something comes into his head and he suddenly commits a poem. At that time, curiously, he does not worry in the least about whether this poem faithfully represents himself, his beliefs, values, tensions, or the absence of all these. He simply writes the poem.

By this ordinary anguish, occasionally relieved in action, a great deal of literature, both good and bad, gets itself produced.

The troubles of this hypothetical or generalized poet will perhaps strike some of you as very literary, overeducated, or even positively neurasthenic, and you may be inclined to say impatiently to him, "Fool, look in thy heart and write," not caring to consider that when Sir Philip Sidney made this excellent recommendation, he was speaking, just like our poet, to himself. And, too, such is the confusion over these things, instructions to look in one's heart and write may turn out translated for practical purposes in weird ways, e.g.: "Look in thy heart and be big, free, and sloppy, like Whitman, who is now becoming fashionable again." There is no end, except for that poem once in a while, to the poet's ability at perverting sound doctrine.

If the foregoing description is even partly applicable to the poetic process, it will be plain that the world will wait a long time for "a declaration of faith" in the poems of this poet. It may also be a consequence of his problem with his identity that a good deal of modern poetry is poetry about the problem, poetry that reveals to interpretation one reflexive dimension having to do with the process of composition itself. This development, where the mind curves back upon itself, may be always a limit, not only for poetry but for every kind of thought, for that "speculation" which Shakespeare says "turns not to itself / Till it hath travell'd, and is mirror'd there / Where it may see itself," adding that "This is not strange at all." But perhaps it has become more strange in the present age, that palace of mirrors where, says Valéry, the lonely lamp is multiplied, or where, as Eliot says, we multiply variety in a wilderness of mirrors, and where the "breakthrough," so pathetically and often discussed in relation to all contemporary arts, is most faithfully imagined in Alice's adventure through the looking-glass, the last consequence of narcissism and "incest of spirit" (Allen Tate, "Last Days of Alice") being the explosion into absurdity, very frequently followed by silence.

Silence, alas, may be preferable to the demand of "educators" that the poet should affirm something (anything?) or the often iterated instruction of certain literary persons that he should *communicate* (what?). But silence, for anyone who has set out to be a poet, is an unlovely alternative, containing in itself some religious (that is, some sinful) implication of being too good for this world, so that many poets accept the disabilities of their elected condition by making many small refusals to prevent one great one. The vanities of publication, these seem to say, are better than the silences of pride. And so, for them, the weary round begins again after every poem, as they seek over and over an image of their being: hermit crabs, crawling unprotected from one deserted shell to the next, finding each time a temporary home which, though by no means a perfect fit, is better at any rate than their nakedness.

It is gratuitous, or even impertinent after all this, and surely offers no defense, to say that they sometimes write good poems in their planetary course from house to house. What can we possibly mean, now, by *a good poem*? Let that be another circle, in another hell. While the present purpose is to say something about the process itself, the kind of relation with the world which results in poetic writings and is an attempt to fix for a moment the swaying form.

When people are impatient with a work of art, they assert their feeling in this way: "What does it mean?" Their tone of voice indicates that this is the most natural question in the world, the demand which they have the most immediate and God-given right to make. So their absolute condemnation and dismissal of a work of art is given in this way: "It doesn't mean anything. It doesn't mean anything to *me*." Only in those plaintive last words does there appear a tiny and scarcely acknowledged doubt of the all-sufficiency of this idea of meaning—that there may actually be meanings, which one does not personally possess.

Now we are all forced to believe about large areas of the world's work that this is so: that all around us physicists, financiers, and pharmacists are conducting complex operations which do have meaning though we do not know what it is. While we may occasionally wonder if those emperors are in fact wearing any clothes, we more usually allow that our bewilderment belongs to ourselves and does not say anything destructive about those disciplines in themselves, even where they do not produce any overwhelmingly obvious practical result such as an atomic explosion. But about works of art we continue to ask that question, "What do they mean?" and regard the answer to it as somehow crucial.

In a realm of contemplation, the question about meaning could, though it generally does not, begin a chain reaction involving the whole universe, since the answer can be given only in terms to which the same question is again applicable. But because we are well-mannered people, or because we haven't the time, or really don't care, or because we are in fact reassured and consoled by receiving an answer—any answer—we know where to stop. So that a large part of our intellectual operations takes inevitably the following form:

A. Why is the grass green?
B. Because of the chlorophyll.
A. Oh.*

So, in a realm of contemplation, meaning would itself be inexplicable. The typewriters rattle, the telephones ring, the moving finger keeps writing one triviality after another, the great gabble of the world goes incessantly on as people translate, encipher, decipher, as one set of words is transformed more or less symmetrically into another set of words—whereupon someone says, "O, now I understand. . . ."

*That is a made-up example, but here is one from actual play, as Fingarette, writing on "The Ego and Mystic Selflessness" (in *Identity and Anxiety: Survival of the Person in Mass Society*, p. 572), quotes a Chinese mystic as saying: "When neither hatred nor love disturb the mind,/Serene and restful is our sleep," and comments: "While this is surely not meant simply in a literal way, we know from Freud that the literal meaning of the image is perfectly apt. Provided one interprets 'hatred' and 'love' as unsublimated aggressive and libidinal instinctual drives, one hardly needs to change a word to consider the verse as a basic psychological truth."

But the question about meaning attests, wherever it is asked, the presence of civilization with all its possibilities, all its limitations; attests the presence of *language*, that vast echoing rattle and sibilance buzzing between ourselves and whatever it is we presume we are looking at, experiencing, being in, and which sometimes appears to have an independent value, if any at all, like the machine someone built a few years back, which had thousands of moving parts and no function. The semanticist to the contrary, words are things, though not always the things they say they are. The painter Delacroix expressed it by saying that Nature is a dictionary. Everything is there, but not in the order one needs. The universe itself, so far as we relate ourselves to it by the mind, may be not so much a meaning as a rhythm, a continuous articulation of question and answer, question and answer, a musical dialectic precipitating out moments of meaning which become distinct only as one wave does in a sea of waves. "You think you live under universal principles," said Montaigne, "but in fact they are municipal bylaws."

Language, then, is the marvelous mirror of the human condition, a mirror so miraculous that it can see what is invisible, that is, the relations between things. At the same time, the mirror is a limit, and as such, it is sorrowful; one wants to break it and look beyond. But unless we have the singular talent for mystical experience we do not really break the mirror, and even the mystic's experience is available to us only as reflected, inadequately, in the mirror. Most often man deals with reality by its reflection. That is the sense of Perseus' victory over the Gorgon by consenting to see her only in the mirror of his shield, and it is the sense of the saying in Corinthians that we see now as through a glass darkly—a phrase rendered by modern translators as "now we see as in a little mirror."

Civilization, mirrored in language, is the garden where relations grow; outside the garden is the wild abyss. Poetry, an art of fictions, illusions, even lies—"Homer," said Aristotle, "first taught us the art of framing lies in the right way"—poetry is the art of contemplating this situation in the mirror of language.

"Only connect ⋮ . . ." is the civilized and civilizing motto of a book by E. M. Forster, wherein he speaks eloquently of meaning, art, and order in "the world of telegrams and anger," and of what exists outside that world: "panic and emptiness, panic and emptiness." W. H. Auden, also very eloquently, writes of the limiting extremes within which meaning means, between "the ocean flats where no subscription concerts are given" and "the desert plain where there is nothing for lunch."

But meaning, like religion, seeks of its own nature to monopolize experience. For example, in children's playbooks there are numbered dots to be followed in sequence by the pencil; the line so produced finally becomes recognizable as a shape. So the lines produced among stars (which can scarcely all be in the same plane) become the geometrical abstractions of a Bear, a Wagon, Orion the Hunter; and by softening or humanizing the outlines, recognizable images are produced, but in the process the stars themselves have to be omitted. So does meaning at first simplify and afterward supersede the world. Poetry, I would say, is, in its highest ranges, no mere playing with the counters of meaning, but a perpetual rederiving of the possibility of meaning from matter, of the intelligible world from the brute recalcitrance of things. Poetry differs from thought in this respect, that thought eats up the language in which it thinks. Thought is proud, and always wants to forget its humble origin in things. In doing so, it begins to speak by means of very elevated abstractions, which quickly become emptied and impoverished. The business of poetry is to bring thought back into relation with the five wits, the five senses which Blake calls "the chief inlets of soul in this age," to show how our discontents, as Shakespeare finely says of Timon's, "are unremovably coupled to nature." So the ivory tower must always be cut from the horn of Behemoth.

The relation of poetry to religion is both intimate and antithetical, for poetry exists only by a continuing revelation in a world always incarnate of word and flesh indissolubly, a world simultaneously solid and transpicuous. At the same time, religion can never really dissociate itself from poetry and the continuing revelation; and its attempts to do so turn it into a form of literary criticism, as the scriptures and sacred books of the world, in comparison with their interminable commentaries, will sufficiently show. Poetry and institutionalized religion are in a sense the flowing and the static forms of the same substance, liquid and solid states of the same elemental energy.

This is a simple thing; it has been said many times and forgotten many times plus one. William Blake says it this way:

The ancient Poets animated all sensible objects with Gods or Geniuses, calling them by the names and adorning them with the properties of woods, rivers, mountains, lakes, cities, nations, and whatever their enlarged and numerous senses could perceive.

And particularly they studied the Genius of each city and country, placing it under its Mental Deity;

Till a system was formed, which some took advantage of, and enslav'd the

vulgar by attempting to realise or abstract the Mental Deities from their objects—
thus began Priesthood;

Choosing forms of worship from poetic tales.

And at length they pronounc'd that the Gods had order'd such things. Thus
men forgot that All Deities reside in the Human Breast.

The poet's business, I would say, is to name as accurately as possible a
situation, but a situation which he himself is in. The name he gives ought
to be so close a fit with the actuality it summons into being that there
remains no room between inside and outside; the thought must be "like
a beast moving in its skin" (Dante). If he does his work properly, there
won't be any other name for the situation (and for his being in it) than the
one he invents, or, rather, his name will swallow up all the others as Aar-
on's rod swallowed up the rods of Pharaoh's wizards.

Sometimes the name so given is a relatively simple one, as when Alexander Pope gave the Prince of Wales a dog, and had inscribed on its
collar

> I am his Highness' dog at Kew.
> Pray tell me, sir, whose dog are you?

And sometimes the name so given, the situation thus identified and brought
into being, is immensely complex, so that one has to refer to it by a tag,
an abbreviation, e.g., "King Lear."

A poem, whether of two lines or ten thousand, is therefore the name
of something, and in its ideal realm of fiction or illusion it corresponds to
what is said of the Divine Name in several significant respects:

> *It is unique.*
> *It can never be repeated.*
> *It brings into being the situation it names, and is therefore truly a creation.*
> *It is secret, even while being perfectly open and public, for it defines a thing
> which could not have been known without it.*

As to the poet himself, one might add this. Writing is a species of *askesis*, a persevering devotion to the energy passing between self and world.
It is a way of living, a way of being, and though it does produce results in
the form of works, these may come to seem of secondary importance to
the person so engaged.

The young writer is always told (he was, anyhow, when I was young) that writing means first and last "having something to say." I cherish as a souvenir of boyhood that honorable and aged platitude, but would like to modify it by this addition: Writing means trying to find out what the nature of things has to say about what you think you have to say. And the process is reflective or cyclical, a matter of feedback between oneself and "it," an "it" which can gain its identity only in the course of being brought into being, come into being only in the course of finding its identity. This is a matter, as Lu Chi says, of how to hold the axe while you are cutting its handle.

I say that writing is a species of *askesis*. But as it works in an ideal or fictional, rather than in a practical, realm, so it purifies not the character but the style. There is, however, a connection between the two, at least in the hope that a charity of the imagination shall be not quite the same thing as an imaginary charity.

That, then, is what I have tried to characterize as "the swaying form," a process of becoming related to nature and the nature of things (*natura naturata* and *natura naturans*). The view here taken suggests that art has some evident affinities with both religion and science on the very simple basis that all three exist in the presumption that the truth is possible to be told about existence; but these affinities themselves also define differences, distances, and intrinsic antagonisms.

As to art's relation with science. The experimental method was defined, by Galileo, I believe, as putting nature to the question, where "the question" meant the judicial process of torture. The definition seems to imply a faith that nature, so treated, will reveal the secret name for a situation; when once that situation has been isolated, treated as a situation in itself, and considered for a moment apart from the flux of all things, nature will, as it were, confess her presumably guilty secret.

Well, the artist, it seems to me, works on a not so different principle, leading from hypothesis—"what will happen to this noble nature if it can be led to believe Desdemona unfaithful?"—through experiment—the question as put by Iago—to result, to "the tragic loading of this bed." In this sense, and not in the fashionable popular sense, art is "experimental," and its methods to a certain extent resemble those of the laboratory; art, too, produces its process under controlled and limiting conditions, cutting away irrelevancies, speeding up or slowing down the reaction under study, so that the results, whatever they may be, will stand forth with a singular purity and distinction. The instruments of science, of course, have as their aim the creation of an objectivity as nearly as possible universal in character; the poet's aim might be thought of as the same and reversed, a mirror image—to represent in the world the movement of a subjectivity as nearly as possible universal in character.

And art is akin to religion, if we will be nondenominational about it, in that the work (though not, perhaps, the artist, oddly enough) is driven by its own composition to the implication of invisible things inherent in visible ones. The subject, the content, of the art work is sorrowful, because life is sorrowful; but the work itself, by the nature of its form, dances. A beautiful passage from Proust's novel will be relevant here. Marcel is thinking of the writer Bergotte, who died of a stroke while contemplating a detail, a piece of yellow wall, in a painting by Vermeer:

> He was dead. Forever? Who can say? After all, occult experiences demonstrate no more than the dogmas of religion do about the soul's continuance. But what can be said is this, that we live our life as though we had entered it under the burden of obligations already assumed in another; there is, in the conditions of our life here, no reason which should make us believe ourselves obliged to do good, to be fastidious or even polite, nor which should make the godless painter believe himself obliged to start over twenty times a detail the praise of which will matter very little to his body eaten by worms—a detail such as the section of yellow wall painted with such skill and taste by an artist forever unknown and scarce identified under the name of Vermeer. All such obligations, which have no sanction in our present life, seem to belong to a different world based on goodness, consideration and sacrifice, a world altogether different from this one, and from which we emerge to be born on this earth, before perhaps returning there to live under the rule of those unknown laws which we have obeyed because we carry their teaching within us though unaware who traced it there—those laws to which every profound work of the intelligence tends to reconcile us, and which are invisible only—and forever!—to fools.

So the work of art is religious in nature, not because it beautifies an ugly world or pretends that a naughty world is a nice one—for these things especially art does not do—but because it shows of its own nature that things drawn within the sacred circle of its forms are transfigured, illuminated by an inward radiance which amounts to goodness because it amounts to Being itself. In the life conferred by art, Iago and Desdemona, Edmund and Cordelia, the damned and the blessed, equally achieve immortality by their relation with the creating intelligence which sustains them. The art work is not responsible for saying that things in reality are so, but rather for revealing what this world says to candid vision. It is thus that we delight in tragedies whose actions in life would merely appall us. And it is thus that art, by its illusions, achieves a human analogy to the resolution of that famous question of theodicy—the relation of an Omnipotent Benevolence to evil—which the theologians, bound to the fixed forms of things, have for centuries struggled with, intemperately and in vain. And it is thus that art, by vision and not by dogma, patiently and repeatedly offers the substance of things hoped for, the evidence of things unseen.

The Poet and the Copy-Writer: A Dialogue

OSRIC, a poet
OSWALD, an advertising man

OSRIC: My hair is falling out, and no one reads my poems.

OSWALD: My liver is bad, and everyone reads my ads.

OSRIC: Alas, I am marginal to the economy.

OSWALD: Alas, I am central to the economy.

OSRIC: Of course, you had to sell your soul.

OSWALD: And you were unable to sell yours; perhaps I could write you an ad? Soul, used but in fair condition, one owner, careful treatment, radio and heater. . . .

OSRIC: . . . spine damaged and binding slightly foxed. I know, I know. Lost, one bard. Small reward. Sentimental value. Or else. . . .

OSWALD: I can see you'd enjoy writing ads once you began. And I'd like to write poems, too, if only they had something definite to sell in them, instead of just truth and beauty, beauty and truth.

OSRIC: The idea that poems consist of beauty and truth is a common fallacy which Criticism has dispelled. You are still, perhaps, in the nineteenth century.

OSWALD: You mean that your poems have neither beauty nor truth?

OSRIC: Oh, well, if you want to make it a personal matter . . . I suppose they do, somewhat.

OSWALD: But you can't sell beauty and truth, either because they're free and everyone has all he needs of them, or because no one can afford them any more at all. With soap and gas and brassières, though, you know where you are. It concentrates the language.

OSRIC: It does *not* concentrate the language. I think your ads are getting more obscure every day, and if it weren't for the manufacturer's name at the bottom I wouldn't know whether you were discussing soap flakes or democracy.

OSWALD: Well, you know, we do like to put one in terms of the other.

OSRIC: In terms of, in terms of. If I hear that stupid phrase again I'll scream. Everyone uses it now. I heard a fashionable young woman say the other day, "I choose my lipstick in terms of my complexion."

OSWALD: Well, you know, it sounds kind of scientific, and everyone likes that.

OSRIC: It sounds poetical—dirty rotten poetical.

OSWALD: Why do you call yourself a poet if you hate whatever is poetical?

OSRIC: Because whatever is poetical, baby, belongs to you. If you keep telling women that without underarm perspiration they will immediately resemble Venus by Botticelli, then I must give up Venus by Botticelli.

OSWALD: But in exchange you get underarm perspiration.

OSRIC: Yes . . . yes, there's a subject you haven't ruined: sweat, shame, secrecy, hypocrisy. . . .

OSWALD: Go on, you might exude an ode.

OSRIC: Armpits! The smoky armpits of the world.

OSWALD: Yes, I envy you your freedom to deal with the seamy side of life. But it makes you rather coarse in your rhetoric, where we should be delicate.

OSRIC: Yah, your delicacy. Sneaky minginess. But you have hit on a real point there: freedom. Poets may be poor, but they are free. A copy-writer is nothing but a slave.

OSWALD: Ah, yes, that precious freedom. Vergil's freedom to laud Augustus, Tennyson's freedom to admire railroads, Dryden's freedom to adore the smallpox sores on Lord Hastings' chin.

OSRIC: There may have been abuses.

OSWALD: Then never mind the abuses. What about the Great Tradition itself—the centuries of edifying, instructing, bringing virtue out on top, purveying manners and morals to the great unwashed masses? What about "purifying the language of the tribe"? I may be a servile copy-writer, but I think it more honorable to sell people soap than to sell them Cleanliness.

OSRIC: How could you sell them soap if we hadn't sold them cleanliness for all those centuries?

OSWALD: So, you admit we're in the same business!

OSRIC: Nonsense. You deal in Things, material commodities, whereas I deal in spiritual values.

OSWALD: Meaning that you insist on Cleanliness without providing soap?

OSRIC: Yes, dammit, I do. Spiritual cleanliness.

OSWALD: With spiritual soap? Soft soap. As a matter of fact, though, it is the poets who are always talking about Things, and the advertisers who deal in spiritual values. "Roses have thorns, and silver fountains mud." Look at all the Things in one quite ordinary line of poetry. We advertisers, of course, would want to dress the whole proposition up a bit: "You wouldn't dream of having mud in your silver fountain—why have thorns on your roses?"

OSRIC: And there in your other hand, all the while, would be a new, patent rose-depilatory.

OSWALD: Quite likely there would. And what would be wrong with thornless roses?

OSRIC: Everything. The morality of the Western world has depended for centuries on the fact that roses have thorns.

OSWALD: And look at the shape the Western world is in now. No, my friend, I tell you—in confidence—that you poets have had your chance and you're through. The future of poetry, I'm afraid, is with advertising.

OSRIC: That's perhaps the funniest thing I've ever heard said. If it weren't, I'd put my head in the oven.

OSWALD: You'll want to try one of our new, fully automatic, self-regulating ovens. You can leave your head in it while you go out, and when you return. . . . Seriously, though, you're through. Poetry is done for, and advertising is the only hope.

OSRIC: But quite apart from one million other possible objections, your advertisements are so terribly dull.

OSWALD: I agree, I agree—though if it comes to that what about *The Faërie Queene*? But ever so many people seem to disagree. At least, they read advertisements every day and practically never read poetry. That's true even of some poets I know, but never mind that just now. The point is, that in almost any magazine you look at the advertisements take far more space than the stories, poems, articles, editorials—than all the stuff we may broadly call Poetry. Not only that, but the advertisements—dull as they are, and I agree they are dull—are frequently more interesting than the poetry.

OSRIC: Yah, it's because they have pictures.

OSWALD: It *is not* because they have pictures. If you weren't prejudiced, you'd allow that the pictures are, if anything, worse than the prose.

OSRIC: I see you call it prose, not poetry.

OSWALD: A feeble defense. Is poetry like *Moby-Dick* and *Urn Burial*? Or is it more like the nearest available sonnet by a lady with three names?

OSRIC: I concede the point.

OSWALD: Then if you'll be quiet for a minute or so, I'll try to explain the present position as we in advertising understand it.

OSRIC: Very well, go ahead.

OSWALD: Now formerly, until not so long ago, buying and selling, and everything we mean by *business*, were considered not to be occupations for a gentleman; they were reprehensible, necessary but suspect, and all the better people pretended that such things didn't happen at all. The reason for this, we find when we go back to the tradition, was that the gentleman's occupations had always been conceived of simply as love and war. Poetry, too, for this reason, and because it was read largely by gentlemen, concerned itself with love and war. And what happened then?

OSRIC: You're telling me, I'm not telling you. Go on.

OSWALD: Buying and selling, because they were necessary, finally became gentlemanly, until now, at the present time, it is believed that these precisely, and especially if conducted on a very grand scale, are fit occupations for a gentleman—if only because a gentleman must have money, and there is practically no other way of ensuring a steady supply. So buying and selling have become respectable, and, more important than that, they are rapidly becoming total, and soon, if the present trend continues (which it will), they will become absolutely the form of morality.

OSRIC: And what a morality. I spit.

OSWALD: That is a very poetical attitude you take. And I observe that, like a true poet, you say "I spit" but you don't spit; a world of significance there. And poetry, indeed, was the last human discipline to be left standing helplessly on the untenable platform which the gentleman himself had deserted a long time before. Poetry was still dreaming of its magical kings and gentle heroes while the real gentleman, having seen the shape of things to come, was out in the marketplace buying and selling as fast as he could.

OSRIC: But things have always been that way. You are deluded with the delusion of those *esprits simplistes* who fancy that Elizabeth and Essex, Drake and Hawkins, habitually talked iambic pentameter and sounded like Desdemona and Macbeth. But I'm willing to skip that if you'll only stop your half-baked theorizing about history and come to the point: what about advertising?

OSWALD: For all practical purposes you could put it this way: that the gentleman, who were accustomed to having poets celebrate their doings, simply hired a new lot of poets when they saw that the old poets wouldn't celebrate. The new poets were pretty awful; not only were they untrained and without competence in a difficult art, but also they were set to work inventing a new kind of poetry to suit the age, since the real poets had refused to bother with the age. As to what you say about history, I'll admit, of course, that the thing didn't happen in the way I have described, being a process largely unconscious and a response to more immediate pressures; but in effect, as we can see now, it might as well have happened that way, since there now exists a new class of poets writing a new kind of poetry called advertising. They are doing it on the whole very badly still, I admit that, but getting better, getting better.

OSRIC: Ingenious enough, and interesting. But how can you "get better" at selling, say, cigarettes? Doesn't the product, in its ineffable dreariness, impose a very low ceiling on your lyrical flights?

OSWALD: I may remind you here that you and your critical colleagues have been telling us for years that subject is of no importance, while imagination is everything. Granted imagination enough, a fine poem may be produced upon a trivial or disgusting subject—isn't that how the old critical song has been going? At any rate, your belief about the true nature of advertising is quite as naïve as my belief that poetry has something to do with the true and the beautiful. Do you seriously still believe that advertising is primarily interested in *selling things*?

OSRIC: I had heard it mentioned now and again.

OSWALD: It is a vulgar error of the age. The kind of advertising you must mean still exists, of course, in great quantities—people selling one another souvenir salt shakers, bronzed baby shoes, rupture appliances, holy water in plastic tears, and so on up the line to liqueurs and luggage and limousines. But that is advertising directed at the consumer, and compares with real advertising as limericks do with iliads. Major modern advertising, like your major modern poetry, goes right over the heads of the private consumers to begin with, and straight to the elite. How many readers of a news magazine, for instance, are really listening when the ball-bearing manufacturer spreads over a full page his delicate mating call to the maker of aircraft? Of those who hear, how many understand? Of those who understand, how many are in a position to do anything with what they understand? Or when a utilities company expounds for two whole pages the strong and subtle bond of metaphor that connects utilities with democracy, what has that to do with your private citizen? No, such advertisements are as privileged as private correspondence, as secure as messages in cipher, as haughty in their doings as any poetry.

OSRIC: But still selling things, really, aren't they?

OSWALD: You're still not althogether clear about the vast differences separating major and revolutionary advertising from the rest. You're still thinking about mere material commodities—it doesn't matter whether they are corsets or rocket planes—while I want you to lift up your mind to spiritual things, that is, to the Way of Life, the Truth and Beauty which make buying and selling possible. For example, we used to sell refrigerators; but now we have realized that if we sell the Way of Life, refrigerators will follow in great plenty—and I will go further than that. . . .

OSRIC: I am afraid you will.

OSWALD: Please treat this as a confidence, will you? What I am about to describe has not yet come to pass. Presently, you see, we shall have double-crossed the manufacturers along with everyone else.

OSRIC: We?

OSWALD: We of the advertising world. They thought they were making use of us, did all those small-minded *practical* men, when all the while we were making use of them, trying our wings until we should be ready to fly away. Who will care, then, if they never sell another refrigerator? Advertising, which began as practical magic, now becomes spiritual and contemplative, autonomous magic, having its end in itself, just as poetry, which you will agree began as practical magic, with curses and charms and casting of spells, at last became spiritual and contemplative and by definition impractical, and turned inward upon itself. Advertising has mirrored itself long enough in the material world of commerce and production, and now begins to turn inward to contemplation—

OSRIC: Staring at its own soft center.

OSWALD: Go on, laugh while you yet may. But the thing is clearly happening. I foresee the time—for advertising men, you see, are vaticinators now, just as poets used to be said to be—I foresee the time, not far in the future, when advertisement will have driven all editorial content from magazine and newspaper. As various heavy industries combine, and as all heavy industry combines with government, all human relations will be expressible as buying and selling—

OSRIC: But I thought you said . . . ?

OSWALD: There's no contradiction. When all human relations are expressible in market values, as buying and selling, there will be no need to talk about buying and selling, since that language will look as natural then as the language of traditional morality does now—that is what I meant when I said that buying and selling would become the very form of morality. In the same way, when advertising becomes the total content of human communication, as you will allow it is very near to doing already, there will be no need to use the somewhat pejorative word "advertising," since this activity need no longer be defined against other modes of speech, which simply will have ceased to exist. Moreover, on account of the very complex coordination of interests as between industries themselves on the one hand, and industry and political power and armed force and education on the other, the advertising writer will develop a much greater freedom in his point of view, simply because everything will be, to the ordinary reader, so dreadfully mixed up.

OSRIC: Quite as usual, in other words. You claim to be describing the future, but as you speak I keep seeing the present. What about this "ordinary reader," by the way—the people, as distinct from those who are so mighty in the buying and selling which you define as the essence of society to come?

OSWALD: The people? I hate to say it, because I'm as good an American as yourself, but I imagine some conditions of light and not very unpleasant servitude will be found for the people. They must, of course, continue to buy and sell, and as they are for the most part already convinced that in buying and selling consists the true meaning of earthly life, I imagine they will have little hardship in adjusting to the last turns of the vise. And their priests, as usual, will assist them in the perception that it is all somehow right and necessary. Their God has been made over in the image of a great businessman; well, now He will become a great advertising man.

OSRIC: In the end will be the Word, is that it?

OSWALD: Very poetically and aptly put.

OSRIC: You make it very clear. As the private interest covers the public interest, as the line between advertising and propaganda becomes indistinct, and both discover ever more *recherché* ways of skinning their cats, advertising will become, for one thing, less imperative and more simply declarative, less urgent and more leisured, less hortatory and more contemplative.

OSWALD: Like poetry.

OSRIC: Yes, and I think I see further than that. There will develop an advertising class, or caste, with hereditary succession, as distinct as the class of scribes in ancient Egypt or China, and this class will have altogether in its hands the composition of odes describing, in a highly specialized way, the mysterious connections on which subsists the mystical body of society: the sinews of metaphor uniting, for example, the university with the debutante with the railroad with contraception with the concrete mixer with high tariffs with race prejudice with universities with debutantes. . . .

OSWALD: Stop, you are being carried away. But yes, that is more or less the way it will work out, though I suppose we shall not live to see it.

OSRIC: Being a vaticinator in my turn, and one, moreover, who is only wise after the event, I will tell you that we are already seeing it. Of course, even when your victory is complete, your stuff will always be deficient as poetry because it will have no real—that is, unsubsidized—acknowledgment of evil. But that will not be noticed, because all genuine poetry will by that time have disappeared.

OSWALD: Ah, you *genuine* poets are proud. On that day, your heads will be the first to fall.

OSRIC: Our heads will have shriveled long before that day comes.

OSWALD: If you would abandon your pride and save yourself, I might be able to find an opening for you with us. We can always use a man who has your skill with words. And you could write your poetry on the side, evenings and week ends.

OSRIC: Thank you ever so much. But really, and it's no matter of pride. I can't believe I'd be talented enough for your kind of work.

OSWALD: Oh, we'd start you off in a small way, of course. But after an apprenticeship on frozen foods and sanitary napkins—what we in the trade think of as the hot-point and cold-spot of it—you'd go quickly up the ladder, I'm sure of it, a man of your brilliance and sincerity and warmth of feeling. It's only a matter of learning to apply those fine human qualities to new objects. After all, as one of your own poets said at the very beginning of his career, "Words alone are certain good." And at the end of that career he also said, speaking directly to poets, "Sing whatever is well made." Cigarettes these days are very well made.

OSRIC: For a man in your line of work, you seem to know an awful lot of poetry.

OSWALD: Ah, my dear man, that is my little secret. I was one of you once, but that is a long time ago. "Who would not sing for Lycidas? he knew / Himself to sing and build the lofty rhyme." Except I didn't, really, or not very well. But I'm certain you'd like it very well with us, we're not at all the vulgar, uncultivated boors that legend makes us out to be; most of the finest minds in the business belong to men who, like myself, started out to be poets. And, of course, as our work has so much to do with truth and beauty, we keep ourselves in shape by much reading, and visits to art galleries.

OSRIC: Sounds a very gloomy life to me. Art galleries remind me of undertakers' parlors, and I very rarely read books. When I hear the word "culture," I take a drink and the feeling passes.

OSWALD: You know, I still write a little from time to time, though I don't like to mention it around the office. I was wondering if maybe you might look over some of my stuff some day, and tell me if you think it's good enough.

OSRIC: Good enough for what?

OSWALD: To publish, I guess, what else?

OSRIC: But I'm not a publisher.

OSWALD: No, you're a snob, that's what you are. You're sneering at my poems without even reading them.

OSRIC: I don't deny being a snob, even my mother used to tell me I was. It doesn't really matter. But I'm not trying to stop you from writing poems, am I? Whereas all that you were saying a while ago indicated that your activities would presently stop me from writing poems, which you seem to think a perfectly happy result. I'll tell you what, suppose instead of reading your poems I read your ads? Is that fair enough?

OSWALD: No, it's not. No wonder the world doesn't care for your verse, since you persist in that snide attitude of yours. Suppose just for the sake of argument that my poetry turns out to be absolutely wonderful, that I really have something to say to the world? What then?

OSRIC: I'm supposing as hard as I can. Why don't you say it, in that case? And I'll read your poems, if you care that much.

OSWALD: Don't imagine I'm afraid of any criticism you might make. After all, my poems are only a hobby, and not important, I am well aware of that.

OSRIC: Do you see that bird over there?

OSWALD: Certainly. It's only a robin.

OSRIC: Just so. And do you know that though it has been called a robin in English for so many centuries, that bird is so stupid it still doesn't know it is a robin?

OSWALD: What are you driving at?

OSRIC: That is the meaning of poetry.

OSWALD: You're only trying to puzzle me, you think it's a smart thing to do.

OSRIC: I will make my meaning clearer in a parable about poets and poetry, which I made up a long time ago, at a very bad time in my life when I thought that one ought not to do anything without having a clear idea of what it was for. This parable has sometimes comforted me in some odd manner, and perhaps it may do the same for you.

OSWALD: Come on, then, get to it.

OSRIC: It is a parable about the monkish medieval poet Caedmon. Caedmon, a stupid man by nature, became a poet by divine visitation in sleep; waking, he found he could remember quite well the verses to the glory of the Creator which he had been inspired to sing the night before, and he wrote them down. He spent the rest of his life versifying passages from Scripture, which others had translated for him—the Exodus from Egypt, the Passion of Christ, and so on. Now, concerning all these things, which the present taste does not even find very beautiful, scholars now believe, first, that they were not written by Caedmon; second, that nothing from his hand has come down to us, and third, that no such person, it may be, ever lived. What remains, then? Poets ought to consider it well. There remains only the voice in the night: "Caedmon . . . sing the beginning of created things."

OSWALD: I'll tell you what your trouble is. You not only don't communicate to an ordinary man like me, but you don't even want to communicate, that's your trouble, and so far as I'm concerned you can go die for it.

OSRIC: But there's more truth than poetry in that.

The Dream of Reason

M any people of more or less my age, having done their forty years in the wilderness and grown somewhat at home there, show signs of regret and even, occasionally, resentment about entering the promised land of science, that ambiguous utopia which is acceptable only as each day's tomorrow. We were much influenced in earlier years by Aldous Huxley's *Brave New World*, in which the proposition was (perhaps for the last time) seriously stated that Shakespeare was not merely preferable but also antithetical to planned parenthood; it was somewhere between our matriculation and our enlistment that the mad scientist came from the comic strip bearing his death rays, incendiary bats, and apocalyptic powders, and the world settled for a career in science fiction. I am being unjust to the scientists among us, but never mind; for the existence of people of my age proves only that in the matter of planned obsolescence Nature was ahead even of General Motors. When I hear that "science says" or "scientists tell us," I still see that serious, white-coated individual frowning from the car cards of the IRT and making nasty statements about the condition of my gums (perfectly true, they were in terrible shape) as a means to purveying his now vanished tooth powder.

The world has gone a long way since then, and I don't know if I came along. The technical pronouncements of scientists about their various trades are frequently quite incomprehensible to me, and even resemble mystical revelations or metaphysical poems (all that about antimatter, for example), while the nontechnical pronouncements of scientists upon the more generally human concerns of religion, culture, civilization—the future—have sometimes an air of strange and only half-intentional comedy: Archimago the guileful great enchanter as he might be if *The Faërie Queene* were done by Walt Disney, which God forbid.

The Darwin Centennial as celebrated at the University of Chicago brought together forty-seven leading biologists and geneticists who, according to William L. Laurence in the *New York Times*, "dealt with all the fundamental questions to which the theory of evolution gave new meaning. How did life begin? What happened before it started? Is the evolution of man completed? Does evolution necessarily mean progress? How did man develop mind? Where did society come from? How does culture shape the future? Is there evolution outside the earth? What is man's fate?"

All these questions, and perhaps especially the last, are of some interest also to the nonscientist, or would be if he were able to understand the answers, and I should like to comment here on "one of the most provocative presentations" of the Centennial, the remarks of Professor Hermann J. Muller, Nobel Prize-winning geneticist. My description of these is drawn from the account given by Mr. Laurence (Science in Review: "A Century After Darwin, a Geneticist Foresees Guided Human Evolution") in the *New York Times* for Sunday, November 29, 1959. It will be sufficiently plain that I am not speaking as a scientist, but perhaps I ought to add that my criticisms have no intention of impugning Professor Muller's scientific work, or his high standing in his own mystery.

Professor Muller's thesis is that evolution has been blind through billions of years, but need no longer be so. "From now on, evolution is what we make it, provided that we choose the true and the good. Otherwise we shall sink back into oblivion."

This is delphic enough to raise doubts: one might think that, given the technical means to transform the biological future, evolution would be what we made it whether we chose the true and the good or the false and the evil. As to sinking back into oblivion, it is unhappily not hard to imagine a clan of sages, with refrigerated genes in either hand, deciding that this was a human condition profoundly to be desired, as against the life of conscience and anxiety, and acting accordingly, so that our descendants would browse on salads in the fields, like Nebuchadnezzar. The power of meddling in the future, as many mythologies will show, is a double and dubious one; the fairy godmother appears at the christening and says of the child, "He may have one Freudian wish."

Still, all moral action is a means of meddling with the future (though none heretofore, unless possibly the project for the Tower of Babel, has proposed itself on so spectacular a scale), and one cannot argue against this particular sample without arguing against the nature of moral action conceived in it. My own doubts concern some of Professor Muller's assumptions about the desirability of what is possible, and about the simplicity with which man, especially scientific man, is able to interpret the true and the good.

'Any relaxation in genetic selection, Dr. Muller said, results in some genetic deterioration by allowing detrimental mutant genes . . . to accumulate to a higher frequency. At the present time, he maintained, modern culture "is giving rein to biological decadence."'*

Again, this is a matter of assumptions. We may note that the term "biological decadence" is unabashedly a moral and political one, scarcely even masquerading as a scientific one; its opposite, which might be used to describe Dr. Muller's remedy, might very well be called "biological Republicanism." It involves the supposition that you know not only what farm hands and factory workers are for, but also what man is for; further, that you are now able to back up your knowledge with effective action, so that if your idea of what man is for is not at present diagnostically true it can be made diagnostically true in the future—by making man over in the image of your idea.

'The only remedy consistent with cultural progess whereby this situation can be met, Professor Muller holds, would be the extension of social awareness and motivation to matters of reproduction—that is, "the increasing recognition by individuals of their responsibility not only for the education and living conditions but also for the genetic endowment of the generations succeeding them."'

To achieve the desired end, he goes on, "some long-entrenched attitudes, especially the feelings of proprietary rights and prerogatives about one's own germinal material, supported by misplaced egotism, will have to yield to some extent. This feeling [sic] does not represent a natural instinct, since there are primitive tribes yet alive who do not have even the concept of biological fatherhood. . . ."

I do not wish to oppose Professor Muller on sentimental grounds; if they are bad, those rights and prerogatives, let them vanish. Nor do I want to make him appear as a monster purposefully propagating monstrosities,

---

*The *Times* account is not invariably clear in distinguishing by quotation marks the boundary between Dr. Muller's words and Mr. Laurence's paraphrase; I shall show the difference as plainly as I can by using double quotation marks for the former, single for the latter.

for the values he wishes to achieve genetically are simply "the same as those already recognized in the bringing up and education of children."

And I do not disbelieve in the power of geneticists to accomplish such miracles; I do have doubts about the propriety of their doing so. The propriety I mean is not simply a moral one, or a delicacy about sexual and reproductive matters, but the propriety of employing so immense a force *as though* its results were predictable if its results are in fact not predictable at all.

Here is the program for the endowment of future generations with "a new morality" made possible by artificial insemination, which, given some little technical improvement, would allow children to be adopted "not merely after birth but even, as it were, before fertilization." ("As it were," so placed in the sentence, is a fine stroke of comedy.) "This will provide the opportunity of bearing a child resulting from the union, under the microscope, of reproductive cells one or both of which may have been derived from persons who exemplified the ideals of the foster parents."

He goes on to say that these reproductive cells would "preferably be derived from persons long deceased" (he doesn't say why; possibly on the Greek theory that one should call no man happy—or wise, or genetically sound—until he is dead), and adds, with a certain dry enthusiasm, that 'this procedure would make the most precious genetic heritage of all humanity—the genetic endowments of the Einsteins, Beethovens, da Vincis, Shakespeares, Lincolns of each generation—"available for nurturing into childhood and adulthood."'

If this were not enough, 'Even more predictability about the nature of the progeny could be attained ... by a kind of parthenogenesis—the duplication of a complete individual either from a male or female germ cell alone.' In this way, 'the offspring will obtain his hereditary equipment entirely from one individual, with whom he will be as identical genetically as if he were his identical twin.' You would take all this hereditary equipment from 'the cell of some preexisting person, chosen on the evidence of the life he or she had led, and his or her tried potentialities.'

'In this manner it would become possible to bring back to life outstanding individuals, long since dead, perpetuating for all future generations large numbers of men and women of genius in all fields of endeavor. This would, in a sense, represent a form of physical immortality.'

And the *Times* article concludes with a solemn augury: 'Experiments along these lines have already succeeded in creating parthenogenetic frogs.'

Let me think first about making available 'the most precious genetic heritage of all humanity—the genetic endowments of the Einsteins, Beethovens, da Vincis, Shakespeares, Lincolns, of each generation.' A noble aim. And yet some questions do come up.

First, I observe that Dr. Muller is reported as speaking about these extraordinary phenomena in the plural, and as occurring in each generation; whereas I should have thought that each of his examples represented something in the last degree singular and unrepeatable, not only in genetic but in historical terms. Even on a less world-shaking scale—if we were to consider making available the genetic endowment not of Shakespeare but of, say Offenbach—might not the prospect of a few hundred Offenbachs in the next generation seem to be absurd and not a little sinister? So much more a gaggle of Shakespeares. And what becomes of the idea of the individual (one of those obsolete misnomers, like "atom," meaning "what cannot be divided")?

In the same connection, consider the historical implications of this device. Would the genes of Beethoven produce new Beethovens who would write—to take it with the most naïve literalism—the sonatas of Beethoven? But we already have those. Well, then, a little less literally, would they write in the style of Beethoven? Imitation Beethoven sonatas? Worse yet (and we already have some of those, too). Assume finally that 'the proper environment and education' would take care of that; there remains the question what all these Beethovens would do in the world; could their genetic equipment comfortably absorb the influences of Wagner, Debussy, Schoenberg? The object, of course, must be that they would do for music in their time what Beethoven did for music in his time (even so, the idea of a lot of them doing it seems odd)—but, to put the extreme question, could their genetic equipment absorb, whether comfortably or not, the influence of Beethoven? He did, after all, exist; and wrote all that music. It appears that the production of an abundance of Beethovens might be only an embarrassment to the world.

Second, is the matter of genetic endowment so simple as all that? Presumably this endowment inseparably contains *all* and not only some of the traits of the person it produces. Would society then settle for the reproduction of numerous Beethovens congenitally gifted with music and syphilis together? Of so many Leonardos in whom painting and pederasty go together? No doubt it is easy to contemplate irritating the oyster to achieve the pearl: but do you deliberately and with a good conscience condemn your Keatses and Kafkas, Mozarts and Schuberts, to suffering lives and early deaths with the object of benefiting from their anguish? Is it so certain, after all, that these disadvantages, whether genetic as with Beethoven's illness, or environmental, as with Mozart's poverty, have nothing to do with art, so that the one may be skillfully detached from the other under a microscope?

Professor Muller is reported as saying that 'an individual with the genetic endowment of a Lincoln, for example, will overcome any obstacle of an unfavorable environment and lack of educational opportunities.' Now, our history books tell us that Lincoln did overcome such disabilities, and that a part of his greatness consists in his having done so; but must you then, following another well-known 'scientific' generalization about history, that of 'challenge and response,' provide your embryonic Lincolns with an unfavorable environment and an ample want of educational opportunities? Cynics would say that we already do so, but that is not the scientific vision.

A third point under this first heading—how do you make up your mind as to which genetic endowment is the most precious? If the selection committee had been required to choose during the period of Beethoven's early maturity, when his reproductive cells would presumably have been fertile, should we not with near absolute certainty have had a progeny of Rossinis instead? Rossinis are a grand and agreeable commodity, but they are not Beethovens.

Again, Professor Muller or his reporter assumes, with a charming kindliness, according to the examples, that the world's loving admiration is extended with a certain uniformity to those contemporaries who will later be renowned for art, science, and statesmanship so far above politics as to resemble a condition of sanctity. But supposing we agreed that "the persons who exemplified the ideals of the foster parents" would be very often the same as the persons whose pictures hang on their walls, whose names are most often and potently in their newspapers, and after whom they do now in fact name their children;—from the past couple of decades what a crop should we not have had, deliberately produced, of Hitlers, Stalins, Maos—balanced, of course, on the cultural side, by thousands of Bing Crosbys, hundreds of Billy Grahams, and a few dozen Immanuel Velikovskys.

Imagine the danger to foster parents, not to mention the children, who had opted for and received likenesses of Stalin, and then had to cross the periods of Beria, Malenkov, and Khrushchev, with those fatal images growing daily more recognizable beside them.

Of course all this will be done, when it is done, with the greatest circumspection and dispassionate wisdom, by committees of—scientists.

My second subject, following Dr. Muller's argument, is parthenogenesis, the duplication of a complete individual either from a male or a female cell alone. By this means, 'even more predictability about the nature of the progeny could be attained' than by the normal procedure of artificial insemination.

As I have already suggested, the idea of 'duplicating' an 'individual' contains a contradiction; but let us allow that to be a fault, or obsolescence, in the nature of language itself, rather than in Dr. Muller's thought, and pass on to ask, concerning the idea of 'predictability,' whether it is possible and whether it is desirable.

I do not doubt the possibility in a technical sense, that is, that what Dr. Muller is able to do with frogs his geneticist descendants will sooner or later, probably sooner, be able to do with us. But once again the theme of history comes in, and in this connection it might be expressed as follows:

History does not really repeat itself; and the world is full of the ruined cities of peoples who believed it did.

It does not contradict, but only affirms, this proposition to say with Marx that everything in history happens twice, once seriously and once as a parody of itself. That is exactly the issue. Perhaps no better recipe for the mass-production of human suffering has ever been found than bringing people up to believe that the world is as their fathers saw it and need only be faced in the same way; perhaps no better recipe for human suffering could ever be found than to produce people so endowed by nature as to be incapable of believing anything else.

Historians are accustomed to see everywhere this elemental and calamitous want of imagination blinding an old world to the existence of a new: in what numbers, through the ages, the deceived children of royalty and success go to the block, the guillotine, the doomed campaign, making stoical and witty remarks as they disappear from the stage in St. Petersburg and Paris, Byzantium and Peking; lamenting so often that they have not been faithful to the ancestral ways, when in fact it is as often this fidelity which has betrayed them. The same judgment is rendered by Shakespeare, whose armored giants blunder and fall in a world which changed while they refused to look: Richard the Second, Gloucester and Lear, Antony, destroyed by new, efficient, somewhat cold men who can use the present because they do not love or want or understand the past. That all this is sad is undeniable, but there may be some objections to instituting a genetic program which shall ensure a constant supply of tragic heroes.

In a limited sense, what Professor Muller proposes is possible, or will foreseeably become so: 'In this manner [he is reported as having said] it would become possible to bring back to life outstanding individuals, long since dead, perpetuating for all future generations large numbers of men and women of genius in all fields of endeavor.'

In this manner it would become possible for a man to make sure not only that his son carried on his business after he was gone, but also that he made the same mistakes in it; and though we here approach mysteries of paradox, it seems included in the genetic argument that the son would carry on his father's business even if it had gone bankrupt in the interim between his conception and his coming of age.

It is admittedly difficult to see how literally we are to take all of this, or how literally Professor Muller takes it. But what is Leonardo to do in the world, given that he is once again Leonardo? What is he to be, if not Leonardo? The line of thought, not at the best free of mythological elements, here approaches the popular Sunday supplement question, What Would Jesus Do If He Returned To Earth Today? The accompanying picture always shows Jesus costumed *de chez* Raphael and Lloyd Douglas, with a streetful of people not unnaturally gaping after Him—their curiosity kindly rather than mocking, of course—and thus suggests by antithesis some reasons for His perhaps being a touch hard to recognize if He did in fact appear.

Again, parthenogenesis, which might be described as incest squared, or as fertile masturbation, or as sexual solipsism ("as if a man were author of himself, and knew no other kin." *Coriolanus*, 5.3.36), would selectively breed traits considered to be valuable, intensifying these and weakening, or finally excluding, others, all in the name of predictability.

But, considering once more the historical question, and the passage of 'real' time over the genetic 'immortality'—how predictable would be the behavior resulting from a determinate set of characteristics in a new situation? If predictability in this meaning extends to the particulars of behavior, we should have to say that Marie Antoinette, supposing her to be repeated in this manner, would somehow manage to get herself guillotined in the twenty-first century or so. Absurd. Granted, it is absurd. But it is not less absurd to think of predictability as not having this meaning, for then it has no meaning at all except that the behavior of what is predictable will not be predictable. Under this condition, imagine rapidly in succession the reproduction in modern circumstances of Beau Brummel, Thomas Aquinas, Cato the Censor: they are not to behave as they did in fact behave, but they are to behave as they would behave, given their—

what shall we say?—characters, personalities, souls, selves, genes, in a situation incalculably altered; and, moreover, with the example of themselves constantly before their eyes; what is so predictable about that, except disaster? Milton, thou shouldst be living at this hour? But if he were, what? And would he read Milton? And if there were more than one of him? From his point of view the situation would be intolerable; not less so from ours. Milton, go home!

It is not considered seemly these days to joke about science, which invites a respectful silence from the lay person, but I am afraid that a number of these jokes make themselves, or have already been made by Professor Muller, and very sorry jokes they are, too. His conclusion about perpetuating the large numbers of dead geniuses by parthenogenesis is a fit punch line; he is reported as having said: 'This would, in a sense, represent a form of physical immortality.'

"In a sense" comes in here with what a comedian would call good timing. The 'sense' is commonly consented to belong in the first place to Plato, who thought the perpetuating of oneself in children an inferior form of immortality, and is no doubt as good as it ever was, though showing as usual a surprising indifference to what people want physical immortality for, that is, to be always happy and never to die. Whether the latter condition would include the former is another thing, as Swift shows in his parable of the Struldbrugs; but perhaps the scientists, who offer the cold consolation of this immortality 'in a sense' rather often, should find some other term for the expression of their meaning.

Now, following on with the argument about parthenogenesis, what traits are valuable, how do you determine the value of a trait abstractly, by itself, and who does the valuing?

Dr. Muller is reported as believing that the traits to be striven for by artificial insemination, and thus by parthenogenesis which is a species of it, are the same as those already recognized as the chief aims in the bringing up and education of children. Among these the following are enumerated: 'more robust health; keener, deeper and more creative intelligence; genuine warmth of fellow feeling and cooperative disposition; and richer appreciation of man's intellectual and spiritual values and its [the appreciation's?] more adequate expression.'

Here doubt gives way to bewilderment. Can he mean that all these things ought to go together in any human being? Can he mean that examples of such a human being already exist, so as to guide us as to the probable conduct of future models? Are there not internal contradictions among the specifications, so that the possession of one would prohibit its accompaniment by another? Jesus of Nazareth Himself might possibly be characterized as having genuine warmth of fellow feeling, as revealed in His crucifixion for the sake of mankind, but had He a really cooperative disposition as it was manifested in his dealings with the Sanhedrin, the Roman authority, the spirit in the wilderness (Luke, 4.) or even His own mother?

Alas, in the mechanics of value as elsewhere you reap what you sow, and output is determined by input.

So the meaning of Professor Muller's list must be that, as all these traits are good ones, it is good to produce human beings who have only some of them, even if you cannot produce human beings who have all of them together. But Genghis Khan was characterized by robust health, while Richard Wagner suffered all his life from constipation. El Greco's rich appreciation of man's intellectual and spiritual values did not prevent him from saying "a nice man, but doesn't know how to paint" about Michelangelo, whom other authorities have seen as a horrible man who knew how to paint extremely well. And so on, indefinitely.

All this in the name of "human control," "predictability," and attitude toward reproduction which shall be "more rational and more socially directed."

We have raised some questions about the possibility of a genetically induced predictability in human character. Now we should ask, assuming the thing to be possible, who wants it? Let us resist the temptation to say, whether despairingly or with cheerful cynicism, that They want it.

But we see that predictability is associated, by those who do want it, with rationality and control; and so far as can be seen from the account of Dr. Muller's talk, no slightest suspicion of the entire benevolence of this enterprise has ever come into his head.

No doubt it is man's earnest and noble desire to control things, to make them accessible to reason, to make them predictable, and thus to change such of them as he finds undesirable. As long as he has to do with things, this object does not conflict with his other great object of freedom; rather, the one increases the other, and that is an excellent reason for valuing very highly indeed the methods and achievements of science. But you cannot long have to do with things, without also having to do with people, and here the matter is less settled. Supposing it to be magically within my power to make you a nicer fellow. Ought not I to do so at once? But of course. On the other hand, what do I mean by a nicer fellow? It is extremely probable that I mean a fellow who will concur in anything I say or do, or at least won't get in my way when he can't. This is not the whole dream of power, but only its first and most moderate form; the gas chambers come later, when the simple existence of other, not so nice fellows, even when not directly in the way, becomes an intolerable itch.

Calmly, please. I am not associating Professor Muller with tyranny in any form; I am only inquiring what happens to the products of the laboratory when once they come out of that austere and pure environment and get into other hands, Tamburlaine's, or Napoleon's, or yours, or mine.

A few years ago, the grand, supranational unity of science was badly ruffled by the discoveries, or the pretensions, depending which side you were on, of the Russian geneticist Lysenko concerning the possibility of modifying mankind by the hereditary transmission of acquired characteristics, so that, for example, a Stakhanovite father might easily be made to conceive a Stakhanovite son, to whom overwork would be natural and instinctual.

The Lysenko crisis is quiet at present (though not necessarily settled; see for example "The Third Stage in Genetics" by Donald Michie, in *A Century of Darwin*, ed. S. A. Barnett, London, 1958), but not the least of its effects while it lasted was the widely disputed question whether there could be not one but two biologies, a Soviet one identified with Stalin and Lysenko fundamentally opposed to a bourgeois or capitalist one identified with Mendel and Weismann (at least not with the head of a state, to be thankful for small mercies). According to the former, you might soon be able to change human beings at will in the space of a generation or so; according to the latter, you would never be able to do any such thing, the germ cells being inaccessible, immortal, a direct heritage from Adam playing no part in the life of their individual bearer, and, in effect, an entity as near being the soul itself as you could have without effectively having it. Which of these theories was correct, assuming that either was, bothered some people less than the frightful suggestion behind it, that science itself, pure and rational though it might seem, was in fact socially conditioned and much given to mythologizing, fulfulling wishes, rationalizing phantasies; it did not make matters any better, from our side, that Marx had already said as much. Shakespeare too had observed that reason panders will, but his observation had not achieved scientific status.

Now, although Professor Muller has not raised the Lysenko heresy— and it is odd how that word *heresy* creeps from field to field, and from one authority to another—has he not by some accident propounded a sinister bourgeois equivalent to the Soviet nightmare? In each vision,

Someone is to decide upon a biological future for man, and do his (doubt-less very effective) best to insure that it shall come to pass. The children of the day after tomorrow, and theirs into remote ages, are to live not merely among the ruined cathedrals and nonsensical superstitions of their progenitors, which is what people do already, but also under a genetical compulsion to repeat indefinitely the shallow virtues, moderate intelli-gences, and doom-ridden phantasies of the same.

Why is this necessary?

Because, says Professor Muller, any relaxation in genetic selection re-sults in some genetic deterioration by allowing detrimental mutant genes to accumulate to a higher frequency. At the present time, modern culture is "giving rein to biological decadence."

The sense in which he employs this term "biological decadence" is probably, in the first place, our failure to embark on a long-range program of breeding with conscious intention as to the results, a failure, in his terms, "to choose the true and the good."

Behind this, however, he passingly recommends his remedy as a 're-sponse to the challenge arising from the modern uses of radiation.'

It is a remedy as staunchly conservative in its human object as it is wildly radical in its scientific means.

But with all good will, I cannot see that the scientist, who has made available 'the modern uses of radiation' which he admittedly is unable to control and does not accept responsibility for, can claim in advance that on account of his responsibility and control of consciously organized breeding of human beings for particular purposes, even if these are thought to be virtuous ones, will not in the same way come into the hands of the possessors of political power.

Let us conclude our discussion with a couple of mottoes to guide all right-thinking persons in their consideration of these great matters. The first is from *The Tempest*:

PROSPERO: I have us'd thee
                   (Filth as thou art) with humane care, and lodg'd thee
                   In mine own cell till thou didst seek to violate
                   The honour of my child.
CALIBAN: O ho, O ho! Would't had been done!
                   Thou didst prevent me; I had peopled else
                   This isle with Calibans.

The second is that one of Goya's *Caprichos* showing a man asleep with his head on a desk; a huge cat raises its head nearby, and from behind him arise many owl-faced, bat-winged creatures who stare at him and ourselves; on the side of the desk the painter has written: *El sueño de la razon produce monstruos*, The dream of reason begets monsters.

The Poetry of Wallace Stevens

I BEGIN with a not very precise sense of difference: that the poetry of
Wallace Stevens is essentially different from almost everything else in
English. If I take at random three or four poets not usually thought of for
their similarities one to the other—Donne, Pope, Tennyson, and Frost,
say—and consider what poetry seems to mean to them and what poetry
seems to mean to Stevens, I find a family likeness among these four and
something like a generic difference in Stevens; not only what he does, but
what he wants to do, is different. Only sometimes in Wordsworth do I
catch some usually tenuous hint of kinship:

> . . . to range the faculties
> In scale and order, class the cabinet
> Of their sensations, and in voluble phrase
> Run through the history and birth of each
> As of a single independent thing.

The resemblance is perhaps neither very close nor identifiable by particulars; if Wordsworth's "voluble phrase" sounds a trifle like a combination
by Stevens ("the most prolific narrative," "life's voluble utterance"), we
feel nevertheless that the former is being earnest in a way that the latter
is not; it is merely that the exact tone of the word "voluble" has changed,
for us, from what it was for Wordsworth. Still, compare this of Stevens:

If the rejected things, the things denied,
Slid over the western cataract, yet one,
One only, one thing that was firm, even
No greater than a cricket's horn, no more
Than a thought to be rehearsed all day, a speech
Of the self that must sustain itself on speech,
One thing remaining, infallible, would be
Enough.

What likeness there is also defines the difference; in Stevens, proportions like the above can take a more abrupt form, and often do: "The deer and the dachshund are one." If Wordsworth is a "philosophical" poet, Stevens is a poet whose favorite disguise (there are several others) is the philosopher, robe, gesture, and speech—the "scholar," the "metaphysician," "Weisheit, the rabbi." And the poems are frequently sermons, lectures, meditations: "Extracts From Addresses to the Academy of Fine Ideas."

All this, though personative certainly, seems far from being otherwise dramatic; and from the idea of drama, of "action," we get these days our greatest pathos as readers of poetry; from the development of particular human fate as the tragic poets and the modern novelists alike teach us to regard it. Yet ideas, like books, have also fates, and Dryden finely says, "Every alteration of the design, every new-sprung passion or turn of it, is a part of the action, and much the noblest, except we conceive nothing to be action till they come to blows." Every alteration of the design—it describes, I think, the "action" in Stevens' poems. This too, of Paul Valéry, is relevant:

Within the mind, there is a drama. Drama, adventure, agitation, all words of this category can be employed on condition that several are used, and are corrected one by the other. Such dramas are usually lost, like the plays of Menander.

That defines something of Stevens' nearly unique preoccupation in poetry: the recording of that subtle drama of inductions of which we lose or throw away a thousand examples daily, so that we have formed the prudent habit of calling it trivial, just as though all that we regard as decisive in the world did not depend precisely on this triviality: "The poem of the act of the mind."

As such considerations begin to define the distinction, so they do the difficulty of these poems, which have about them an "impenetrable lucid-

ity," a brilliance of surface that defeats sometimes the kind of explication
that works tolerably well on a good deal of English poetry. That is, we are
sometimes compelled to wish a little wistfully for a moment requiring
esoteric knowledge, as with Eliot, or the sorting-out of syntax or complex
metaphor, as with Donne, Yeats, and a number of others; but Stevens is
most difficult at precisely the moments of greatest simplicity, where the
world, so far as meaning is concerned, is summed up and destroyed in a
phrase usually balanced upon the point of the verb "to be": "The law of
chaos is the law of ideas," "Ideas are men," "Building and dream are one,"
"Life is a bitter aspic," "The point of vision and desire are one," "The mind
is the great poem of winter," etc. Moments of this kind seem to stand, in
his poetry, for the arbitrary in all thought; they catch the mind in its fantastic act of deciding; and the same element is present in his argumenta-
tive, dialectical habit of phrase: "Suppose ...," "Say that ...," "For example. ..." In a way, it is quite true to say that a poetry of this sort cannot
be dramatic, because it begins just where thought has arrived at "the ratio
of all things," and has only two developments open to it: the closing of the
circle, or the transcending leap into something other, which will be something arbitrary—the leap, for instance, from generality to particulars—
and either mystical or absurd, if we still care to distinguish those two
terms. So metaphor also becomes arbitrary, mystical, or absurd, since particulars may be said to resemble generalities as it were helplessly, whether
or not the mind can trace the details of the resemblance:

> The dress of a woman of Lhassa,
> In its place,
> Is an invisible element of that place
> Made visible.

To which we can only sigh assent. Sometimes it works, and sometimes it
doesn't; but Stevens had a gift for making it work at great deal of the time.

This principle of composition, which revokes at once all other principles and makes something uniquely recognizable of Stevens' figures, is
given us more or less diagrammatically at the beginning of a poem called
"Connoisseur of Chaos":

> A. A violent order is disorder; and
> B. A great disorder is an order. These
> Two things are one. (Pages of illustrations.)

The subsequent illustrations—"If all the green of spring was blue, and it is"—play at developing the theme of "a law of inherent opposites, / Of essential unity," which is "as pleasant as port, / As pleasant as the brush-strokes of a bough, / An upper, particular bough in, say, Marchand." The tone is that of philosophic conversation or meditation, but the sense is, with a touch of gentle contempt for philosophic simplicities, that philosophy is over and done with, and of no interest *except* as the poetic act of the philosopher, the poem of the act of the mind:

> After all the pretty contrast of life and death
> Proves that these opposite things partake of one,
> At least that was the theory, when bishops' books
> Resolved the world. We cannot go back to that.
> The squirming facts exceed the squamous mind,
> If one may say so. And yet relation appears,
> A small relation expanding like the shade
> Of a cloud on sand, a shape on the side of a hill.

The poem continues to debate these contrasts, which dissolve and re-form themselves in being debated—"Just one more truth, one more / Element in the immense disorder of truths,"—and concludes on a figure which for once is rigorously traditional in its combination:

> The pensive man. . . . He sees that eagle float
> For which the intricate Alps are a single nest.

That the poet's view of metaphor, or analogy as he more usually calls it, is such as I have said, is demonstrated not only in the poems but at many places in his very beautiful essays on poetics (*The Necessary Angel*, 1951), from one of which I will draw a somewhat extended passage as evidence:

First, then, as to the resemblance between things in nature, it should be observed that resemblance constitutes a relation between them since, in some sense, all things resemble each other. Take, for example, a beach extending as far as the eye can reach, bordered, on the one hand, by trees and, on the other, by the sea. The sky is cloudless and the sun is red. In what sense do the objects in this scene resemble each other? There is enough green in the sea to relate it to the palms. There is enough of the sky reflected in the water to create a resemblance, in some sense, between them. The sand is yellow between the green and the blue. In short, the light alone creates a unity not only in the recedings of distance, where differences become invisible, but also in the contacts of closer sight. So, too, sufficiently generalized, each man resembles all other men, each woman resembles all other women, this year resembles last year. The beginning of time will, no doubt, resemble the end of time. One world is said to resemble another.

To talk this way is to treat metaphor very largely—handsomely, but largely. Through my bewilderment about a gesture so sweeping I feel that all the *things* mentioned in the passage have in reality but one element common, and that their being *things thought*; they all participate the climate of the mind, and it is that which gives them such resemblance to one another as they may have. On this, I begin to think of, or hear some echo of, Plato—"First, then, as to the resemblance between things in nature"— and I reflect that the philosopher whose robes this poet wears is none other: "the ultimate Plato," "a large-sculptured, platonic person free from time," and so on. There are things, and there are ideas of things; the cross-relations between these are manifold and mysterious, enough to poetize upon perhaps endlessly:

> Poet, patting more nonsense foamed
> From the sea, conceive for the courts
> Of these academies, the diviner health
> Disclosed in common forms. Set up
> The rugged black, the image. Design
> The touch. Fix quiet. Take the place
> Of parents, lewdest of ancestors.
> We are conceived in your conceits.

That is suggestive. But it is not enough. Plato is in the poet's mind, but cannot be there without being modified any more than the theories of "bishops' books" can be there without being modified. One further comparison may be attempted, anyhow.

I have no firsthand acquaintance with the school of existential thought known as phenomenology, but a description of some of its elements by Albert Camus (*The Myth of Sisyphus*, 1955) struck me as immediately relevant to this exposition. Again I must quote at length:

Originally Husserl's method negates the classic procedure of the reason. . . . Thinking is not unifying or making the appearance familiar under the guise of a great principle. Thinking is learning all over again how to see, directing one's consciousness, making of every image a privileged place. In other words, phenomenology declines to explain the world, it wants to be merely a description of actual experience. It confirms absurd thought in its initial assertion that there is no truth, but merely truths. . . . Consciousness does not form the object of its understanding, it merely focuses, it is the act of attention, and, to borrow a Bergsonian image, it resembles the projector that suddenly focuses on an image. The difference is that there is no scenario, but a successive and incoherent illustration.

(Compare Stevens' "Just one more truth, one more / Element in the immense disorder of truths.") Camus goes on to develop the phenomenological leap from the above position back once again into a world of significances:

For Husserl speaks likewise of "extra-temporal essences" brought to light by the intention, and he sounds like Plato. All things are not explained by one thing but by all things. I see no difference. . . . There is no longer a single idea explaining everything, but an infinite number of essences giving a meaning to an infinite number of objects. The world comes to a stop, but also lights up.

And a few pages later he enforces the relation of phenomenology to Neoplatonism by suggesting that the whole attitude already exists in Plotinus' contention that there is not only an idea of man but also an idea of Socrates. With this, I think, we are again in Stevens' realm, where the compositions of analogy touch upon the absurd because particulars and generalities are really in a certain sense incompatible, and our pages of illustration therefore more or less arbitrary.

To see that this is so is not to accomplish anything essential; there is about the perception a reassurance largely academical. We are left still with the nature of the poetry, the nature of the world it composes; and in a way we have always known that the arbitrary is the beginning of poetry, and suspected it of being the beginning of worlds. Nevertheless, this may now be said about the figurative center of Stevens' poetry: that every object, in the poet's mind, becomes the idea of itself, and thereby produces the final illumination which in the Platonic philosophy would have been produced by the view of the archetypes themselves; save that this illumination, final as it is, is meaningless, repetitious as prayer, yet "responsive as a mirror with a voice"—the epiphany not of what is real, but of the self poetizing. This is our reality, that "we believe without belief, beyond belief," that "Life consists / Of propositions about life," and that "The poem must resist the intelligence / Almost successfully."

> Yet to speak of the whole world as metaphor
> Is still to stick to the contents of the mind
> And the desire to believe in a metaphor.
> It is to stick to the nicer knowledge of
> Belief, that what it believes in is not true.

What follows from the principle of poetics which I have attributed to Wallace Stevens is this, that the poet's art constitutes the world. This contention is also, I think, the chief subject of his poems, which meditate the ambiguity, old as Genesis, whether this poetic act is a creation *ex nihilo* or the ordering and making perceptible in language the immense possibilities of chaos, the establishment of what Joyce called "the ineluctable modality of the visible." The dominance of this subject, which makes the freedom and particular strangeness of Stevens' poetry—since all objects may be exalted into poems, the act of looking at them being what is at issue—also sets their limits and is responsible for their repetitive and sometimes bemused character—since the meditation is endless, or ends only with death (an end but no solution):

> Or if the music sticks, if the anecdote
> Is false, if Crispin is a profitless
> Philosopher, beginning with green brag,
> Concluding fadedly, if as a man
> Prone to distemper he abates in taste,
> Fickle and fumbling, variable, obscure,
> Glozing his life with after-shining flicks,
> Illuminating, from a fancy gorged
> By apparition, plain and common things,
> Sequestering the fluster from the year,
> Making gulped potions from obstreperous drops,
> And so distorting, proving what he proves
> Is nothing, what can all this matter, since
> The relation comes, benignly, to its end?

> So may the relation of each man be clipped.

It remains to characterize by illustrations the recurring elements and continuing preoccupations of the poetry. First, as to the ambiguity just spoken of, the poet does not usually think of a creation out of nothing, but sometimes nevertheless comes close to suggesting it; so that even in thinking of "the Idea of *Order* at Key West" he views the singing girl as making the world by her song, and not merely as arranging it; the sea, here, is primordial chaos, the deep, just as in Genesis, "The water never formed to mind or voice," and it becomes something other than itself in her song:

> She was the single artificer of the world
> In which she sang. And when she sang, the sea,
> Whatever self it had, became the self
> That was her song, for she was the maker.

Generally, however, the poem creates by organizing the chaos of experience, "the storm," "the dreadful sundry of this world," producing from it "the mute, the final sculpture," the center, the focusing image which, remaining itself, orders the world about it:

> I placed a jar in Tennessee
> And round it was, upon a hill.
> It made the slovenly wilderness
> Surround that hill.

Yet it is not the establishment of such an image, in Platonic domination, that is the theme; it is, rather, the act of establishing, considered in itself, "the blessed rage for order," the act of seeing the lights which "Mastered the night and portioned out the sea," the act of seeing such things in silence and stasis, "as in the powerful mirror of my wish and will." This act, or spell cast upon chaos, is never final and must always be repeated, since "It can never be satisfied, the mind, never." The tension between mind and world may be harmonized in innumerable ways, on the "harmonium," the "clavier," "the blue guitar," and these precipitated harmonies are poems:

> I know my lazy, leaden twang
> Is like the reason in a storm;
>
> And yet it brings the storm to bear.
> I twang it out and leave it there.

But the resolution so produced, while in its way final, is meaningless and not allegorical, it tells us nothing beyond itself. It brings the storm to bear, but the storm continues, and the use of poetry is, by repeated charms, to

create perpetually resolving, dissolving equations between composition
and the storm. Thus in "Valley Candle":

> My candle burned alone in an immense valley.
> Beams of the huge night converged upon it,
> Until the wind blew.
> Then beams of the huge night
> Converged upon its image,
> Until the wind blew.

The principle of composition, whereby—to put it very roughly—all
particulars may "represent" all general statements, makes for an immense
variety of apparently individual subjects and images; yet I have been able
to make out some strains of iterative and thematic imagery whereby the
central tension is composed many times, and I will indicate briefly the
most important of these.

The chaos of the actual is represented, as I have said, in sea, storm,
wind, darkness; also in the figure of the jungle: Venezuela, Africa, Brazil,
Yucatan, "Florida, Venereal Soil," the Everglades, and (epitomizing its
qualities) "that alien, point-blank, green and actual Guatemala," whose antithesis, in a sadly satiric poem, is the Waldorf,

> Where the wild poem is a substitute
> For the woman one loves or ought to love,
> One wild rhapsody a fake for another.

Most often, though, the jungle of immediate experience is placed over
against the image of the statue, which may appear in very various forms:
the snow man, the Founder of the State, allegorical emblems of Fides,
Justitia, Patientia, Fortitudo, "those sovereigns of the soul / And savings
banks," Belshazzar, Stalin, Xenophon, etc. We may note that in an essay,
"The Noble Rider and the Sound of Words," the poet's image for the meeting place of imagination and reality is Verrocchio's *Condottiere*.

Now this image has many resources central to Stevens' purpose. It is
often treated satirically, as "gross effigy and simulacrum," but the satire
itself runs into reverence for something too large for human purpose:
"The well-composed in his burnished solitude, / The tower, the ancient
accent, the wintry size." The statue, like the jar in Tennessee or the valley
candle, orders the wilderness (usually a park) in which it is set, providing
a center and focus for all that green; but beyond that it alludes to all that

is dominating and heroic, all that is too big for man, until, in its remotest ranges, it becomes indistinguishable, with Platonic piety, from the One, and is identified with soldier, giant, hero, captain—"outer captain, inner saint," "a large-sculptured, platonic person, free from time," "the soldier of time grown deathless in great size."

It is between these extremes of the jungle and the monumental hero that the poet produces—with a wistful, hankering eye on the One—his transformations, "As of a general being or human universe," whereby the most random experiences are to be reflected mythically in "the central man," "the impossible possible philosophers' man,"

> our oldest parent, peer
> Of the populace of the heart, the reddest lord,
> Who has gone before us in experience,

with the foredoomed, ruefully Platonic object of "The essential poem at the centre of things."

It is part of this poetical bargain with the world, of course, that one does not bring forth the essential poem at the center of things. The poet, as musician and clown, as Crispin, Peter Quince, Man with the Blue Guitar, must daily renew the contest with chaos which he cannot win; the tenacity with which Stevens held himself at this frontier between the actual and the mind characterizes both the successes and the failures of his genius. Beginning where he began, development was impossible except as abstraction, progressive refinement, development to a stripped simplicity; it is as though what he developed was primarily the sense of what he was about, the simplifying consciousness of his poetry as an assault upon conventions of meaning, conventions of language, upon those people who, as Valéry once wrote, are so little aware of the pains and pleasures of vision that they have invented *beautiful views.*

It is the tragedy of poetry so conceived that, in a certain sense, it produces beautiful views despite itself; and a greater tragedy that all success is briefly sustained upon failure. I must make allowances for the fact that my affection to the poems of Stevens' early and middle periods owes something extra to my having grown up on *Harmonium*, *Ideas of Order*, *The Man with the Blue Guitar*, and certain poems from *Parts of a World* which appeared before that volume. And two major works after that, *Esthétique du Mal* and *Notes Toward a Supreme Fiction*, kept still their majesty and power as summaries of an argument of which, however, one had already heard a great deal. Nevertheless, the works of the poet's last few years seem to me most often to represent a falling-off and a repetition at a diminished pitch—for two reasons chiefly. First, a conscious endeavor to purify the terms of the parable: the pages of illustration, in those final volumes, seem more perfunctory than before. Second, a corresponding loss of tension, since the *particulars* of experience, with their resistance to the mind, formed one element in his process, and these particulars were now being treated as though, so to say, they were already dissolved in generality.

I should be sorry to have my reader take this opinion as pontifical, for in a certain, generally undervalued sense poetry is what you like. If there was a failure, it followed many noble poems, and followed them not merely in time but as their consciously accepted consequence in the difficult art of a man who, so far as thought is concerned, may prove to have been the only truly *modern* poet of his time. In considering the sense of his own parable, "How the honey of heaven may or may not come, / But that of earth both comes and goes at once," he rejected all easy solutions, and may be said to have found his artistic life still where he found his profession, in the investigation of surety claims.

> There was no fury in transcendent forms.
> But his actual candle blazed with artifice.

The Bread of Faithful Speech—
Wallace Stevens and
The Voices of Imagination

IN BOOKS left by the old magician we find many things, things ill-assorted and not particularly well catalogued according to any scheme we are familiar with. It is as though a supreme identity were turning out the contents of its wallet, going through the desk, the filing cabinets, the closets, preparatory to moving elsewhere, or being other. Here are the licenses and registrations of the self, its snapshots of single raindrops in distant towns, its myths of creation, spells which worked on one occasion only, receipted bills from Guatemala and the Waldorf, inventories, formulae, annotations on unidentifiable texts; one sarcophagus containing one owl, statues of clowns, rabbis, soldiers, invocations of an uncertain someone variously called the outer captain, the inner saint, Don John, John Zeller, St. John, The Backache, turbulent Schlemihl, and so forth. A quiet and final remark, "Wisdom asks nothing more," is followed by a recipe for Parfait Martinique: "coffee mousse, rum on top, a little cream on top of that." Sometimes it seems as though toward the end he gave up doing magic in favor of meditating on its procedures, and he said: "As a man becomes familiar with his own poetry, it becomes as obsolete for himself as for anyone else." Or perhaps everything by this time had been transmuted into magical substance, so that he could say: "Life consists of propositions about life." Or a doubt would arise, so that he said: "Life is an affair of people not places. But for me life is an affair of places and that is the trouble."

Now he is gone the inheritors rummage through what is left, taking various views of their legacy. Some see only a cabinet of curiosities got together by a traveled uncle. Others, understanding they have come into the possession of a gold mine, nevertheless resent his not having had the ore refined so as to be turned in at the treasury for honest paper money that anyone can understand and use immediately. A few young nephews and nieces are upset because when they say the spells nothing happens. And the earnest amateurs of theology search the remains for the single phrase that will transform the world. He would perhaps have said to them:

> It is to stick to the nicer knowledge of
> Belief, that what it believes in is not true.

The true inheritance, if we are able to see it, is a world already transformed, the lucid realization of one among infinite possibilities of transformation, of projection from the shadowy presence at the center. Concerning this he quoted from Whitehead these rather cryptic words: "In a certain sense, everything is everywhere at all times, for every location involves an aspect of itself in every other location. Thus every spatio-temporal standpoint mirrors the world." His comment on this consists of a translation of Whitehead's observation so that it becomes recognizably characteristic of himself and the elegantly slapdash chiaroscuro notation which identifies his voice, his style, and with these the world they alone express: "These words [he says] are pretty obviously words from a level where everything is poetic, as if the statement that every location involves an aspect of itself in every other location produced in the imagination a universal iridescence, a dithering of presences and, say, a complex of differences."

The voice of his poetry is that of a man thinking, a man studying how I may compare this prison where I live unto the world. But it is not philosophical poetry, though it may often adopt the air and gesture of some myth about a philosopher philosophizing. And if it is the poetry of a man thinking, it is nevertheless not "intellectual poetry," not the poetry of "a beau language without a drop of blood," for what the man thinks about is, at last, expressiveness itself, the mystery of the phrase in its relation to the world. There is a difference, which he described, for himself, as the change from a young man to an older one:

> Like a dark rabbi, I
> Observed, when young, the nature of mankind,
> In lordly study. Every day, I found
> Man proved a gobbet in my mincing world.
> Like a rose rabbi, later, I pursued,
> And still pursue, the origin and course
> Of love, but until now I never knew
> That fluttering things have so distinct a shade.

The fluttering things, which in that poem make such a dithering of presences, were pigeons, and he returned to them for an image at the close of another poem, where they have the same expressive function of relating the light and the dark, somewhere between things and the ambience of things, things and the thought of things:

> in the isolation of the sky,
> At evening, casual flocks of pigeons make
> Ambiguous undulations as they sink
> Downward to darkness, on extended wings.

In this poem, which meditates the mysteries of incarnation, of how things come to be and cease to be, the pigeons are as thoughts, or as the manner of our perceiving thoughts between the bright emptiness above and the generative dark beneath, mediators which without solving resolve. In some way, such a poem cannot end, it can only stop at the finish of a cadence, satisfactory for the moment but recognizably inconclusive. A dithering of presences, a complex of differences. All is to do again.

The voice of his poems is the voice of the poet. Even in the poem I have just been quoting from, which begins as though in prospect of a dramatic monologue, it is the poet and not the lady who carries the burden of meditation; she says something once in a while, and he develops the thoughts which she might appropriately have.

This voice has a great consistency over the whole range of the poetry: it is learned, for "poetry is the scholar's art"; it is humorously eccentric, given to French phrases (for in poetry "English and French constitute a single language"), sorrowful and somewhat fatigued, its tone and feeling much affected by the weather and changes of season; it has a balanced gravity owing something to many repetitions; it is a considerate voice, its altitudes of grandeur and nobility are achieved perceptibly in despite of weariness and a leaning toward resignation. It is a poet's voice; or, you might say, it is the voice of wisdom as this might be heard by a poet.

Nor is this so unusual. For whatever our view of the personative, or dramatic, element in lyric poetry, it very often happens that the poet, a middle-aged or an old man thinking of his life and the approaching end of it, of its poetry and whatever all that may mean, projects these thoughts upon the more or less mythified figure of a middle-aged or an old man thinking of his life, and so on. He not so much, that is, bespeaks for himself on the occasion a fictitious character, as he generalizes out the character he has, or thinks he has, or wants to have; often enough he will make this voice of his poem—"as of a general being or a human universe," our poet says—older than himself. For among the poet's ambitions is this unseemly one, to become wise by sounding wise, to be a hermit scholar in a tower first, and only after that find something to study. How odd that it should ever even seem to work.

In this process, the amount of distancing and dignifying that almost necessarily goes on may make it seem that the daily self and the self in the poem are absolutely unlike; thus Yeats and his famous theory of the creation of character from the opposite: "It is perhaps because nature made me a gregarious man, going hither and thither looking for conversation, and ready to deny from fear or favour his dearest conviction, that I love proud and lonely things."

In Yeats's poetry the equivalent thought demonstrates this process of dignifying and distancing by its loftier arrogance of phrase, and by the poet's assigning to Dante what he wished to believe about himself:

> I think he fashioned from his opposite
> An image that might have been a stony face . . .

relating the austere pilgrim of the poem directly with a worldly life of lechery and cynicism.

For some poets, then, the writing of poetry may become an elucidation of character, a spiritual exercise having for its chief object the discovery or invention of one's character: Myself must I remake, Du musst dein Leben ändern, &c. Something of this sort appears in our poet also, and he said about it: "It is the explanations of things that we make to ourselves that disclose our character; the subjects of one's poems are the symbols of one's self or of one of one's selves."

We have said so far, a little foolishly, that the poet's voice is the voice of the poet; and added that the poet hears this voice as that in which the wise might speak, the old and wise and a little foolish, an aged eagle, an old philosopher in Rome, the man in the golden breastplate under the old stone Cross, the magician opening his folio by candlelight in the lonely tower.

To view the poet as a magician is fair, if we remember that magicians do not really solve the hero's problems, but only help him to confront these; as Merlin may be said to have helped Arthur, not so much by doing magic as by being for him a presence and a voice, a way of saying which indicated a way of being. Of this relation our poet said that the soldier is poor without the poet's lines, adding this in explanation:

> How simply the fictive hero becomes the real;
> How gladly with proper words the soldier dies,
> If he must, or lives on the bread of faithful speech.

We observe here, in an aside, that some poets, ours not among them, believe, or pretend to believe, in a magic that more directly affects the world. These poets are like the Friar in the ballad, where the girl fears she will go to hell if she lets him seduce her:

> Tush, quoth the Fryer, and do not doubt,
> If you were in hell I could sing you out.

This has often been the poet's false pride about his magic; but he resembles the Friar in another way, for he too will end up in the well, without the girl.

Our proper magic is the magic of language, where the refrain of the riddling verse, "Sing ninety-nine and ninety," is simply not the same thing as singing a hundred and eighty-nine. It is also the magic of impersonation, and not without its sinister aspect, the being possessed by spirits, or by the spirit. Combining the two, it is being possessed by the word, and about this there is a certain mystery, which we are able to describe, though not to solve, as follows.

We are fond of saying that poetry is personative, hence dramatic. To say this is probably true enough, if not conspicuously helpful, for it does give at any rate our sense that the I of the poem is not quite the poet, even if we have the lingering sense also that this I is not quite not the poet either. It is a problem in style, the beginning of a problem in identities. Browning gives us an idea of Bishop Blougram, but it is an idea we cannot hold without holding at the same time an idea that the Bishop is Brown-

ingesque along with Andrea del Sarto and others. Prufrock is distinct from
Tiresias, but both recognizably belong to Mr. Eliot, just as Michael Ro-
bartes and Crazy Jane sound like themselves and like Yeats; as all the dead
of Spoon River sound like Masters, and so on. In the drama itself, the
problem is aggravated, or dismissed: either they all sound like Shakespeare, or none of them does. Proust puts it this way, that all the sitters to
one painter have a family likeness in their portraits, greater than the likeness they share with members of their own families.

So the poet's sounding like others may be his way of sounding like
himself. And there is a range of possibilities here, between the impossible
extremes of sounding exactly like oneself and entirely other than oneself.
The limits of this range are given by Keats: the "chameleon poet," on one
side, who has no character because he is constantly impersonating someone else; and on the other side the Wordsworthian, or Egotistical Sublime.

Through the other, the poet impersonates the self, his own self or one
of his selves, and there are two "voices of poetry." But it doesn't stop there,
for we read the poem, and then it speaks in our voice as well; this too is
mysterious. When I say over some lines,

> Every thread of summer is at last unwoven.
> By one caterpillar is great Africa devoured
> And Gibraltar is dissolved like spit in the wind.

And when I go on, saying these lines that follow,

> Over all these the mighty imagination triumphs
> Like a trumpet and says, in this season of memory,
> When the leaves fall like things mournful of the past,

> Keep quiet in the heart, O wild bitch. O mind
> Gone wild, be what he tells you to be. . . .

When I say over these things, I say them as myself and not myself, as a
possibility of certain grandeurs and contempts in the self which the poet
alone has been able to release, and I ask whether the voice that speaks at
this moment is more his or mine, or whether poetry is not in this respect
the most satisfactory of many unsatisfactory ways we have of expressing
our sense that we are members of one another. That voice, which I add
by reading, or which the poet adds to me when I read, a voice which in
some way belongs to neither of us personally, is a third voice of poetry.
Our poet, who thought of these things, said of this: "The poet seems to

confer his identity on the reader. It is easiest to recognize this when listening to music—I mean this sort of thing: the transference."

And there is still one further voice of poetry to be considered, though we can say little enough about it except that at certain times it is there. That is the voice of an eternally other, the resonance that in our repetition of the poet's words seems to come from the outside, when "the shadow of an external world draws near"; as when our poet, calling himself for the occasion Ariel, and speaking in the voice of this Ariel, says of Ariel's poems:

> It was not important that they survive.
> What mattered was that they should bear
> Some lineament or character,
>
> Some affluence, if only half perceived,
> In the poverty of their words,
> Of the planet of which they were part.

Our poet thought also and often about this last voice, of which he said: "When the mind is like a hall in which thought is like a voice speaking, the voice is always that of someone else."

His magic, ever more insistently, was a magic to open this world and not another, but this world as an imagination of this world, a transformation where "what is possible replaces what is not"; for that impossible which was replaced, for "man's mind grown venerable in the unreal," he had at most a half-friendly, half-mocking nostalgia; and of that other, the last voice of all, and the one all poetry seeks to hear, he said: "The mind that in heaven created the earth and the mind that on earth created heaven were, as it happened, one."

We say it over and we feel, as it happens, better.

Composition and Fate in the Short Novel

THE writer attempting for the first time a short novel must face, I should think, nothing but problems, the first, though probably the least, of which is, What are short novels? For the writer who is by habit of mind a novelist they must represent not simply a compression but a correspond-
· ing rhythmic intensification, a more refined criterion of relevance than the one he usually enjoys, an austerity and economy perhaps somewhat compulsive in the intention itself. For the writer who habitually thinks in short stories—a bad habit, by the way—the challenge is probably greater: he will have to learn as never before about the interstices of his action; he will have to think about a fairly large space which must be filled, not with everything (his complaint against the novelist), but with something definite which must be made to yield in a quite explicit way its most reserved and recondite ranges of feeling; he will have to think, for once, of design and not merely of plot. To both writers it must soon become apparent that a short novel is something in itself, neither a lengthily written short story nor the refurbished attempt at a novel sent out into the world with its hat clapped on at the eightieth page.

I am speaking, perhaps, ideally, and about the ideal; it is difficult not to. For quite apart from technical considerations, the tradition of the short novel—perhaps because for so long it was commercially useless and un-
acceptable—is a tradition of masterpieces; further than that, the compos-
ers of this tradition of masterpieces are almost without exception the com-

posers of still greater works, such as *Moby-Dick, War and Peace, The Possessed, The Magic Mountain*, and so on, from which their short novels differ, in fact, by a kind of intensification of art, by a closed and resonant style of composition suggestive of the demonstrations of mathematics or chess.

The writer proposing to himself a short novel probably ought not to scare himself with the thought that he is entering that kind of competition; once he begins, of course, he will resolutely forget all about those great men and their works, and pay his exclusive attention to the business in hand. Again, though, the game is scarcely worth playing without an ac-knowledgment of its specific difficulties; the specific difficulties, if they can be identified, are what define the form—without them it is not a form but only so and so many thousand words—and in a discussion like this one I see no way of approaching the matter at all except by attending to the ideal so far as it can be deduced from great examples.

The material economy of the short novel, and its strict analogical style of composition, seem to be functions one of the other. The epitome of the first point, material economy, I must fetch from far away; it seems bril-liantly expressed in a discussion of variety in the creation, by Thomas Aquinas, who says that although an angel is a better thing, objectively con-sidered, than a stone, yet a universe composed of two angels is inferior to a universe composed of one angel and one stone. A variousness so strictly limited and identified as that characterizes, as though by satiric exaggera-tion, the universe of the short novel. As to the strict and analogical style of composition, I shall quote a somewhat extended but very rewarding an-ecdote from the autobiography of a most admirable novelist, Vladimir Na-bokov:

The place is . . . Abbazia, on the Adriatic. About the same time, at a cafe in nearby Fiume, my father happened to notice, just as we were being served, two Japanese officers at a table near us, and we immediately left—not without my hastily snatch-ing a whole *bombe* of lemon sherbet, which I carried away secreted in my aching mouth. The year was ·1904. I was five. Russia was fighting Japan. With hearty relish, the English illustrated weekly Miss Norcott subscribed to reproduced pictures by Japanese artists that showed how the Russian locomotives—made singularly toy-like by the Japanese pictorial style—would drown if our Army tried to lay rails across the treacherous ice of Lake Baikal.

But let me see. I had an even earlier association with that war. One afternoon at the beginning of the same year, in our St. Petersburg house, I was led down from the nursery into my father's study to say how-do-you-do to a friend of the family,

General Kuropatkin. To amuse me, he spread out a handful of matches on the divan where he was sitting, placed ten of them end to end to make a horizontal line and said, "This is the sea in calm weather." Then he tipped up each pair so as to turn the straight line into a zigzag—and that was "a stormy sea." He scrambled the matches and was about to do, I hoped, a better trick when we were interrupted. His aide-de-camp was shown in and said something to him. With a Russian, flustered grunt, Kuropatkin immediately rose from his seat, the loose matches jumping up on the divan as his weight left it. That day, he had been ordered to assume supreme command of the Russian Army in the Far East.

This incident had a special sequel fifteen years later, when at a certain point of my father's flight from Bolshevik-held St. Petersburg to southern Russia, he was accosted, while crossing a bridge, by an old man who looked like a grey-bearded peasant in his sheepskin coat. He asked my father for a light. The next moment each recognized the other. Whether or not old Kuropatkin, in his rustic disguise, managed to evade Soviet imprisonment, is immaterial. What pleases me is the evolution of the match theme; those magic ones he had shown me had been trifled with and mislaid, and his armies had also vanished, and everything had fallen through, like my toy trains that, in the winter of 1904–05, in Wiesbaden, I tried to run over the frozen puddles in the grounds of the Hotel Oranien. The following of such thematic designs through one's life should be, I think, the true purpose of autobiography.—*Speak, Memory*, 1951, pp. 15–17.

A good deal that characterizes the composition of short novels is summed up and lightly demonstrated in this passage, even to a certain ruthlessness: "Whether or not old Kuropatkin . . . managed to evade Soviet imprisonment, is immaterial." And "the evolution of the match theme," with the problems attendant on it, is my proper subject here. But before going on to discuss examples I will try to suggest, without wasting time on attempts at unexceptionable definition, some of the things, other than length, which seem to set the novella apart from the short story and the novel. For the term "short novel" is descriptive only in the way that the term "Middle Ages" is descriptive—that is, not at all, except with reference to the territory on either side. And just as historians exaggerate the darkness of the Dark Ages and the brightness of the Renaissance, I shall exaggerate some elements of the short story and the novel, to make the middle term more visible.

The short story at present is a way of transacting one's fictional business which is shiny, efficient, and inexpensive; consequently it has become very attractive to nonartists. If publishers tell us despite this that collections of short stories rarely succeed, that is probably because everyone is too busy writing his own to be able to read anyone else's. To write a fine short story may be harder now than it has ever been, but there is no indication that large numbers of short story writers are aware of the fact. There are many honorable exceptions, perhaps, submerged in the flood of junk—commercial junk, high-literary junk, undergraduate junk, much of it competent and even attractive, but bearing too much the mark of the machine to give, even at the best, any deep pleasure. Short stories amount for the most part to parlor tricks, party favors with build-in snappers, gadgets for inducing recognitions and reversals: a small pump serves to build up the pressure, a tiny trigger releases it, there follow a puff and a flash as freedom and necessity combine; finally a Celluloid doll drops from the muzzle and descends by parachute to the floor. These things happen, but they happen to no one in particular.

Of many possible reasons why this fate has overtaken the short story, one must be the vast quantity of such stuff produced every day of every week and published in newspapers and magazines, on radio and television (for those "dramas" are either adapted from short stories or made up with the same requirements in mind). That so much of our experience, or the stereotype which passes for it, should be dealt with by means of the short story is perhaps the symptom, not unnoticeable elsewhere in the public domain, of an unlovely cynicism about human character, a propensity to see *individual* behavior as purely atmospheric—*colorful*, as they call it—and accordingly to require stereotyped behavior for everything having to do with the essential action. To invent an example: our hero is individual to the point of eccentricity, he is weirdly named Cyrus Pyracanth, he suffers from hemophilia, keeps pet snakes, and smokes a nargileh; but when it comes to the point, none of this has anything to do with the action his author requires him to perform, for the sake of which he might be called Mr. X and live in Bronxville on an average income and a moral equipment supplied by *Time* magazine or some other leading wholesaler. What has happened to him in the short story is not that he has lost his inwardness; only that for all practical purposes (the writer's purposes) it has ceased to matter.

It is natural that the mass production of short fiction should exert great pressure to bring the story down to its mechanically imitable elements, so that it provides solutions at the expense of problems, answers to which no one has asked the question; there is, indeed, a certain aesthetic pleasure to be gained from the contemplation of simple and pretty combinations purified, as in the detective story, of human complication and human depth; but it is a pleasure easily exhausted. The story gets its power from a whole implied drama which it does not tell aloud; its neglect of that implication reduces it to clever trickery. There is much to be said for clever trickery as a contributing means to great works, nor do great novelists often neglect this part of art which is purely artifice—but when there is little or nothing else, and when in addition all the tricks have been played so many times . . . ?

This is not simply a question of length, but much rather a question of depth; when a short story's action comprises, by brilliant symbolic reflection, the whole of a life, it becomes novelistic. I think in this connection of two stories by Kay Boyle, "Keep Your Pity" and "Dear Mr. Walrus." Neither exceeds thirty pages, but those pages are written throughout with the kind of attention sometimes held to be proper only for poetry (I do not mean what is called "poetic prose," rather the reverse), whereas short stories such as I have been talking about usually betray themselves as having been written only with a view to the ending.

The word *novel* will cover a multitude of sins. I can think of an author "writing" a novella, but this simple term will not do for a novel, where I have to think of him "sitting down at his desk" and "addressing himself to the task." I think of lavish productions, casts of thousands, full technicolor, photographed against authentic backgrounds, and so on. Not all of this is accurate, or it need not be, but I emphasize it for the sake of a contrast; besides, when faced with the need for a commanding generality on this topic, I find myself to have forgotten all the novels I have ever read. The contrast I want to bring out is this: for many novelists, all but the simplest element of compositional art (the plot) is destroyed by observation, by detail work, by reality which keeps poking its head in. The leisure, the "warm earthy humanity," of the novel owes itself to this consideration: people read novellas, but they tend to live in novels, and sometimes they live there very comfortably indeed: thus you have descriptions which are nothing but descriptions, thus you have philosophical excursions, set-pieces, summaries, double plot, and full orchestration, not to mention that all the chairs are heavily upholstered and even the walls padded. Stendhal provided benches for the reader to sit down on, but many novelists erect hotels for the same laudable accommodation.

Let me try to bring this distinction back down to the ground. The master novelist is Shakespearean in combinative skill, if not in language: he handles actions which are long, complex, serious, and explicitly generalized through the social and political fabric, e.g., *The Possessed, War and Peace, The Red and the Black, Remembrance of Things Past.* The authors of such works are masters in parable and reality simultaneously. Then there are masters in parable, and I would only indicate the range of this art by mentioning together the names of Jane Austen and Franz Kafka; if I say that *Emma* and *The Trial* are, for me, like short novels in spite of their length, that will suggest my feeling that the name "short novel" does not exactly discriminate, and that some such terms as *simple* and *complex* novels might be used instead. A few lesser examples may help here: Mrs. Compton-Burnett writes short novels at whatever length, as do Graham Greene and Henry Green and Virginia Woolf. I need hardly say that the distinction is not one of quality any more than it is one of length. *The Counterfeiters* means to be a novel, so does *Point Counter Point*, so does *Nostromo*, so does *Tender is the Night*, but I do not prefer them before *Lafcadio's Adventures, After Many a Summer Dies the Swan, The Secret Agent*, or *The Great Gatsby*, which are examples of the other kind.

I favor this distinction of the simple and complex, the Greek drama and the Shakespearean, over the other which seems to be based purely on length. Simple novels will normally be shorter than complex ones anyhow, though not always—I notice for instance that Cyril Connolly refers to *Gatsby* and *The Spoils of Poynton* together as short novels, and I, sharing his feeling or mistaken memory as to the latter, was surprised to find it just twice as long as *Gatsby*. But I shall not insist on these terms, simple and complex, and will draw my illustrations in the following discussion from novels generally allowed to be *short* ones.

We have, after all, only two ways of thinking about literary composition. In one, general ideas are illustrated by appropriate particulars; in the other, the contemplation of particulars produces general ideas. Perhaps neither of these species can ever be seen in purity and isolation in any given work, especially since the work as we read it offers no certain guide to the means of its composition, so that all literary composition appears as a combination of these extremes, possibly to be characterized by the dominance of one or the other. The pure state of the first kind, in which the author determines first upon a more or less systematic arrangement of general notions, then devises particular appearances for them, would be allegory of the most rigorously scientific sort, like an equation; literary allegories can never be quite that rigid, because every particular does more than illustrate, it modifies the general idea. The pure state of the second kind would exist only if the contemplation of particulars quite failed to produce general ideas and systematic meanings, but produced only the intense view of particulars as themselves the *irrational* demonstration of the nature of things: symbolism is a way station on this road which runs further to expressionism, surrealism, dada, and the riddles of the Zen Koan.

It is fashionably believed at present that the artist belongs finally to the irrational, that his is the ecstasy of the unique, the individual and irreducible, the opaque detail existing in and for itself; conversely, that reason, construction, architecture of general ideas, will destroy him as an artist. It is a theme which I shall not develop at large in this place, but the tradition of the short novel offers a good deal of evidence for the opposite view. The most striking element shared by almost all the great pieces in this genre is their outright concentration upon traditional problems of philosophy, the boldness of their venture into generality, the evidence they give of direct and profound moral concern. We are not entitled to suppose, of course, that such works were composed from the point of view first of general ideas and philosophic problems and paradoxes, even though sometimes—as with the *Notes from the Underground*, for example—it is tempting so to suppose. What we may insist is that these works combine with their actions a most explicit awareness of themselves as parables, as philosophic myths, and almost invariably announce and demonstrate the intention of discursive profundity—the intention, it is not too much to say, of becoming sacred books: final instances, exhaustively analyzed, of a symbolic universe of whose truth we can be persuaded only by fictions. The result for composition is that problem becomes the center of the short novel, which with a peculiar purity dramatizes conflicts of appearance and reality (*Benito Cereno*), freedom and necessity (*Notes from the Underground*), madness and sanity (*Ward Number Six*); all these are of course forms of a single problem essential and not accidental to the genre, which I shall try to illustrate by describing and giving examples of one theme which is pervasive to the point of obsession in the short novel.

The theme is broadly speaking that of *identity*, and the action deriving from it may be generalized as follows: the mutual attachment or dependency between A and B has a mortal strength; its dissolution requires a crisis fatal to one or the other party; but this dissolution is represented as salvation.

It is clear from many examples that the story of the Passion itself, with its suffering and dying Redeemer, sin-eater, scapegoat, is explicitly thought of in connection with this theme, which may be told as a religious parable, an adventure story, a fantasy, a psychological novel, often with strong homosexual or narcissistic emphasis.

1. The most literal form of this attachment occurs in the conclusion of *St. Julian the Hospitaler*, which Flaubert adapted from the *Gesta Roma-*

norum (though the story embodies even older materials, such as the legends of St. Hubert and St. Christopher). Julian's final penance is to lie down in the embrace of the leper, who turns into a bright angelic being and takes him to heaven.

2. In *The Private Memoirs and Confessions of a Justified Sinner*, by James Hogg, the self-righteous man is seduced and destroyed by the Prince of Darkness who appears as his double; whether his repentance speaks much for self-knowledge may be doubtful enough, but there is a redemptive note in the circumstance that he ends his life in a manger, "a byre, or cowhouse ... where, on a divot loft, my humble bedstead stood, and the cattle grunted and puffed below me."

3. Melville's short novels, those combinations of the most baldly stated symbolism with the most mysterious ambiguousness of resolution, explore this theme. Captain Delano in his benign unworldliness and innocence becomes responsible for Benito Cereno, through whose sufferings and death he is enabled to perceive, beneath appearances, how things really are. The Master in Chancery becomes liable personally, morally, religiously, and at one point legally, for Bartleby. His final phrase of sorrowful commiseration—"Ah, Bartleby! Ah, humanity!"—gains a certain force of revelation from being compared with some of his earlier statements, e.g., "I am a man who, from his youth upward, has been filled with a profound conviction that the easiest way of life is the best." *Billy Budd* is a somewhat more complex rendering. Billy and Claggart are represented as eternally fated to one another; beyond that it is Captain Vere who suffers the "mystery of iniquity" of this predestinated encounter. Billy suffers as Adam tempted and fallen, as Cain whose brother (Claggart) is preferred before him, as the Son of God whose death redeems to order an unruly people (the mutinous Navy), but who is publicly misrepresented in history (the newspaper article) and art (the ballad). Other, less religious interpretation is possible, but enough has been said for the present purpose.

4. In Conrad's *The Secret Sharer* the story is told with a particular purity as well as a rare optimism (in other examples where the disappearance of one party is allowed to do for his death, that disappearance is usually into an insane asylum). The young captain, irresolute and uncertain in his first command, comes face to face with his double: "It was, in the night, as though I had been faced by my own reflection in the depths of a somber and immense mirror." By protecting Leggatt (a legate from the darkness of the sea outside and the self within), by sharing his identity, by experiencing in homeopathic amounts the criminal element in his own nature, by at last liberating, or separating, this other self from his own at the risk

of shipwreck, the young man gains a "perfect communion" with his first command.

Marlow says of Kurtz, "It was written I should be loyal to the nightmare of my choice," and he is loyal to the final extent of lying for him, though "there is a taint of death, a flavor of mortality, in lies." The view of Kurtz as scapegoat, as evil or fallen savior, is generalized throughout, notably in what Marlow says to his audience, those nameless masters of the world, the Director of Companies, the Lawyer, the Narrator: "You can't understand. How could you?—with solid pavement under your feet, surrounded by kind neighbors ready to cheer you or fall on you, stepping delicately between the butcher and the policeman, in the holy terror of scandal and gallows and lunatic asylums—how can you imagine what particular region of the first ages a man's untrammeled feet may take him into by the way of solitude—utter solitude without a policeman—by the way of silence—utter silence, where no warning voice of a kind neighbor can be heard whispering of public opinion. These little things make all the great difference." So Kurtz is an instance of absolute power corrupted absolutely, yes, but this power is further characterized as that of the impulsive, archaic life liberated, which no man can bear and live, which Marlow himself nearly died of the briefest and most homeopathic contact with, and which in some sense is the force that makes history and makes civilization.

5. The theme we are describing is of the first importance to Dostoevsky, who intensifies both the psychological penetration of the treatment and its ultimate religious or metaphysical expansions. The typical bond, between the worldly man and his sinister, underworld, epicene counterpart—his "poor relation," as the Devil is called in *The Brothers Karamazov*—occurs in the major novels in such double figures as Ivan and Smerdyakov, Ivan and the Devil, Christ and the Grand Inquisitor, Stavrogin and Pyotr Stepanovich, and, with a quite different tonality, Muishkin and Rogozhin. Two of the short novels concentrate exclusively on the development of this theme. *The Eternal Husband* ties together the seducer and the cuckold in a relation characterized as ambiguously homosexual and sadistic, a comedy agonizing enough but hardly more so than that of *The Double*, which relates how poor, stupid Mr. Golyadkin, portrayed from the outset as suffering symptoms of paranoia, comes face to face with his double, Golyadkin, Jr., who behaves insufferably, calls him "darling," pinches his cheek, embarrasses him in every way public and private, until the original Golyadkin, what remains of him, is driven off to the asylum. In this last scene several people run after the carriage, shouting, until they are

left behind, and "Mr. Golyadkin's unworthy twin kept up longer than anyone . . . he ran on with a satisfied air, skipping first to one and then to the other side of the carriage . . . poking his head in at the window, and throwing farewell kisses to Mr. Golyadkin."

6. Without giving any further examples in detail I may merely mention a few more short novels in which this theme is developed: in Chekhov's *Ward Number Six*, Andrew Ephimich and the young man Ivan Dimitrich Gronov; the young soldier and his captain in Lawrence's *The Prussian Officer*; Aschenbach and Tadzio in Mann's *Death in Venice*, Mario and Cipolla in his *Mario and the Magician*; the condemned man and the officer in *In the Penal Colony* by Kafka; Howe and Tertan in Lionel Trilling's *Of This Time, of That Place*; Wilhelm and Dr. Tamkin in Saul Bellow's *Seize the Day*.

My intention is to discuss composition in the strict sense, rather than to consider the interpretation and historical placement of this thematic insistence. Yet it is worth pausing here to observe in how many of these stories the theme is employed to show the man of the middle class, rational, worldly, either rather stupid or of a somewhat dry intelligence and limited vision, plunged into the domain of the forbidden, extravagant, and illicit, the life of the impulses beneath or the life of compulsive and punitive authority above, both of them equally regions in which every detail gains fatal significance, every perception is excruciatingly intensified, and every decision for salvation or doom: so it happens, in various ways, to Captain Delano, the Master in Chancery, Ivan Ilyich, Gustave Aschenbach, Velchaninov, Gregor Samsa, the Woman Who Rode Away, Andrew Ephimich. . . . And it is remarkable, too, how often, by the device of the double, ·the incubus as it were, their sufferings and perceptions seem to invade them ambiguously from the world outside and the self within. I am tempted to think that the characteristic economy of the short novel, its precisely defined space, the peculiar lucidity and simplicity of its internal forms—two or three persons, a single action, equal tension among the persons, each of whom has a fate—tends to involve the artist more overtly than usual in trying to.expound by fantasies what he himself is and what he is doing in his art. Indeed, this is perhaps cryptically hinted to us by Flaubert, when he makes his Félicité suffer the lash of a coachman's whip on the road between Honfleur and Pont l'Eveque, where he himself, riding in a carriage, suffered his first attack of epilepsy, or serious hysteria. And by Melville, who sees his scrivener—unwilling to copy the writings of others—as having had the previous job of handling dead letters "and assorting them for the flames"—this in the year after a fire at the publishing house had destroyed the plates for Melville's own works. Less cryptically by Mann, who sees his artist-heroes by turns as diseased aristocrats, confidence men, and monstrous tyrants (Savonarola, Cipolla). For the fullest meaning of the theme, most minutely expounded, we should have to refer to Proust, who by the most intricately woven analogies throughout his immense work characterizes the moral isolation of the poet as, on the one hand, that of the invalid, the pervert, the criminal, the Jew, the traitor, and, on the other hand, that of the hero, aristocrat, doctor or surgeon, and commander of armies in the field.

Whether what I have tried to describe is the product of a limited historical tradition or of a tragic circumstance as near eternal as that witnessed to in Greek tragedies or in the Book of Job I am unable to say certainly and must not stop to debate here. So far as the theme results in actions typical of the short novel—actions simple and decisive, generally mortal in fact, and involving few persons—the following points of compositional interest arise.

Whereas the short story tends to rest upon action, a combination of circumstances to which the characters must very readily conform, while the novel, especially in English, goes toward the opposite pole and tends to produce "characters" as an independent value, the short novel strikes a very delicate and exact balance between motive and circumstance; its action generally speaking is the fate of the agonists, and this fate is regarded as flowing demonstrably and with some precision and in great detail from their individual natures, which accordingly are developed at considerable length. I need barely mention examples: the portraits, as distinct from the stories, of e.g., Aschenbach, Captain Delano, The Man from Underground, Gabriel Conroy, John Marcher. . . . What happens to all these persons, and ever so many other protagonists of the short novel, happens expressly to them and because they are as they are; perhaps the simplest instance is that of Captain Delano, whose innocence is represented precisely as the condition of his survival in a naughty world: "a person of a singularly undistrustful good nature, not liable, except on extraordinary and repeated excitement, and hardly then, to indulge in personal alarms, any way involving the imputation of malign evil in man. Whether, in view of what humanity is capable, such a trait implies, along with a benevolent heart, more than ordinary quickness and accuracy of intellectual perception, may be left to the wise to determine."

The same balance is maintained by the authors of these compositions, in the exact division of their attention to the inside of things and the outside, between knowledge of the ordinary, undramatic world, and imagination of the drama which takes place under its exacting conditions. How this is so may be seen most simply from *Notes from the Underground*, where the argument and its dramatic equivalent are given separately; oftener, however, the two strands are concurrent, and occasionally, in very sophisticated and elegant works, they are identical; as in *Un Coeur Simple*, which may be read as the plain product of observation, as though a "sketch of provincial life," and read again, or simultaneously, as a structure of great intricacy and density, entirely musical and contrapuntal in the laws of its being, and consequently forming a world all its own, rhythmic, resonant, symmetrical, in which every detail balances another so as to produce great riches of meaning not so much symbolically in a direct sense as by constellation and patterning, the method James called the figure in the carpet. In this connection I would mention once again Kay Boyle as possibly the foremost modern practitioner of this subtle style, especially in two short novels, *The Crazy Hunter* and *The Bridegroom's Body*.

It is this balance, so like that of the poetic drama, the balance between the appearance and the motive, the observed world and the world of law, which I conceive to be more exactly drawn and maintained in the short novel than elsewhere, that gives to works in this genre the characteristic of ruthlessness I referred to before. The ideal, that every detail should at once seem freely chosen by probable observation, and be in fact the product of a developing inner necessity, confers on these tales something of the air of demonstrations; so that, for example, when Andrew Ephimich is first drawn to visit Gronov in the asylum it is as though the chess master announced mate in twelve—we neither doubt the result nor see at all how it is to be accomplished. In this sense we sometimes feel the protagonists of short novels to be the victims not of fate or of the gods so much as of literary styles and laws of composition—that strict style of composition discussed by Adrian Leverkühn, himself such a victim, in Mann's *Dr. Faustus*.

This again is a subject I must be content to leave implicit: whether the idea itself of the "art work" any longer has anything to do with anything; whether, being based at last on religious valuations, magical sanctions, and the sense of a universe at once "real" and "symbolic," a universe of signatures, the work of art can continue to interpret human experience. I merely note that this theme is disturbingly *there*, and pass on to safer ground.

The characteristic balance I am speaking of reflects itself very distinc-

tively in the treatment of detail in short novels; more so, or more perspic-
uously so, than in long ones. A few instances will serve to conclude this
discussion.

There are two kinds of relevance in literary composition, and I think
they are both readily observable in principle although it is doubtful whether
they can always be distinguished in the work itself. One kind has to do
with the temporal succession of events, as though the single point of the
idea must be viewed in an added dimension as a straight line: in order to
tell how a distinguished German author dies in Venice we must get him
to Venice, keep him there, and supply a disease for him to die of. He will
doubtless see many things, and think many things, on his journey—what
things? We need another kind of relevance, having to do with association,
symbol, metaphor, as well as with probable and realistic observation; while
the distinguished author is in Venice it occurs to him, waking, that his
situation is like that discussed in the *Phaedrus*, and, dreaming, that his
situation is like that of King Pentheus in *The Bacchae* of Euripedes.

The first kind of relevance you may call external, the second internal;
or, better, the first is linear, and progresses in time, while the second is
radical and comes at every instant from the central conception. The difference between them, practically speaking, is that the story could be told
without the contribution of the symbolic details and could not be told
without the succession of events. It will be objected, perhaps, that without
the symbolic details, or with other symbolic details, it would be a different
story and an inferior one, and that is true enough but for compositional
purposes irrelevant. What is more important is that neither kind in itself
accounts for the story, what makes it worth our while to hear that the
distinguished German author went to Venice and died there—for that we
require something that binds both sorts together, and makes the temporal
and ideal situations the subject of the same decision: in this instance the
figure of the boy Tadzio, who according to the first kind of relevance is
the motive for Aschenbach's remaining in Venice long enough to contract
his fatal disease, and according to the second kind plays Dionysus to his
Pentheus, Phaedrus to his Socrates, inspires highly relevant reflections on
love and morality, beauty and disease, form and corruption, aristocratic
control and chaos, and so on.

The tensions of these two criteria of choice in the short novel tend to
make the selection of details extraordinarily fateful; especially it seems
that everything which is symbolic, associational, metaphorically relevant,
is multiply determined, as the details of a dream are said to be, and thus

gains a dramatic prominence and a kind of luminous quality. I will try to illustrate by a few examples.

When Aschenbach dies, there by the shore, we are told that the weather was autumnal, the beach deserted and not even very clean; suddenly we are given this: "A camera on a tripod stood at the edge of the water, apparently abandoned, its black cloth snapped in the freshening wind." That is all, our attention is given to Tadzio, Aschenbach's death soon follows, the camera is never mentioned again.

Crudely speaking, this camera is unnecessary and no one could possibly have noticed anything missing had the author decided against its inclusion; yet in a musical, compositional sense it exquisitely touches the center of the story and creates a resonance which makes us for a moment aware of the entire inner space of the action, of all things relevant and their relations to one another.

Our sense of this is mostly beyond exposition, as symbolic things have a way of being; but some of its elements may be mentioned. About the camera by the sea there is, first, a poignant desolation, the emptiness of vast spaces, and in its pictorial quality it resembles one of the earliest images in the story, when Aschenbach, standing by the cemetery, looks away down the empty streets: "not a wagon in sight, either on the paved Ungererstrasse, with its gleaming tramlines stretching off towards Schwabing, nor on the Föhring highway." Both pictures are by Di Chirico. The camera's black cloth reminds us of the gondola, "black as nothing else on earth except a coffin," and the repeated insistence on black in that description; also of the "labor in darkness" which brings forth the work of art. For we perceive that the camera stands to the sea as, throughout this story, the artist has stood to experience, in a morally heroic yet at the same time dubious or ridiculous or even impossible relation of form to all possibility, and that at the summer's end, in the freshening wind, the camera is abandoned. It would be near forgivable, so full of Greek mysteries is this work, if we thought the tripod itself remotely Delphic.

Here is another example. At the beginning of *The Secret Sharer* Conrad gives us an image which at that time, perhaps, we cannot see as anything but pictorial: the young man, looking out across the sea, sees "lines of fishing stakes resembling a mysterious system of half-submerged bamboo fences." But when we have finished the story we may see even that image in the first sentence as compositionally resonant, as a cryptic emblem set up at the gateway of the action. This emblem suggests to us how the conscious distinctions, the property rights, of reason and society, extend also beneath the surface (of the sea, of the mind) and are in fact rooted down there: precisely what is learned by the narrator who before his adventure "rejoiced in the great security of the sea as compared with the unrest of the land, in my choice of that untempted life presenting no disquieting problems, invested with an elementary moral beauty by the absolute straightforwardness of its appeal and by the singleness of its purpose"— fine phrases, on which the story, like its opening image, comments in sympathetic, pedagogic irony.

Another example. In *The Death of Ivan Ilyich*, Tolstoy shows us the funeral service and a colleague of the dead man going in to visit the widow, who is under three several necessities which exclude one another: of showing terrible grief, of passing ashtrays to prevent the guest's spoiling the rug, of discussing the payment of her husband's pension. The visitor sits down "on a low pouffe, the springs of which yielded under his weight." The widow, however, catches her shawl on the edge of a table, so "Peter Ivanovich rose to detach it, and the springs of the pouffe, relieved of his weight, rose also and gave him a push. The widow began detaching her shawl herself, and Peter Ivanovich again sat down, suppressing the rebellious springs of the pouffe under him. But the widow had not quite freed herself, and Peter Ivanovich got up again, and again the pouffe rebelled and even creaked." A page later, as the widow approaches the subject of the pension, "Peter Ivanovich bowed, keeping control of the springs of the pouffe, which immediately began quivering under him."

This comically autonomous pouffe represents not merely the social obliquities of the interview, nor merely that inanimate objects continually mutter their comments to the detriment of human dignity and solemnity, but also how such objects may tend actively to push us where we do not wish to go, to represent some implacable hostility in the world of objects, especially those meant for our convenience. Death occurs with just the same independence of human volition, and we are emblematically informed—"As he sat down on the pouffe Peter Ivanovich recalled how Ivan Ilyich has arranged this room and had consulted him regarding this pink cretonne with green leaves"—of something we learn more explicitly later, that Ivan Ilyich's interest precisely in such things, in "decoration," caused his death: "when mounting a stepladder to show the upholsterer, who did not understand, how he wanted the hangings draped, he made a false step and slipped. . . ."

This species of inner determination produces, in the short novel, not single details only but chains and clusters of iterative imagery also, such as we usually identify with the poetry of Shakespeare; and sometimes, as in *Un Coeur Simple*, it is the elegant patterning and constatation of such groups of images which alone, implicitly, supply the meaning, or meanings: an interested reader may trace on his own, for example, the provenience of the parrot-paraclete Loulou, not in the action alone, but in the far-ranging associated imagery—how it is gradually prepared for before its appearance by much talk of jungles and far places, by the geography book given the children by M. Bourais, by Félicité's childish ideas of distant places and times, by Victor's voyages and death, by Mme. Auban's dream after the death of Virginie, and so on.

I have tried to describe the short novel, according to the examples I am most familiar with, not as a compromise between novel and short story, but as something like the ideal and primary form, suggestively allied in simplicity and even in length with the tragedies of antiquity, and dealing in effect with equivalent materials. No doubt in dealing with this subject I have slighted somewhat the complex novel and, even more, the short story; that has to do in part, as I said, with making the middle term visible, but perhaps in even greater part with my lasting delight in short novels, which I will even go so far as nearly to identify with tragic art in our fictional tradition. What is accomplished by the works I have been speaking of may be given the sanction of science as well as magic or religion in the following words of Sir D'Arcy Wentworth Thompson in the introductory chapter of his work *On Growth and Form*: "Like warp and woof, mechanism and teleology are interwoven together, and we must not cleave to the one nor despise the other; for their union is rooted in the very nature of totality. We may grow shy or weary of looking to a final cause for an explanation of our phenomena; but after we have accounted for these on the plainest principles of mechanical causation it may be useful and appropriate to see how the final cause would tally with the other, and lead towards the same conclusion." It is this double exploration which, I have contended, is undertaken in the short novel more than in other sorts of fiction. Even the matter of the length or brevity of such works ought not to be beneath discussion as "merely" mechanical; in the book I quoted from before, Vladimir Nabokov says something which I shall repeat for a conclusion to this matter. Discussing ways of seeing—the lantern slide, the microscope—he says, "There is, it would seem, in the dimensional scale of the world a kind of delicate meeting-place between imagination and knowledge, a point, arrived at by diminishing large things and enlarging small ones, that is intrinsically artistic."

Themes and Methods in the Early Stories of Thomas Mann

THE art work has, to begin with, its own form, its own finish, and represents an achievement in itself. Retrospectively, however, each work by a master has an additional significance as an episode or chapter in the development of his art; that voyage of discovery whose three-fold goal is to liberate, elucidate, and universalize the author's characteristic obsession with certain figures, materials, means of composition.

The reader's retracing the steps of this journey, though he profit, like any historian, solely from the wisdom of hindsight, is a process not without interest; one gets a view, even if it is a fictive view, of things which had seemed deep and hidden in each individual work, but which now become apparent in the whole series; one gets a view of the necessity within what had looked arbitrary; it is an exercise in the "reading of destinies." The reader is privileged to make, rapidly and with some ease though at greatly diminished intensity, some of the discoveries which his author must have made painfully and laboriously over many years; and he thus participates vicariously, as well as he may, in the idea of creation. For the author himself does not begin with "a world," ready-made and waiting only to be described; he begins rather with an impulse, a tendency, a secret which is secret also from himself and can express itself only indirectly, in the work, by means of the work.

Rapidly and very generally resuming Thomas Mann's career in fiction, from the somber naturalism of *Buddenbrooks* through the symbolic and allegorical fabrics of *The Magic Mountain* and *Doctor Faustus*, the triumphant "God-invention" of *Joseph and His Brothers*, the miracle tales of *The Transposed Heads* and *The Holy Sinner*, to the satyr play of *Felix Krull* which crowns and in a sense redeems the entire *oeuvre*, we are struck not only by the immense reach of this author's development, but also by the great constancy at all times dominant over it. Beginning with original sin in the shape of the artist's expulsion from a nineteenth century bourgeois Eden, the fatally corrupting flaw of knowledge, the reflexive splitting-off of consciousness from self, becomes the dialectical instrument for re-creating history, gradually expanding to take in the furthest realms of power, politics, and the practical life. To say something of the beginnings of all this, of how much of it, to hindsight at any rate, is already present at the start, is the object of this essay.

Disappointed lovers of life and the world, those whose love has turned to hatred or to cynicism, those whose love is an abject and constantly tormenting surrender in the face of scorn, those whose love masquerades as indifference and superiority which a chance encounter will destroy— such are the protagonists of Mann's early stories.

Perhaps the simplest expression of the type occurs in "Little Herr Friedemann" (1897). Deformed by an accident in infancy, Friedemann learns by the age of sixteen that love is not for him. Very well, he will settle for what remains when that is subtracted: the innocent pleasure one takes in nature; the almost equally innocent pleasures afforded by books, music, and especially the theater. And so he lives quietly until he is thirty, when he meets a woman whose beauty becomes his obsession, and whose scorn for his humpbacked, pigeon-breasted self causes him to take his own life. But her scorn can gain this final power only after her kindness has broken through his carefully constructed defenses:

"Thirty years old," she repeated. "And those thirty years were not happy ones?"
Little Herr Friedemann shook his head, his lips quivered.
"No," he said, "that was all lies and my imagination."

With the help of "lies and imagination" he has composed for all these years a disciplined, critical life not without elegance, a life based precisely upon his infirmity and what it has forbidden him. In this life, love is characterized as "an attack," and associated with physical symptoms of fever

and fatigue. It is not so much the woman Gerda who destroys Herr Friedemann, as it is what she evokes from within him in the way of the forbidden, the long-buried will-to-live which is for him a mortal sickness. There
is in this figure, with his masochistic stoicism, his deliberate self-limitation,
his rigid intelligence, already much of Aschenbach, whose more elaborate
destiny in "Death in Venice" is similarly grounded on the clash of archaic
impulses with the prohibitions of civilization, art, and intellect, to say nothing of a certain physical debility.

The same revelation, the same knowledge of scornful betrayal on the
part of the beloved, destroys the hero of "Little Lizzy" (1897), the lawyer
Jacoby, whose disability in life it is to be enormously, grotesquely, painfully fat, and to despise himself on this account. His life is an endless
apology, a will to humiliation (in this he a little resembles, as he does also
in some physical respects, Chekhov's Andrew Ephimich in "Ward Number
Six," and compare the figure of Wehsal in "The Magic Mountain"), and he
is most abject in his love for his wife, who betrays him with a musician,
Alfred Läutner. It is the sudden knowledge of this betrayal which brings
about Jacoby's death, as his wife and her lover compel him to participate
in some amateur theatricals as "Little Lizzy," "a *chanteuse* in a red satin
baby frock."

It is worth dwelling in some detail on the crisis of this story, because
it brings together a number of characteristic elements and makes of them
a curious, riddling compound obscurely but centrally significant for Mann's
work.

The wife, Amra, and her lover are both savagely portrayed, she as incarnate sensuality, "voluptuous" and "indolent," possibly "a mischief maker,"
with "a kind of luxurious cunning" to set against her apparent simplicity,
her "birdlike brain." Läutner, for his part, "belonged to the present-day
race of small artists, who do not demand the utmost of themselves," and
the bitter description of the type includes such epithets as "wretched little
poseurs," the devastating indictment "they do not know how to be wretched
decently and in order," and the somewhat extreme prophecy, so far not
fulfilled: "They will be destroyed."

The trick these two play upon Jacoby reveals their want not simply of
decency but of imagination as well. His appearance as Lizzy evokes not
amusement but horror in the audience; it is a spectacle absolutely painful,
an epiphany of the suffering flesh unredeemed by spirit, untouched by
any spirit other than abasement and humiliation. At the same time the
multiple transvestitism involved—the fat man as girl and as baby, as co-
quette pretending to be a baby—touches for a moment horrifyingly upon

the secret sources of a life like Jacoby's, upon the sinister dreams which form the sources of any human life.

The music which Läutner has composed for this episode is for the most part "rather pretty and perfectly banal." But it is characteristic of him, we are told, "his little artifice," to be able to introduce "into a fairly vulgar and humorous piece of hackwork a sudden phrase of genuine creative art." And this occurs now, at the refrain of Jacoby's song—at the point, in fact, of the name "Lizzy"—a modulation described as "almost a stroke of genius." "A miracle, a revelation, it was like a curtain suddenly torn away to reveal something nude." It is this modulation which reveals to Jacoby his own frightful abjection and, simultaneously, his wife's infidelity. By the same means he perceives this fact as having communicated itself to the audience; he collapses, and dies.

In the work of every artist, I suppose, there may be found one or more moments which strike the student as absolutely decisive, ultimately emblematic of what it is all about; not less strikingly so for being mysterious, as though some deeply hidden constatation of thoughts were enciphered in a single image, a single moment. So here. The horrifying humor, the specifically sexual embarrassment of the joke gone wrong, the monstrous image of the fat man dressed up as a whore dressing up as a baby; the epiphany of that quivering flesh; the bringing together around it of the secret liaison between indolent, mindless sensuality and sharp, shrewd talent, cleverness with an occasional touch of genius (which, however, does not know "how to attack the problem of suffering"); the miraculous way in which music, revelation, and death are associated in a single instant—all this seems a triumph of art, a rather desperate art, in itself; beyond itself, also, it evokes numerous and distant resonances from the entire body of Mann's work.

When I try to work out my reasons for feeling that this passage is of critical significance, I come up with the following ideas, which I shall express very briefly here.

Love is the crucial dilemma of experience for Mann's heroes. The dramatic construction of his stories characteristically turns on a situation in which someone is simultaneously compelled and forbidden to love. The release, the freedom, involved in loving another is either terribly difficult or else absolutely impossible; and the motion toward it brings disaster.

This prohibition on love has an especially poignant relation to art; it is particularly the artist (Tonio Kröger, Aschenbach, Leverkühn) who suffers from it. The specific analogy to the dilemma of love is the problem of the "breakthrough" in the realm of art.

Again, the sufferings and disasters produced by any transgression against the commandment not to love are almost invariably associated in one way or another with childhood, with the figure of a child.

Finally, the theatrical (and perversely erotic) notions of dressing up, cosmetics, disguise, and especially change of costume (or singularity of constume, as with Cipolla), are characteristically associated with the catastrophes of Mann's stories.

We shall return to these statements and deal with them more fully as the evidence for them accumulates. For the present it is enough to note that in the grotesque figure of Jacoby, at the moment of his collapse, all these elements come together in prophetic parody. Professionally a lawyer, that is to say associated with dignity, reserve, discipline, with much that is essentially middle-class, he is compelled by an impossible love to exhibit himself dressed up, disguised—that is, paradoxically, revealed—as a child, and, worse, as a whore masquerading as a child.* That this abandonment takes place on a stage, during an "artistic" performance, is enough to associate Jacoby with art, and to bring down upon him the punishment for art; that is, he is suspect, guilty, punishable, as is anyone in Mann's stories who produces *illusion*, and this is true even though the constant elements of the artist-nature, technique, magic, guilt, and suffering, are divided in this story between Jacoby and Läutner.

It appears that the dominant tendency of Mann's early tales, however pictorial or even picturesque the surface, is already toward the symbolic, the emblematic, the expressionistic. In a certain perfectly definite way, the method and the theme of his stories are one and the same.

Something of this can be learned from "The Way to the Churchyard" (1901), an anecdote about an old failure whose fit of anger at a passing cyclist causes him to die of a stroke or seizure. There is no more "plot" than that; only slightly more, perhaps, than a newspaper account of such an incident would give. The artistic interest, then, lies in what the encounter may be made to represent, in the power of some central significance to draw the details into relevance and meaningfulness.

The first sentence, with its platitudinous irony, announces an emblematic intent: "The way to the churchyard ran along beside the highroad, ran beside it all the way to the end; that is to say, to the churchyard." And the action is consistently presented with regard for this distinction. The highroad, one might say at first, belongs to life, while the way to the churchyard belongs to death. But that is too simple, and won't hold up. As the

*We may compare the sufferings of Leopold Bloom in Nighttown.

first sentence suggests, both roads belong to death in the end. But the highroad, according to the description of its traffic, belongs to life as it is lived in unawareness of death, while the way to the churchyard belongs to some other form of life: a suffering form, an existence wholly comprised in the awareness of death. Thus, on the highroad, a troop of soldiers "marched in their own dust and sang," while on the footpath one man walks alone.

This man's isolation is not merely momentary, it is permanent. He is a widower, his three children are dead, he has no one left on earth; also he is a drunk, and has lost his job on that account. His name is Praisegod Piepsam, and he is rather fully described as to his clothing and physiognomy in a way which relates him to a sinister type in the author's repertory—he is a forerunner of those enigmatic strangers in "Death in Venice," for example, who represent some combination of cadaver, exotic, and psycho-pomp.

This strange person quarrels with a cyclist because the latter is using the path rather than the highroad. The cyclist, a sufficiently commonplace young fellow, is not named but identified simply as "Life"—that and a license number, which Piepsam uses in addressing him. "Life" points out that "everybody uses this path," and starts to ride on. Piepsam tries to stop him by force, receives a push in the chest from "Life," and is left standing in impotent and growing rage, while a crowd begins to gather. His rage assumes a religious form; that is, on the basis of his own sinfulness and abject wretchedness, Piepsam becomes a prophet who in his ecstasy and in the name of God imprecates doom on Life—not only the cyclist now, but the audience, the world, as well: "all you light-headed breed." This passion brings on a fit which proves fatal. Then an ambulance comes along, and they drive Praisegod Piepsam away.

This is simple enough, but several more points of interest may be mentioned as relevant. The season, between spring and summer, belongs to life in its carefree aspect. Piepsam's fatal rage arises not only because *he* cannot stop the cyclist, but also because God will not stop him; as Piepsam says to the crowd in his last moments: "His justice is not of this world."

Life is further characterized, in antithesis to Piepsam, as animal: the image of a dog, which appears at several places, is first given as the criterion of amiable, irrelevant interest aroused by life considered simply as a spectacle: a dog in a wagon is "admirable," "a pleasure to contemplate"; another wagon has no dog, and therefore is "devoid of interest." Piepsam calls the cyclist "cur" and "puppy" among other things, and at the crisis of his fit a little fox terrier stands before him and howls into his face. The ambulance is drawn by two "charming" little horses.

Piepsam is not, certainly, religious in any conventional sense. His religiousness is intimately, or dialectically, connected with his sinfulness; the two may in fact be identical. His unsuccessful strivings to give up drink are represented as religious strivings; he keeps a bottle in a wardrobe at home, and "before this wardrobe Praisegod Piepsam had before now gone literally on his knees, and in his wrestlings had bitten his tongue—and still in the end capitulated."

The cyclist, by contrast, blond and blue-eyed, is simply unreflective, unproblematic Life, "blithe and carefree." "He made no claims to belong to the great and mighty of this earth."

Piepsam is grotesque, a disturbing parody; his end is ridiculous and trivial. He is "a man raving mad on the way to the churchyard." But he is more interesting than the others, the ones who come from the highroad to watch him, more interesting than Life considered as a cyclist. And if I have gone into so much detail about so small a work, that is because it is also so typical a work, representing the germinal form of a conflict which remains essential in Mann's writing: the crude sketch of Piepsam contains, in its critical, destructive, and self-destructive tendencies, much that is enlarged and illuminated in the figures of, for instance, Naphta and Leverkühn.

In method as well as in theme this little anecdote, with its details selected as much for expressiveness and allegory as for "realism," anticipates a kind of musical composition, as well as a kind of fictional composition, in which, as Leverkühn says, "there shall be nothing unthematic." It resembles, too, pictures such as Dürer and Bruegel did, in which all that looks at first to be solely pictorial proves on inspection to be also literary, the representation of a proverb, for example, or a deadly sin.

"Gladius Dei" (1902) resembles "The Way to the Churchyard" in its representation of a conflict between light and dark, between "Life" and a spirit of criticism, negation, melancholy, but it goes considerably further in characterizing the elements of this conflict.

The monk Savanarola, brought over from the Renaissance and placed against the background of Munich at the turn of the century, protests against the luxurious works displayed in the art shop of M. Bluthenzweig; in particular against a Madonna portrayed in a voluptuous style and modeled, according to gossip, upon the painter's mistress. Hieronymus, like Piepsam, makes his protest quite in vain, and his rejection, though not fatal, is ridiculous and humiliating; he is simply thrown out of the shop by the porter. On the street outside, Hieronymus envisions a holocaust of the vanities of this world, such a burning of artistic and erotic productions as his namesake actually brought to pass in Florence, and prophetically he issues his curse: "*Gladius Dei supra terram cito et velociter.*"

Hieronymus, like Piepsam, is alone, withdrawn, a failure, ugly, dressed in black; a representative of spirit in the sense that one manifestation of spirit is pure negation based on the conviction of one's own and the world's utter sinfulness. He is like a shadow on "radiant" Munich—again it is early summer, the time belongs to Life—with its elegance, unconventionality, loose morals, its emphatically Renaissance and Italianate ambition of viewing life altogether as "art." On this scene he cannot fail to appear graceless, awkward, depressing; nor can any remark of his, in this context, be other than ridiculous. To a salesman he says that the painting of the Madonna "is vice itself . . . naked sensuality," and that he has overheard how it affected two simple young people and "led them astray on the doctrine of the Immaculate Conception"; to which the salesman replies: "Oh, permit me—that is not the point," and goes on to "explain" that "the picture is a work of art."

This parable is similar to that of "The Way to the Churchyard" in posing against the brilliant, careless commonplace of the world a rebellious figure who insists with all his being that all around him is a vicious sham, and that the truth of life consists in suffering, misery, failure. But in the figure of the monk this attitude is much enriched, complicated, and, accordingly, compromised.

Like Friedemann's life, and Jacoby's, that of Hieronymus is based with Freudian piety on what is forbidden, on denial; and his catastrophe amounts to a return of the repressed. The painting of the Madonna, which he objects to as blasphemous and tending to the corruption of morality, has become his erotic obsession: always with him, even in church, "it stood before his outraged soul." "And no prayer availed to exorcise it." (Compare the treatment of the theme in "Fiorenza," where Savonarola's religious hatred of Lorenzo's mistress is depicted as the consequence of his unrequited lust.) The ambiguous reference of beauty, to the ideal on one side, to the flesh on the other, to the spiritual and the sexual equally, is the stumbling-block for many of Mann's characters: "Beauty alone . . . is lovely and visible at once . . . it is the sole aspect of the spiritual which we can perceive through the senses, or bear so to perceive." Thus Aschenbach, in "Death in Venice," feverishly recollecting Socrates in the *Phaedrus* and characteristically stressing the implication that the spiritual, in becoming visible, also becomes compromised and corrupted.

Hence the problem of art, with its double allegiance to the spirit and the senses inextricably and at once. Hieronymus' rage is not inchoate like Piepsam's; at first, anyhow, it is orderly, eloquent, as well intellectual as impassioned, and directed especially against the affinity of art for elegance, decoration, illusion, laxness and luxury; he would reject that art in favor of an art bent on spiritual knowledge, "in which the passions of our loathsome flesh die away and are quenched." For him, "art is no conscienceless delusion, lending itself to reinforce the allurements of the fleshly. Art is the holy torch which turns its light upon all the frightful depths. . . ." One notes that this definition equably accepts it that art is in the service of knowledge, and that knowledge in turn is in the service of negation and utter annihilation: illuminate to destroy. The agon upon this question continues to be played out, in varying forms, with varying results, through all Mann's works.

An element of composition, of method, also of enduring significance, makes its first appearance here. The central figure is as it were not an "individual" at all, but is based on a prototype from history; he is Savonarola, somewhat clumsily taken over in all his features and attitudes from fifteenth century Florence; and this identity is accented: "Seen in profile his face was strikingly like an old painting preserved at Florence in a narrow cloister cell whence once a frightful and shattering protest issued against life and her triumphs." This circumstance raises some odd questions about the relation between character and deed, will and fate, the actor and his part; it introduces for the first time that further question, so poignant for Mann's art, whether and in what sense the work has to do with life, how the one is fitted, if it is, to interpret the other; how far the idea of destiny, for example, is nothing more than a law of literary composition, having no more status in reality than the device of a magician. For the moment, it is enough to note the early presence of this question, deferring the discussion of it until we shall have collected other examples, in which this "taking over" of the historical, legendary, or literary extends beyond the persons to the action of the drama itself.

The examples we have so far considered share one dominant trait, and that is the doomed impotence of the lonely protagonist against a world which is cruel, mocking, or indifferent; a world in which the inevitable end of his attempt either to live more fully or to overcome life is defeat: his humiliation, followed three times out of four by his death. Whether this death be literally suicide, as with Friedemann, or the result of a stroke of some sort, as with Piepsam and Jacoby, it comes from within; it is a product of self-knowledge, and somehow suggestive of a fulfillment of a wish; one might say that the suppressed erotic nature in these persons reaches out and forces the world to destroy them. For the solitude in which they live is an absolute one; their efforts to break the charmed circle of their isolation appear as impulses to self-destruction.

There is another, and somewhat more fruitful, sort of isolation exhibited in these works, and the examination of some instances of this sort may serve to conclude our discussion of the early stories and sketches.

This is the isolation of the artist, the being who has some not altogether satisfactory yet not necessarily fatal way of responding to the world. Like the other kind, that of Piepsam, Friedemann, etc., it is an enforced loneliness often associated with disease and death; it ends not in violence, however, but rather as a dream, distancing itself and losing itself in the distances; its tonality is different from that of the other. The suffering protagonist may be viewed with some mockery, may even view himself with contempt ("Disillusionment," "The Dilettante"), but upon the whole he is regarded with sympathy by the author, perhaps because he has some insight into his own sufferings ("The Hungry," "A Weary Hour").

In "The Wardrobe" (1899), Albrecht van der Qualen, though still a young man, is mortally ill; doctors have given him only a few more months to live; we scarcely need his name to relate him with agonies and torments. Traveling on the Berlin-Rome express, he yields to impulse and gets off at a way station, a town whose name he does not know. Here, he reflects, he is free; he experiences what Hans Castorp will later know as "the advantages of shame": "Honest unhappiness without charity," thinks Van der Qualen, "is a good thing; a man can say to himself: I owe God nothing."

In this nameless town he rents a room; in the room is a wardrobe; from the wardrobe appears to him at night a girl* who tells him sad, ballad-like stories, and also, in a fevered phantasy somewhere between dream and reality, sweetness and shame, becomes his mistress . . . and that is all, there is no more "story" than that. But that any of it ever "really" happened is a matter of doubt to the author. "Would any of us care to take the responsibility of giving a definite answer?"

This lonely traveler, diseased, bemused, on a journey without beginning or end (he never gets to Rome and we are specifically told that Berlin

---

*She appears from the wardrobe. Piepsam hid his bottle in the wardrobe and went on his knees before it. One might thoughtfully continue to look for wardrobes, cupboards, closets, which turn into tabernacles. Consider, for example, the cupboard from which Hans Lorenz Castorp reverently takes the christening basin.

had not been the beginning of his trip), is the embryonic form of the artist hero; more exactly, the bourgeois artist hero. One observes that Van der Qualen has a first-class compartment, just as his fellow artists and fellow sufferers do: the writer-narrator of "Railway Accident," Tonio Kröger, Gustave Aschenbach. Tonio Kröger supplies the reason, which is that "anyone who suffered inwardly more than other people had a right to a little outward ease." While Tonio Kröger goes North "to the polar bear" and Aschenbach South "to the tiger," Van der Qualen gets off somewhere in between, where nothing has a name . . . and he vanishes, is without issue. His muse of eros, pathos, pathology, tells him stories, but he doesn't write the stories down; and his status in reality is that of a dream, a nineteenth-century dream reminding us of lonely streets in the lost cities of Balzac and Stendhal.

Though Van der Qualen's isolation, like that of the others, is associated with melancholy, illness, boredom, disgust, and though it is once again primarily the inwardness of the character which is stressed, the idea of art, however ineffectual, unreal, fevered, is represented as an alleviation of his condition; it is identified with erotic fulfillment, though also with guilt (his mistress-muse, after yielding to him, tells no more stories for some time); and by the sweet remoteness of its melancholy this little sketch seems to hint that art, a kind of ideal equivalent or substitute for sexuality (perhaps at once the equivalent and the antithesis of masturbation?), is the possibility of escape from the world, a transcendence of it if not its redemption.

Together with and over against this portrait of the artist as sufferer there must be placed the antithetical figure of the artist as illusionist, cynic, or even charlatan; the artist as virtuoso and actor. While we see such persons as Van der Qualen, Spinel, Detlev, Kröger, Aschenbach, and the anonymous protagonists of "The Dilettante," "Disillusion," "Railway Accident," as almost invariably alone, or at most engaged in private conversation, the Greek boy, Bibi, of "The Infant Prodigy" (1903), is depicted in the fullest glare of publicity, giving a concert. He is of course not less alone than the others; but his loneliness is public, aggressive, confident, and assured of mastery.

This most interesting piece is scarcely a story in any usual sense; instead of plot we have a kind of rudimentary musical organization of anecdote. Several themes are introduced and dismissed, only to return in variations. The major contrast of the work is between Bibi's thoughts about his own performance and the thoughts evoked by this performance in the minds of selected members of the audience. These latter take the form of variations on the theme which connects the idea of art simultaneously with the secret-erotic and the composition of society: Bibi's virtuosity arouses in his hearers sexual and forbidden thoughts, while his innocence, or the innocence which they presume in the fact that he is a little boy, makes these thoughts permissible and even rather religious.

Just at the finish a decisive point is made in the confrontation, after the concert, of an elegant young lady accompanied by her officer-brothers, and a bohemian, or early beatnik, couple, a gloomy-looking youth and "a girl with untidy hair." This girl has just said, "We are all infant prodigies, we artists," causing an old gentleman who overhears her to think that "she sounds very oracular"; now, however, she looks after the beautiful and aristocratic girl ("steel-blue eyes," "clean-cut, well-bred face") and her brothers: "she rather despised them, but she looked after them until they turned the corner."

This compound of eros, art, delicate envy, and social climbing is not arbitrarily introduced at all, but forms the climax to a number of preparatory references. Bibi's performance, which he himself regards with a cold pleasure from the technical point of view, in terms of cleverness, calculation, intelligence, virtuosity, arouses warmer sentiments in his hearers, from the old gentleman who compares Bibi to the Christ child, thinking that one could kneel before a child without being ashamed, to the young girl who thinks of kissing the little musician because what he is playing "is expressive of passion, yet he is a child." And she asks herself, "Is there such a thing as passion all by itself, without any earthly object, a sort of child's play of passion?"

The meaning of such reflections is brought out when the impresario climbs on the stage and, "as though overcome," kisses the little boy, "a resounding kiss, square on the mouth." "That kiss ran through the room like an electric shock, it went direct to people's marrow and made them shiver down their backs. They were carried away by a helpless compulsion of sheer noise." A music critic thinks: "Of course that kiss had to come— it's a good old gag. Yes, good Lord, if only one did not see through everything so clearly—." And when Bibi finishes with a piece incorporating the Greek national anthem this critic goes on: "I think I'll criticize that as inartistic. But perhaps I am wrong, perhaps that is the most artistic thing of all. What is the artist? A jack-in-the-box. Criticism is on a higher plane. But I can't say that."

This remarkable composition plays with great though quiet effect on subjects which remain central to the author's work throughout his career. "The Infant Prodigy" is Mann's first representation of some sinister qualities belonging to the underside of the artist nature. A figure like Van der Qualen, with his fever, near to death, and with his sexual muse, might be thought quite sinister enough, but in comparison with Bibi and his like he looks innocent and sympathetic. Here for the first time art is explicitly related to childhood, to perverse sexuality, to a kind of cynical innocence, and to power. Also to criminality, fraud, and imposition. For though Bibi is not a fake, he really can play the piano, we have only to compare his concert to the fake violin concert given by the child Felix Krull on a fiddle with greased strings, to see that the latter is but an intensification of meanings already present in the former: Krull's parents, for instance, profit socially by their son's "little joke." And the "realism" of Krull's performance does depend, we are told, on his being truly inspired, "enchanted" by music. Thus the fraudulent is not completely so, but rooted in real feelings; and the artistic performance, however real, is to a degree fraudulent, depending on illusion; people applauded, we are told, before Bibi played a note, "for a mighty publicity organization had heralded the prodigy and people were already hypnotized, whether they knew it or not." Art, then, takes place in a mysterious realm where nothing is either true or false; the realm of Van der Qualen's dreamy, nameless town, the realm of the theater where in some sense only the child is at home, while the adult must suspect in himself those real feelings which are evoked by means of illusion, and subject these to criticism, that is, to the reservations of shame and guilt.

This relation of art to the theatrical goes very deep in Mann's work, and develops very far. We may observe, about the stories we have been considering up to this point, that the theater is in some way always present. Some of them, like "The Infant Prodigy" and "Little Lizzy," have theatrical performances for their subject. But the ambulance men take Piepsam away smoothly and efficiently, "as in a theater"; Friedemann "loved the theater most of all," and he falls in love at a performance of *Lohengrin*; "Gladius Dei," though chiefly concerned with painting, contains several references to the theater, and Hieronymus' vision of doom has for a background Theatinerstrasse, Theater Street.

Anticipating, it is possible to see the relation of Bibi to the development of those artist figures most involved with evil, with "the questionable" and the powers of darkness: Cipolla, artist and illusionist of the political-erotic; Leverkühn, the artist as Faust, compacted for his powers to the devil; Krull, the artist as criminal, working directly on life. Many minor episodes and vignettes deal with the same compound of beauty and its dubious beginnings: for instance, Tonio Kröger's anecdote about the banker whose talent for short stories emerged only when he served a prison sentence; Felix Krull's horrifying sketch contrasting the actor Muller-Rosé's appearance on stage and off; the ambiguous characterization of art in *The Magic Mountain* and in *Doctor Faustus* as "alchemical," as inorganic imitation of the organic; as bound up with the *illusory* (or *spiritual*: the doubt is everpresent) transmutation of lower into higher: of nothing into matter; matter into life; life into thought; those successive quantum jumps of creation which are characterized also as intensifications of shame and guilt.

There are thus already revealed two views of the artist. In one he is the lonely sufferer of the dark horror of the world; in the other he is the cynical magician whose illusionistic powers enable him somewhat coldly to exploit his own suffering and that of others, for ends which may possibly be redemptive but which are always regarded by the author with much misgiving, at the least because they are remote from the ends of practical life—"poetry is a kiss one gives the world," says Goethe in *The Beloved Returns*, "but kisses get no children"—and at the worst because it is the nature of art to lend a certain prospective reality to dangerous and impermissible phantasies.

Over against both views of the artist there is the commonplace view of "the beautiful," relating it to amusement, entertainment, health; as with the lieutenant in *Tonio Kröger* who "asks the company's permission to read some verses of his own composition." The disaster, says Kröger, was the lieutenant's own fault: "There he stood, suffering embarrassment for the mistake of thinking that one may pluck a single leaf from the laurel tree of art without paying for it with his life."

Thomas Mann's Faust Novel

THOMAS MANN'S *Doctor Faustus* may be seen as a magnificent grotesque, a final parody perhaps not only of the novel but of art generally; it may be likened to a cathedral whose proportions strain so to the overt and exact, to an ideal elegance, as to witness of a god at least as mighty as the one worshipped inside. The long allegiance of Mann's art to music, to the expressly "pure" and solely "formal," has here issued in the story of the musician-hero Adrian Leverkühn, where the tension between Apollo and Dionysus may be localized as that between Bach and the Bacchic; yet the essence of the dialectic was already present in the story of Gustave Aschenbach, the "morally valiant" hero whose art took for its ideal the figure of St. Sebastian: "The conception of an intellectual and virginal manliness, which clenches its teeth and stands in modest defiance of the swords and spears that pierce its side." Pain and disease disguised in form—form as itself the noble concomitant of disease, they are already here in "the aristocratic self-command that is eaten out within and for as long as it can conceals its biologic decline from the eyes of the world." D. H. Lawrence, reviewing *Death in Venice*, spoke of Mann as "the last sick sufferer from the complaint of Flaubert," who, like Flaubert, "feels vaguely that he has in him something finer than ever physical life revealed." This and Lawrence's related complaints (*Phoenix*, pp. 308–13) seem inaccurate inasmuch as they do not account for Mann's further irony, his understanding of the position, whereby Aschenbach's fate (and Leverkühn's too, I think) is made splendidly implicit in the description of his discipline:

Was it perhaps an intellectual consequence of this rebirth, this new austerity, that from now on his style showed an almost exaggerated sense of beauty, a lofty purity, symmetry, and simplicity, which gave his productions a stamp of the classic, or conscious and deliberate mastery? And yet: this moral fibre, surviving the hampering and disintegrating effect of knowledge, does it not result in its turn in a dangerous simplification, in a tendency to equate the world and the human soul, and thus to strengthen the hold of the evil, the forbidden, and the ethically impossible? And has not form two aspects? Is it not moral and immoral at once: moral in so far as it is the expression and result of discipline, immoral—yes, actually hostile to morality—in that of its very essence it is indifferent to good and evil, and deliberately concerned to make the moral world stoop beneath its proud and undivided sceptre?

The fascination and danger of form, of purity, of the rigorous and extreme, is a theme many times debated in Mann's work; it forms a dialectic most productive of paradoxical counterpositions where the individual and the "anonymous and communal," the ideas of "harmonic subjectivity" and "polyphonic objectivity," may change places or be seen as ultimately one, as single nature's double name. In *Doctor Faustus* this theme has so operated as to produce a work that seeks, as it were, to draw all its subject up into form, to leave, as Adrian says, "nothing unthematic"; and in some sense the novel itself develops according to those laws of composition which form one expression of its hero's fate. Just as in music there is something the layman does not hear, an entire dimension not in the least concerned with making pleasing noises and that in fact he would just as lief not hear, so in a "novel" of this sort the expression of internal laws of development entirely takes the place of "psychology," observation of behavior, naturalistic creation of event; the inside is turned outward, like the creatures Adrian Leverkühn's father speaks of, who wear their skeletons like overcoats. And the *leitmotiv* method, whereby in Wagner music vulgarized itself in the direction of literature, now in a fantastic efflorescence becomes a means whereby literature approximates to the condition of music—not a Wagnerian music, however, but a strict counterpoint, a polyphonic objectivity, the solution of a problem.

This extreme, if not in this particular form, not infrequently characterizes the late development of a style, as it does for example in Melville's *Pierre*, where the art to conceal art seems deliberately to have been rejected; as it does in late Shakespeare, where divine revelation is given the figure of artistic management; as it does toward the end of *A la recherche du temps perdu*, where Proust untiringly insists that the whole business of

art is the discovery of general laws governing appearances. Art itself replaces the world it sought to observe, or regards itself lovingly in that
world as in a mirror:

> For speculation turns not to itself,
> Till it hath travell'd and is mirror'd there
> Where it may see itself.
> —*Troilus and Cressida* III. iii. 109.

The distinguishing feature of this development is a majestic yet somewhat sinister contempt for the devices by which art customarily pretends
to the casualness of life (concealment of technique, apparent liberty of
action and development, all effort to make the surface of things look "natural"). The artist, as the god of his world, deliberately exposes the perpetual laws of its being, and suggests by bold analogy how in our "real world"
the two great antagonists, freedom and necessity, may move in constant
harmony to produce the one result.

To illustrate the method of this late style we may compare the making
of certain connections in *The Magic Mountain* with the way in which similar connections are made in *Doctor Faustus*. The relations of spirit and
desire, disease and knowledge are imaged in the earlier work as they are
in the later; the operation of these images in the life of Hans Castorp is
most carefully and circumspectly worked out with a high regard for plau-
sibility and naturalism, in terms of the appearances of life: entire chapters,
long meditations, exhaustive recollections of the past, of childhood, are
employed to demonstrate a certain predestined character of life with
which the will accords, whence it is clear that Clavdia is the evoked image
of the schoolboy Pribislav, that the disease itself is founded on the erotic
experience in the then and the now. In *Doctor Faustus*, on the other hand,
these relations constitute the given, and not that which is to be shown.
They are hurled at the reader in absolute, rigidly jesting and ironical open-
ness, with the most terrible candor not altogether unlike contempt, in
terms of a contrapuntal arrangement and variation of similar material in
erotic, political, artistic, theological, and pathological realms or, better,
voices of a work written in fugue. The Leverkühn house of Adrian's childhood is duplicated in the Schweigestill house where he passed his later
years; the dog Suso becomes then the dog Kaschperl; Adrian inherits his
father's migraine and also, transmuted into art and intensified, his father's
timid concern with that part of inorganic nature that so perfectly imitates
the organic; the Devil remarks on the reentrance of the daemonic into

Europe simultaneously under two forms: the Reformation and the spiro-
chetes. The operation of law, then, is here to be made visible and explicit,
according to the idea expressed by Adrian (p. 191) that freedom "becomes
the principle of an all-round economy that leaves in music nothing casual,
and develops the utmost diversity while adhering to the identical material.
Where there is nothing unthematic left, nothing which could not show
itself to derive from the same basic material, there one can no longer
speak of a 'free style.'" It will be apparent that the essential question of
aesthetic here has clearly political resonances, and I propose that the general subject of this work properly may be spoken of as the relation of
subject and object, of freedom and necessity. This relation is for Mann
extremely subtle, complicated, and liable to inversion; irony, far from being,
as Settembrini would have it be, a direct and classical device of oratory,
becomes the end, or at least the last known objective, and man's nature is
seen as a "between" nature whose best choices cancel out each other. Now
the in-betweenness of irony is on the one hand "sane, noble, harmonious,
humane"—it is the golden mean of wisdom—but again it has in it something of the cruel and contemptuous (as in the portrait of Goethe in *The
Beloved Returns*), of being too good for both sides, refusing to involve
oneself with either party out of a feeling of pride and absolute superiority;
and again it may be seen as contemptible also, as a craven refusal to join
the eternal war, a refusal masquerading under this "above the battle" superiority—thus Dante's feelings about the trimmers, *a Dio spiacenti ed a
nemici Sui*, and thus it was said to the Laodiceans, "I know thy works, that
thou art neither cold nor hot. . . . So then because thou art lukewarm, and
neither cold not hot, I will spew thee out of my mouth." And thus in the
hell described by Mann's Divel, in a brilliantly ironic image, the sinners
have their choice only between extreme cold and extreme heat, they fly
from the one into the other and can never quite get between; yet the
tension between their wish and their reality makes out that they are always
between.

As for a detailed analysis of the fabric of this novel, this metaphysical
poem, fugue, theology, or whatever, it is difficult even to find a way in;
should one start with the "utmost diversity" or with the "strictest economy," the "basic material" from which it is produced? If my notion has
anything right about it, the analysis of a work in which there is "nothing
unthematic" will be impossible short of an exposition of the entire contents of the work according to a different order of presentation, an abstract
schema something like the synopsis of Burton's *Anatomy*; but I hope with-

out going to that length to show at least something of the method of composition. And this method itself in a way makes the job possible, for in a texture so closely and relevantly woven one might conceivably start at any point and by firm probability reach any other, assembling on the way some picture of the whole.

Though the narrator, Serenus Zeitblom, pretends to naïveté perhaps more than is properly his, and especially about the length and order of his chapters, pretending them to be disposed more or less in a random order within a loose frame of necessity, one nevertheless detects some attraction to the magical and formal quality of numbers; the work is divided into forty-seven chapters and an epilogue, the acknowledgment of the covenant with the Divel coming pretty closely in the center, and Schleppfus, that early Satanic "incarnation," is with reverent propriety given the thirteenth chapter all to himself; probably no number in this work, however, has anything like the importance of the number seven in *The Magic Mountain*. But I do think to discover six "voices," each carrying the theme in a different realm of experience, each relating with the others so as to produce the theme (which it is our business so far as may be to define) as an existence independent of any voice; and I like to be fancifully (and not very relevantly) reminded of the great second Ricercar of the *Musikalische Opfer*. These six voices may be named as follows: biological-chemical, or the relation of the organic and inorganic; pathological; theological; erotic; political and historical; aesthetic.

It is only seldom possible to hear these voices in entire isolation; the texture is generally too complicated. But simple combinations of two are very frequent: the identification already mentioned of the spirochete and the Reformation as "daemonic," Adrian's syphilitic corruption of speech referred to his archaizing fondness for the old German of Luther's time, the repetition of the symbols of Hetaera Esmeralda in musical notation as an example of the strict style—in such instances we recognize the most elementary effects of this resonant, echoing, and musically conceived manner of composition. To explore a little further into the last example: Hetaera Esmeralda first appears in Jonathan Leverkühn's "speculation of the elements" as the name of a butterfly "in transparent nudity, loving the duskiness of heavy leafage." The discussion here is generally about camouflage and concealment in nature, a question is asked about the purpose of such devices, and a new example is introduced, of a butterfly not only large but strikingly colored, highly visible, which is "tragically safe" because its secretions are so revolting no animal would eat of it: "We . . . asked ourselves whether this security had not something disgraceful about it, rather than being a cause for rejoicing." And the reader learns that Adrian could not control his laughter over this perverse manifestation. But Esmeralda is the name he gives the whore from whose body he contracts syphilis, and the brief musical "signature" of this name is found to be of strikingly frequent occurrence in the fabric of his music, and may be seen as an example of the strict style inasmuch as it elevates an extraneous and literal consideration into a first principle of composition. In this syndrome we perceive a harmony based primarily upon polyphony, where continuing voices allude to each other and so produce passing chordal effects, the erotic, the aesthetic, the pathological, the question asked of nature about the design of things: these momentarily meet and form a nexus of meaning, then continue their many narratives.

For the narrative is at once one and many, the one theme varied by the voices; so that there exists a clear sense in which Adrian is Germany ("the German soul," "the Kaisersaschern soul"), in which the development of his disease and his talent, his pact with Satan and Germany's pact with the daemonic archaism of the Nazi mythology, are one. Adrian is finally stricken in 1935; in 1939 he is all but dead, "a picture of the utmost spirituality, just there whence the spirit had fled"; in 1940 he dies. But his confession and collapse, his withdrawal from the world and from music, express that degree of *contritio cordis* based on absolute despair that is found in his last work, the "Dr. Fausti Wehe-klag," whose text, strictly bound to the twelve tones of the chromatic scale, is formed of the twelve syllables, "For I die as a good and as a bad Christian."

This counterpoint of the musical, theological, and political is nowhere more clearly put than in the conversations of Chaim Breisacher, the German Jew and polyhistor, who by making the worse appear the better reason confounds the conservative and radical, the archaic and the late-decadent together, and makes of history and all development the magic circle and "the crossway in the Spesser's wood." Thus "the softening, the effeminizing and falsification, the new interpretation put on the old and genuine polyphony . . . had already begun in the sixteenth century, and people like Palestrina, the two Gabrielis, and our good Orlando di Lasso . . . had already played their shameful part in it." And "in this decline, right in the middle of it, belonged the great Bach from Eisenach, whom Goethe quite rightly called a harmonist." Dr. Breisacher's audience is confused at this, but more so at his treatment of the next subject:

King David, King Solomon, and the prophets drivelling about dear God in heaven, these were the already debased representatives of an exploded late theology, which no longer had any idea of the old and genuine Hebraic actuality of Jahve, the Elohim of the people; and in the rites with which at the time of genuine folkishness they served this national god or rather forced him to physical presence, saw only "riddles of primeval time." (p. 281)

Here, and in Dr. Breisacher's characterization of Solomon as "a progressivist blockhead, typical of the back-formation of the cult of the effectively present national god, the general concept of the metaphysical power of the folk, into the preaching of an abstract and generally human god in heaven," one sees, ironically enough, the German implicit in the Jewish situation, the situation which would be "remedied" by the Nazi atavism.

One more illustration will perhaps serve to exemplify the method, and lead on as well to a further consideration: Hans Christian Andersen's tale of *The Little Mermaid,* which Adrian "uncommonly loved and admired," forms the center from which many essential matters radiate. References to her, both direct and extremely devious, occur at many places in the text, but only at the end we learn that the Devil had given her to Adrian for mistress in a "divelish concubinage" in compensation of that *clausulum* in the pact that forbade his love to humankind; we learn further that Adrian regards his sister's son, Echo, as the child of their union, the human-divine child, their Euphorion in fact, and so bound to death by the father's damnation. This liaison, like other elements in Adrian's fate, has amply if indirectly been predicted; for example in the stories told by Schleppfuss (an early devil-avatar) about the relations of young men with succubi. And there are remoter echoes no less important: In Andersen's tale, the world at the bottom of the sea is described, a strange dead world with trees and plants "so supple that they move as if they were alive." And to reach the palace of the witch, the sea-maid must swim through a wood of polyps. These details are represented early in *Doctor Faustus,* in that underwater world, the dead but heliotropic creation of chemistry at which Adrian so laughed when his father displayed it as the result of "osmotic pressure," the melancholy yearning of the inorganic toward life.

But the radiations go further than this, for the Divel speaks thus of the works Adrian will produce under the exaltation of the pact, which is the disease: "Then shall osmotic growths *sine pudore* sprout out of the Apothecary's sowing . . ." and at Adrian's rebuke he says:

Oh, thy father is not so ill placed in my mouth. He was a shrewd one, always wanting to speculate the elements. The mygrim, the point of attack for the knife-pains of the little sea-maid—after all, you have them from him. . . . Moreover . . .

osmosis, fluid diffusion, the proliferation process—the whole magic intreats of these. You have there the spinal sac with the pulsating column of fluid therein, reaching to the cerebrum, to the meninges, in whose tissues the furtive venereal meningitis is at its soundless stealthy work. But our little ones could not reach into the inside, into the parenchyma, however much they are drawn, however much they longingly draw thither—without fluid diffusion, osmosis, with the cell-fluid of the pia watering it, dissolving the tissue, and paving a way inside for the scourges. Everything comes from osmosis, my friend, in whose teasing manifestations you so early diverted yourself.

It will be seen that we are here brought to a center of the work, the question of the alchemy of art ("has the sun better fire than the kitchen?" asks the Divel) and whether it indeed is organic or merely gives the illusion: "What then does 'dead' mean, when the flora grows so rankly, in such diverse colors and shapes? And when they are even heliotropic?" So that our consideration of the role of the sea-maid might from this place be taken anywhere in the work, since it has brought us so rapidly to the essence, the matter of life and death which are called by the names of God and Satan; "for the light shineth in darkness; and the darkness comprehended it not." This figure of Hyphialta, the sea-maid, speaks in all the voices, of lust and disease, of the pact with the Devil and the exaltation thus produced in art, and of the relation of death to life; if the political has not been touched on so explicitly, it may at any rate be seen in the equation of Leverkühns disease, pact, music, with the rigid and death-bound form imposed upon life—a "strict style of composition," surely—by the Nazi regime, of whose concentration camps the Divel reminds us in his description of hell, the *spelunca*, the *carcer*, where all terrors happen "unrecorded, unreckoned, between thick walls."

"Au commencement était le scandale."

This Faust, in life a cheap-jack charlatan as ever was, according to the sources (and if Rembrandt drew him right), more than Christ has given his name to our modern folk, being the instance and image of an honor rooted in dishonor, a striving to the One but nourished by the Other, man blessed by the blessings of heaven and of the deep that lieth under—there is no end to the possible translations and accommodations of his figure. The parable of Job, according to some, teaches that order is broken up in the depths of being only to be more firmly established in the end, that good can have only evil for material to operate upon; and the Divel, the oldest theologian, says to Adrian, "Life is not scrupulous—by morals it sets not a fart. It takes the reckless product of disease, feeds on and digests it, and as soon as it takes it to itself it is health." But St. Paul asks whether we should continue in sin that grace may abound, and replies "God forbid." This is perhaps the deepest question we ask of Faust's covenant. For morality has about it something of the safe, the mediocre ("Virtue," observes Kafka, "is in a certain sense disconsolate"), and mediocrity, as Adrian says, "has no theological status." The traditional, reasonably supported, and already conventionalized fictions by which man lives are seen, according to the Divel, as unsatisfactory also in music:

The pretence of feeling as a compositional work of art, the self-satisfied pretence of music itself, has become impossible and no longer to be preserved—I mean the perennial notion that prescribed and formalized elements shall be introduced as though they were the inviolable necessity of the single case.

We cannot get by this by calling the devil a romantic expressionist in music and a Manichaean in matters of faith. Shall we continue in disorder that truth may abound? ("Only the non-fictional is still permissible, the unplayed, the undisguised and untransfigured expression of suffering in its actual moment.") Shall we continue in disease that health may abound? (". . . the lads will swear by your name, who thanks to your madness will no longer need to be mad"). It is not possible for Adrian to reply to this with the pious "God forbid."

For the Satan, the questioner, is within and without; before and after his apparition to Adrian we have his avatars and reminders, some overt and direct, some equivocal. I have already mentioned Schleppfuss the theologian, or psychologist of theology (who perhaps did really drag one foot, according to Serenus Zeitblom), and Dr. Chaim Breisacher who could make beginnings appear as ends; and may add to the list not only the porter who leads Adrian to his Esmeralda ("a small-beer Schleppfuss," he is called), and the impresario Saul Fitelberg who comes, he says, "to show you the kingdoms of the earth and the glory of them" (Luke IV. 5–6), and "Professor Akercocke," name of horrible derision; but also those neutral or even benign figures of the biography, one or more of whose characteristics is presently found in Adrian under diabolic auspices: Johann Conrad Beissel, the musician-priest of Ephrata, whose tyranny of the "master" and "servant" notes is found, "ghostlike," in Leverkühn's *Apocalypsis cum Figuris*; Wendell Kretschmar, who told Beissel's story, and whose uncon-

trollable stutter eventually affiliates itself with Adrian's pathologic and ar-
chaistic corruption of speech; and Jonathan Leverkühn, who provided the
migraine and the urge to "speculate the elements." It is the effect of the
method to make Adrian's life seem extraordinarily fate-laden and significant at every instant, all detail being as in a dream multiply-determined,
both a *vis a tergo* and a teleological motivation, so that it is at last difficult
enough to say what is will and what is fate, what is harmonic-subjective
and what polyphonic-objective; even of the Divel, when he appears, all
that can be said is that his real existence, if he exists, is horrible, but not
more so than if he exists as a delusion produced by the sick soul.

What is the Divel? He is death, he is deceit as he is death pretending
to life, he is himself what he sponsors so theologically, the osmotic growth
sine pudore. But he is not mediocrity, not Laodicean or trimmer. And
therefore, as Schleppfuss was at such pains to emphasize in his lectures,
sanctity must take its chance with him: "The temptation that one withstood
was indeed no sin; it was merely a proof of virtue. And yet the line between temptation and sin was hard to draw, for was not temptation already
the raging of sin in the blood, and in the very state of fleshly desire did
there not lie much concession to evil? Here again the dialectical unity of
good and evil came out, for holiness was unthinkable without temptation;
it measured itself against the frightfulness of the temptation, against a man's
sin-potential."

The Divel is deceit, and he, who would not serve, appears to man in
the likeness of a servant, a position of unique power because it is at once
and already the expression of a wish. It is the wish to go beyond the
limitations of the human, the wish for "the breakthrough," an impulsion
to freedom which dialectically makes its own chains, since man enslaves
himself to his servant and his power becomes his sickness.

The apparition to Adrian Leverkühn plays boldly upon a similar scene,
the apparition to Ivan Karamazov (who suffered, one remembers, with
symptoms very like Adrian's, though from Dostoevsky's favorite disease,
that mysterious "brain fever"), and even contains hints of a dialogue with
it; the world for Dostoevsky is a journal to which the Devil must write the
"column of criticism," but Mann's Divel denies it outright—"a man of destructive criticism? Slander, and again slander, my friend!" There are more
general parallels: the horrible bantering tone, the fact that both visitors
are seen as social inferiors, the careful attention given in this regard to
their clothing, the recurrent debate about their reality, the use they make
of their hosts' secret thoughts. But Ivan's Devil seems by far the less hor-

rible; almost he is merely the Satan of the Book of Job, questioning, "writing the column of criticism," "pre-destined to deny" without much hope of ultimate success—he regards himself somewhat sadly as a scapegoat, and he is to Ivan almost an occasion of salvation: "I shall sow in you only a tiny grain of faith and it will grow into an oak tree . . . you'll wander into the wilderness to save your soul." Whereas in *Doctor Faustus* he is to the full evil, powerful, the antagonist in a still undecided battle, the very Prince of Lies at whom Martin Luther threw the inkpot.

For Dostoevsky the mystery of Christianity lies in freedom, which necessarily involves the freedom to do evil. Berdyaev works out the dialectic thus:

Free goodness involves the freedom of evil; but freedom of evil leads to the destruction of freedom itself and its degeneration into an evil necessity. On the other hand, the denial of the freedom of evil in favour of an exclusive freedom of good ends equally in a negation of freedom and its degeneration—into a good necessity. But a good necessity is not good, because goodness resides in freedom from necessity.—Nicholas Berdyaev, *Dostoevsky.*

Mann, too, is concerned with this theme, but entrusts its exposition primarily to Schleppfuss, who sees here "a certain logical incompleteness of the All-powerfulness and All-goodness of God; for what He had not been able to do was to produce in the creature . . . the incapacity for sin. That would have meant denying to the created being the free will to turn away from God." And the Divel too plays upon this freedom and uses it as a temptation: "Have you forgotten what you learned in the schools, that God can bring good out of evil and that the occasion to it shall not be marred?" It is as though Mann, at such points, would take back the vision of Dostoevsky as Adrian would take back "the good and noble . . . what we call the human, although it is good and noble . . . the *Ninth Symphony*."

Yet not entirely so. Though the "Lamentation of Dr. Faustus" is conceived as the melancholy counterpart, the formal negation, of the Beethoven *Ninth*, it is yet expressly a "religious" work, "a conversion, a proud and bitter change of heart," the "prideful *contritio*" earlier debated with the Divel, and at its end the last melancholy tone becomes "a hope beyond hopelessness, the transcendence of despair—not betrayal to her, but the miracle that passes belief," and this tone "changes its meaning; it abides as a light in the night." And as with the music, so with the novel, when at its conclusion Serenus Zeitblom, whose name speaks of "the fullness of time" (Ephesians I. 10), speaks of the miracle beyond belief, the light of hope out of the utmost hopelessness.

Doctor Faustus is a noble and melancholy work, and a melancholy hope it expresses there at the end, a hope almost in the strict style of composition—that is, will the dialectic pull us through? The question so long ago debated between Naphta and Settembrini, whether man is "natural" or against nature, in despite of nature, has extended its ground to nature itself: Is nature "natural" even in its perverse osmotic manifestations? Is the sea-maid a monster, or "a complete and charming organic reality" as Adrian held her to be? And so too with art, that "calculation raised to mystery"—can it be organic, or is it Divel's work with magic squares and osmotic pressure? These are questions not to be answered without some sort of intimate relation with the "dubious and questionable"; that they are asked shows the depth of our predicament.

Tragedy exists in tension between ritual and ethic, magic and religion; the hero as he suffers is both punished and sacrificed, and the humanist may well misdoubt himself, in such an ambiguous operation, to be paid by the wrong master. The scapegoat is laden with sin and driven into the wilderness to save the people, as Adrian upon his confession was deserted by his friends, but possibly it is only the scapegoat who is saved out of it all. If the tension cannot be maintained, that is Armageddon or the coming of the Kingdom, either one but in any case the end; for it is with us as it is with music: "Her strictness, or whatever you like to call the moralism of her form, must stand for an excuse for the ravishments of her actual sounds."

Bottom's Dream: The Likeness of Poems and Jokes

THE poetic attempt to say the world, to name it rightly, is perhaps a matter altogether too mysterious to be talked about. When someone, behaving "poetically," looks into the landscape and tries to speak it, this mystery turns inward and takes the form of an anxious searching and striving, until (sometimes) the mind by some wild reach having an evident relation with insanity produces a phrase, and this phrase—somehow—*expresses* ... whereupon some quiet click of accurate conjunction tells us that what has happened is somehow reasonable.

Yet this moment of expressiveness itself occurs at a crossing point, and tells us that something in language is not linguistic, that something in reason is not reasonable. It speaks of a relation between inside and outside, an identity between inside and outside, but this relation, this identity, is itself unspeakable:

Suddenly, I saw the cold and rook-delighting heaven. . . .

That has no meaning, strictly, that can be expressed otherwise, or translated. How, then, to someone who for a long time entertains the phrase as a sort of empty and objectless talisman, a piece of jade turned over in the hand, does it—suddenly, as the poet says—come to identify one alone sort of weather, one alone sort of poetry, that quality the poet wanted, he said elsewhere, of "cold light and tumbling clouds"?

Echo answers. Which is not to say that nothing answers, for it may be by a species of radar that intelligence moves through the world. We might say of expressiveness itself, of the irreducible phrase, that first it is, and then it finds a meaning in the world. Or else: Whatever the mind invents, it also discovers. Or again: Whatever is revealed, in poetry, plays at being revealed.

It is that element of play that I wish to talk about as an essentially poetic quality. This quality, I think, somehow exists in all language, in language considered as an unstable fusion of practicality and dream, in language which is in so large part an instrument for repeating, but in some small part an instrument for inventing and discovering what is invented—which is only to say, perhaps, that epic poems and systems of theology are all written by people who, whatever their talents, could not have been the first to say "cat," because it had already been said for them.

Though this poetic quality exists in all language, it will most often and most easily be visible in expressions which time or custom has set free from the urgencies of exhortation and the immediate claims of life: inscriptions on tombs, the proud dominations of antiquity, Ozymandias in his desert—surely the superfluity I mean has its relations equally with the ideal and the idea of death. Yet it may as certainly be identified in the most trivial examples. If you remove, say, the headline from an advertisement and let it dry in the sun until it shrivels out of context, it will grow other and rather surprising relations:

> . . . new shades of youth. . . .

Its valency, standing thus alone, is other than what it is when you put it back in its intentional place as an incitement to buy something called Ogilvie Creme Hair Color Foam. The tonality of *shades*, for instance, is more Stygian.

So in seeking to identify, if possible, something of the quality of expressiveness called "poetic" you might start, not with the sublime, but down at the humble end of the scale, with such things as that, with appearances of this quality in misprints, newspaper items, jokes . . . working your way up in Horatio Alger style to see how far your descriptions will take you (whether in the end you will marry Sophia, holy wisdom, the boss's daughter). In doing this we shall rely on the help of Freud—in some particulars on his fine joke book, "Wit and Its Relation to the Uncon-

scious," and in general on his attempt to demonstrate systematically how
mental life is continuous with itself in all its manifestations, from slips of
the tongue to systems of philosophy and the visions of religion.

Also of Shakespeare, who in giving a title to these remarks gives also
an instance of the quality we are trying to say something about. When Nick
Bottom wakes in the forest from the true dream in which he wore an ass's
head and was adored by Titania, he speaks of what has happened in language whose comic effect has much to do with its tone of reverence, its
being so full of garbles from scripture, and so on; and he says:

It shall be called Bottom's Dream, because it hath no bottom.

Probably there can be no better definition of poetry—no better definition, I am tempted to say, of anything that matters to us—, though all
the same it is clearly better for Bottom than for the rest of us.

Something of the quality I mean may be discovered in misprints. The
mathematical probability must be quite large that any misprint, such as
the omission or addition or substitution of a single letter, will produce
merely a moment of nonsense in the result, and indeed that happens often
enough. But given this preponderant possibility it is surprising to notice
how often misprints make a curious other sense, and surprising, too, how
economically such transformations may be effected. Here are a few examples:

a. The Russians are dredging what will be "the largest man-maid lake
in the world." Nearly nonsense, and not quite; though not quite witty,
either. Between man and lake the idea of mixed bathing has intervened
to pervert the spelling by the nicest economy so that it gives another sense
which hovers between the appropriate and the absurd; perhaps this secondary sense is not quite strong enough, and that may have to do with the
fact that we cannot hear the difference but have to see it or spell it.

b. A reviewer of one of Kinsey's reports was made to say, "The sexual
urge in females is demonstarted by".... Who would bother reading the
rest of the sentence? Not only does "demonstarted" make sense instead of
nonsense; it makes a sense which is as it were subversively appropriate to
the serious discussion which was supposed to be going on.

c. A girl escaping from East Berlin "swam the icy river to be with her
finance in the West." One imagines a Communist reading this with deepest

satisfaction, since it confirms what he has always believed about love and money in the West. And the compositor was so taken with his invention that he used it again in the next sentence, while giving the finance's name. One observes, too, that the pertness of the criticism is enhanced by the somewhat ballad-like romance of the subject.

The effect common to all three examples is that one reality gives place to another, and a tension is revealed between them: the world of information and, we might say, the symbolic world, reflect one another in this tension. Moreover, the reality revealed by inadvertence is in each instance subversive of the reality intended; this is not so surprising in the first example, since we generally expect the sexual to be the hidden reality in statements, as it is in the second and third, where sexual and marital concerns themselves give way to themes of deeper mystery and deeper obsession still, theology of sorts, and money.

As to the relation of all this with the quality of the poetic, which many have called "vision," it is the first effect of Freud's demonstrations, on errors, dreams, jokes, to show that vision begins with a fault in this world's smooth façade.

The examination now of a few rather more complicated and elaborated examples will perhaps enable us to go further in our description of this quality and its mechanisms.

In "A Handbook of Arms and Armor," by Bashford Dean, I read that Japanese feudal warfare was especially rough on horses because they were not armored; there followed this sentence: "Not until the Tokugawa period, when warfare disappeared, was the horse given adequate armor."

This statement takes the mind away from arms and armor, but not entirely away. It combines with the subject another subject, of symbolic reflexions and resonances, in which the sentence bears a sadly ironic truth (everything is always too late) without in any way losing its pleasant and somehow Oriental flavor of bland paradox calmly mastered (as in the report of an English-language Japanese newspaper, that "the entire aircrew climbed out on the wing of the burning plane and parachuted safely to their death"). It would be possible, no doubt, to appreciate intellectually the wit of the proposition alone, dismissing all that was not abstract as irrelevant; but that would be to lose the nice particularity of "the Tokugawa period," the elegant coup de grâce given in "adequate," and the fine intricate play of sounds (r and w especially) and internal rimes (like that between "period" and "disappeared") which stitches the words together and gives decisive character to the entire statement.

The second example is an AP dispatch reporting that a former lawyer of Al Capone's is convicted of income tax evasion. "I have in mind that you've suffered enough," said the judge, who also said, "Ten years ago . . . you were a well-to-do man. Now you're a man without means because of the debts you incurred in paying off the taxes. You've lost your law practice. This is a strong reminder that the power to tax is the power to destroy."

Something here, maybe the biblical austerity of the last sentence especially, strikes me as bearing the quality of expressiveness I am after; something both tragic and funny, featured by the judge's deadpan style— is he aware, right there, of the comparison implied between gangsters and governments?—and the whole rather complicated situation of the feelings wants only a touch of arrangement, a little bit of pointing, to be brought out. I imagine the former lawyer brooding on what has been said to him:

> Ten years ago, I was a well-to-do man,
> Now I am a man without means.
> I have received
> The strong reminder.
> The power to tax is the power to destroy.
>
> The lesson of the State's Do What you Can,
> That is what the law means
> Though we are deceived,
> O strong reminder
> Of Alcatraz, my master, my joy.
>
> Out here beyond the average life span
> The end no longer means
> What it did. Reprieved
> By the strong reminder,
> I get up the ante and go to destroy.

My last example is also a news item, reporting that a jet plane was shot down by its own gunfire. It is probably interesting enough to know that we live in a world in which this has become possible, but the thing sticks in the mind as well as the throat. An admiral and what the *Times* called "other Navy experts" explain: "The shells left the cannon traveling 1,500 feet a second faster than the airplane. After entering their trajectory they immediately began to slow down and fall because of air resistance and gravity. Meanwhile, (the pilot), going into a steeper dive, began a short cut across the shells' curved course. About two or three miles from the point at which the shells were fired, they reached the same point the plane had achieved. . . ."

This may already be a poem, finished and impossible to meddle with, though the newspaper's account is a little dispersed on the page for my entire satisfaction, and stuffed with irrelevant details. All the same, the relations expressed between murder and suicide are splendidly and as it were secretly there: "a short cut across the shells' curved course" is in itself a fine piece of virtuosity, giving the truth of the human situation with a decisiveness not so easily matched in poetry, though surpassed in this of John Webster: "Like diamonds we are cut with our own dust."

So it seems that this episode of the jet shot down by its own gunfire may be only the last playable variation on a theme poets have constantly handled; the particular comparison which comes to mind is with Hardy's "The Convergence of the Twain (Lines on the loss of the 'Titanic')" where the likeness and prospective identity of ship with iceberg are guaranteed at last by their literally coming together: the point of the joke, which Hardy calls "consummation."

Not trying for the moment to demonstrate the relation of such things to poetry, I shall say instead what characteristics my examples have in common.

Each is a thing in itself, a something decisive which the mind easily recognizes and detaches from the context in which it occurs. To say almost the same thing in another way, each example has the intention of giving information, but is received by the mind as giving something else; the statement, as it is made, crosses over from the practical realm into another, the realm of the superfluous and ideal, where it becomes a focus for meditations on the human condition under the figure of armored horses, aged lawyers, jet pilots who shoot themselves down.

This crossing over, this relation between two realms and the process of moving between them, is perhaps comparable with the relation, in poetry, between letter and allegory, between the picturesque and the symbolic.

The examples have, though in varying degrees, a reflexive character or one in which contradictions resolve; they are, again in varying degrees, increasingly from first to last, about retributive justice, and it may be this which gives them their quality of decisiveness and finish. This reflexive character could be put another way, as a principle of economy: they use their materials twice. And they all three, rather unexpectedly, exhibit the pathos of the obsolete, or obsolescent; they are all about something's being caught up with, something's being over.

Our next step will be to see if the mechanism of a joke in any way illuminates that of a lyric poem; we shall limit ourselves to brief examples.

One critical resemblance between the two will be clear to anyone who has ever tried to make up either—(by the way, how do jokes get made? I do not know that anyone has seriously studied this question)—and this is the problem of the ending. Anyone can begin a poem, anyone can begin a joke (the pointlessness of doing that is very clear, it seems, but many people begin poems). As Plato says in the Laws, "The beginning is like a god, who while he lives among men redeems all." There is a grand feeling of liberty about beginning anything, for it looks as though any gesture in the whole world will do. But, in the difficult world of forms, the gesture you elect will entail consequences good and bad, seen and unseen. Sooner or later, you have to ask yourself how to stop, what it means to stop, what it is that has finished. This is the question we will now examine, first with reference to a few jokes.

a. A riddle. How do you catch the lions in the desert? Answer: you strain off the sand, and the remainder will be lions.

b. From Shipley, "Dictionary of Word Origins," s.v. Strategy. A Chinese general sent his advance guard up to the edge of a forest. To find out if the enemy were in ambush there, he ordered each man to throw a stone into the forest, and if birds flew up there were no men there, so that it would be safe to advance. All this was done, birds flew, the army marched forward—and was captured. For the opposing general, also as it happened Chinese, had said to *his* soldiers: Men, I want each of you to grab a bird, and let it go when they throw those stones.

These instances are perhaps directed against the intellect's character-istic wish to simplify situations so as reductively to bring out logical struc-ture at the expense of everything else in experience, the wit being that this same essentializing structure is employed to bring out the absurdity of logic in this world. Both jokes make use of the same almost absolute economy, using as much as possible in the response what was given in the stimulus, merely revising the elements of the relation in an "impos-sible" way.

The pleasure we get must come from the fulfillment of an expectation that the resolution in both instances will make use very purely, indeed exclusively, of the given materials, plus our surprise at the use made, which as straight men for the occasion we should not have thought of. But note that although we should not have thought of the reply, the very fact of its employing *only* terms already used gave us a not quite explicit sense that we might have thought of it in another instant; that though we did not in fact think of it, our minds were playing with the possibilities of lions-deserts, stones-birds, so that the answer, as a matter of timing, seemed "right" or "inevitable," responsive to a wish on our part for symmetry and economy together with a certain shock, the compounded fulfillment of fairly definite formal expectations with a material surprise. We might compare what happens with what happens in music, eighteenth-century music, say, where to a strict and relatively narrow canon of harmonic possibility, including certain clichés of cadence, is added the composer's originality at handling his materials within the convention.

c. From Freud, "Thoughts for the Times on War and Death" (1915). A husband to his wife, "If one of us should die, I would go and live in Paris."

Here we observe, as with so many jokes, and especially those bearing on sex and marriage, that the sentiment itself is about as unfunny as it could be, setting the death of one partner against the pleasure of the other and leaving no doubt of the choice that would be made. The wit, we suppose, the element which allows us to laugh, comes from two circumstances: first, that the wish expressed is one very widely entertained but usually concealed; second, that it breaks from its concealment so economically, using as its means a very slight grammatical displacement of the solemn, "objective" statement, with its air of entertaining the worst contingencies, which the husband must have consciously intended.

Thus, like our misprints earlier, this remark makes a revelation of sorts. A revelation can be only of that which is hidden, what is hidden is secret, what is secret is so because it is, or is thought to be, evil, shameful, taboo (sacred); finally, this evil represents something we believe to be true. So that the revelation is subversive of the usual order of appearances, beneath which it shows another order, one that gains its reality from the comparison of the two.

d. A last example, not a joke, but from Freud's analysis of one of his own dreams. He dreamt of a place called Mödling. No amount of personal association gave any reason for its presence in the dream, until he went through the following process of dream etymology or even archeology: Mödling, from earlier Mödelitz, from the Latin *Mea Delicia* (my joy) = *mein Freud*.

Though not strictly a joke, this instance purely illuminates a vital quality of wit, which takes the longest way round only as the shortest way home, whose beginnings and endings seem to be disposed upon a circle, not a straight line. This quality has to do with that economy we mentioned earlier in connection with our first two examples, to which it adds, however, the further consideration that this economy may tend to be reflexive, to turn back on itself and use itself again in a new sense (here quite literally a translation into another language and back). This is in itself a very poetical idea about the nature of forms, that they are like human beings who in seeking the world find themselves, like Odysseus who encompassed a vast world simply by trying to get home (this aspect of the journey is finely brought out in a beautiful poem by Cavafy, "Ithaka"). So also Donne, "Thy firmnesse makes my circle just, And makes me end where I begunne." (The example suggests another and more recondite possibility, that dreamer, poet, and wit are somehow endeavoring to say the world as a form of their own name. "When Thou has done, Thou hast not Donne." This would only rarely, if ever, be demonstrable, though I have observed my own name, only slightly concealed, in my contention that the poet is a "namer of" the world. But it is in this sense that Shakespeare, with a "profound" or "abysmal" pun, has Bottom say of his night in the enchanted wood, "It shall be called Bottom's Dream, because it hath no Bottom.")

Summing up what we have so far: our examples tell us about the effect and mechanism of jokes that they depend on a strictly limited material, which they resolve surprisingly in terms of itself. Freud would remark that this economy is itself a source of our pleasure, and adduce such terms as remembering, recognition, recurrence, as analogous; and would add, what we discovered from one of our examples, that hostility may also be a pleasure-bearing part of wit. For, after all, a smile, physiologically speaking, is a step on the road to a snarl and a bite (cf. "sarcasm," a "biting remark").

So we have: economy of materials.
        sudden reversal of the relations of the elements.
        introduction of absurdity, but
        the apparent absurdity, introduced into the context of
            the former sense, makes a new and deeper sense;
        the hidden is revealed.

We may suspect that makers of jokes and smart remarks resemble poets at least in this, that they too would be excluded from Plato's Republic; for it is of the nature of Utopia and the Crystal Palace, as Dostoevsky said, that you can't stick your tongue out at it. A joke expresses tension, which it releases in laughter; it is a sort of permissible rebellion against things as they are—permissible, perhaps, because this rebellion is at the same time stoically resigned, it acknowledges that things are as they are, and that they will, after the moment of laughter, continue to be that way. That is why jokes concentrate on the most sensitive areas of human concern: sex, death, religion, and the most powerful institutions of society; and poems do the same. We might consider in this connection how grave a business civilization must be, to require professional comedians. Or, as Mr. Empson said (in a poem), "The safety valve alone knows the worst truth about the engine."

In general, to succeed at joking or at poetry, you have to be serious; the least hint that you think you are being funny will cancel the effect, and there is probably no lower human enterprise than "humorous writing." Still, there are poems which clearly also are jokes, yet by no means light verse, and one of these may serve for a bridge between the two realms; the inscription on the collar of a dog which Alexander Pope gave the Prince of Wales:

> I am His Highness' dog at Kew.
> Pray tell me, sir, whose dog are you?

This couplet possesses fully the characteristics we have distinguished in jokes: the sentiment itself is tendentious, might even come near to being savage were it not spoken by a dog with an air of doggy innocence; by cleverness it gets away with the sort of revelation of how societies exist which might at various times and in various realms cost a man his life or liberty; it works economically, by transformation of the given material. Probably, to be pedantic, the wit consists in getting us to accept the literal meaning of "dog" in the first line, so that we receive the metaphorical "dog" of the second line with surprise, but a surprise conditioned by expectation, for it is after all the same word.

The example raises another point, that one mechanism of economy in joking is the pun, either in the use of one word in two senses, as here, or in the use of two words of similar sound which mean different things but still somehow establish a resemblance beyond that of the sound. Notice that in the archaic economy of poetry it frequently happens that a resemblance in sound is, though cryptically, a resemblance in sense, as in the kind of logical connection hinted by a rime, or in these examples:

> For ruin hath taught me thus to ruminate (Shakespeare)

> Oh Attic shape! Fair attitude! (Keats)

We may add this as well. The "purely formal" arrangements of poetry, such as measure, rime, stanza, which it appears not at all to share with the joke, are in fact intensifications of a characteristic we have already noticed in jokes: the compound of expectation with a fulfillment which is simultaneously exact and surprising, giving to the result that quality sometimes thought of as inevitability, or rightness. Observe, too, that many jokes show a rudimentary form of stanzaic progression, by being arranged in a series of three, with similar grammatical structure, so that the hearer correctly anticipates the punchline as coming the third time a character says something, does something, and so forth.

Here is an example in which the humor is overtly savage, and any responsive smile might be accompanied by some gnashing of teeth; it is from Swift's "Satirical Elegy on the Death of a Late Famous General"; he means the Duke of Marlborough:

> Behold his funeral appears,
> Nor widow's sighs, nor orphan's tears,
> Wont at such times each heart to pierce,
> Attend the progress of his herse.
> But what of that, his friends may say,
> He had those honours in his day.
> True to his profit and his pride,
> He made them weep before he dy'd. . . .

What is possibly the oldest joke in the world says, "With friends like that you don't need enemies." Its present form seems to be Jewish, but I have found it in Tacitus, who remarks on the persecutions under Nero, "Those who had no enemies were betrayed by their friends."

And now, to climax this sequence, an example from whose grim strength all the laughter has fallen away; and yet it seems that the mechanism of the joke remains unchanged. It is Housman's "Epitaph on an Army of Mercenaries."

> These, in the day when heaven was falling,
> The hour when earth's foundations fled,

> Followed their mercenary calling
> And took their wages and are dead.

> Their shoulders held the sky suspended;
> They stood, and earth's foundations stay;
> What God abandoned, these defended,
> And saved the sum of things for pay.

Among so many fine things here, we single out the splendid economy of wit which remembers "and took their wages" from the first stanza to bring it back in a savage reversal as "the sum of things."

But by now you may have the serious objection that I am being unduly free with the idea of a joke. Engrossed in my pedantries, I seem to have forgotten that the first thing to see about a joke is that it makes us laugh; whatever doesn't do that cannot really be likened to a joke.

I should reply as follows. There is a great range of jokes whose intent is indeed to make us laugh. But can you really distinguish these as absolutely separate from and in no way resembling the range, at least as great, of such artifacts of speech as: riddles, proverbs, aphorisms, epigrams, gnomic sayings, anecdotes, parables. . .? Jokes, it is reasonable to claim, have often been the instruments of moral teaching, and even religious revelation. Their humor may be far indeed from laughter (consider the other meaning of "funny": strange, wrong), or may be close to it without invoking it, as in the riddles of the Zen Koan or those Tales of the Hasidim collected by Martin Buber. To take one example only, with what sort of laughter does one respond to this joke by Nietzsche: "The last Christian died on the Cross?"

I think I may continue to claim that poems and jokes resemble one another, laughter or no; and that the essential characteristic, in virtue of which the resemblance obtains, is not the laughter but, far rather, the quality of decisiveness and finish, of absolute completion to which nothing need be added nor could be added: not laughter, but the silence with which we greet the thing absolutely done.

You may go on with examples from a more ambiguous realm, where the quality of the response may be hovering and doubtful. Here is Herrick, on Julia weeping:

> She by the River sate, and sitting there,
> She wept, and made it deeper by a teare.

Its delicacy, its reticence, are not without humor; probably its miniature aspect asks for a smile. And yet, to even a moment's contemplation, it grows very large, and the thin, molecular film of that tear spreading over the river is enough to express the world's sorrow; just exactly as in that saddest joke of all, where one rabbi comes to another who is weeping for the death of his son.

> "Why do you weep," asks the one, "seeing it does no good?"
> "That is the reason," says the other, "I weep because it does no good."
> And the first rabbi sat beside the other, and wept with him.

There are poems by William Blake in which the feeling seems to be resolved actually by ambiguity, or by the maintaining a tension (a balance?) between two possibilities of feeling. This is difficult to explain, but less difficult to demonstrate. In "The Chimney Sweeper," a boy is the speaker; he tells of his and his friend Tom's wretched life, and of Tom's beautiful dream, in which an Angel opens the coffins of all the chimney sweeps and sets them free; then the poem ends:

> And so Tom awoke and we rose in the dark
> And got with our bags & our brushes to work.
> Tho' the morning was cold, Tom was happy & warm,
> So if all do their duty, they need not fear harm.

My point is this: one first reads the last line as spoken by the child, and spoken straight. Yet one cannot fail to catch, I believe, another voice, that of William Blake, who is also speaking the same line at the same time, in a tone of righteous indignation, in a snarl of woe against Church and State. And the same thing happens in "Holy Thursday," where, after describing the poor children being walked to church by beadles, and how their songs were "like harmonious thunderings the seats of heaven among," he finishes with the moral: "Then cherish pity, lest you drive an angel from your door." Again, you can read it straight: pity the poor children, for their angelic prayers really are powerful in heaven; or it is possible to sneer it, as if it meant to say: what sort of pity is it, that allows children to be poor? If you try reading the poems aloud, I think you will see that this tension is there. It is a tension which Blake expresses explicitly in one of his jokes, one of those quatrains which read like nursery rimes until they explode in your face, taking most of the moral world with them:

> Pity would be no more,
> If we did not make somebody Poor;

And Mercy no more could be,
If all were as happy as we.

The course of an argument will normally be thus, that many matters from the roots come together in a single trunk, a thought which can for a certain time be sustained; but inevitably, at last, the trunk divides in branches, the branches in twigs, the twigs bear leaves, and the leaves fall. Perhaps we are just now arriving at the place where the trunk divides and becomes several instead of one, and I ought to say here that I am not trying to show that jokes and poems are one and the same thing throughout the range. We have the same problem with metaphor generally, where the assertion that A is like B implies that A is also other than B, and not the same thing at all. "To thee the reed is as the oak." The poet meant, not that there was no difference, nor that both reed and oak are plants, but that the differences, to Imogen as dead, were a matter of indifference.

Or else you might say that at a certain point in an argument the thought, which had seemed identifiably one, begins to become indistinguishable from a good many other thoughts—as though we had gone a long way round only to discover ourselves back in quite familiar territory. Here are some of the landmarks of that territory, which perhaps our journey at best has but allowed us to see for a moment as though they were new.

The real resemblance, the illuminating one, is that poems and jokes to succeed must do something decisive; which may seem to mean that their endings are somehow contained in their beginnings. This of course is precisely the magical, illusionist, or religious character of art, which has customarily rested on the assumption that God in creating the world did something coherent although mysterious, and that therefore history, at the last great day, would be seen as "like" a drama. So that poetic art has concerned itself characteristically with doubleness, and with what oneness can possibly or impossibly be made out of doubleness: with freedom and necessity, with changelings, with going out and coming back, with echo, mirror, radar, with serious parody; here we approach Aristotle's notions of recognition and reversal, and may see them operant not only in the major forms of tragic poetry, but also and equally in the minute particulars of the poet's art, e.g.,

With eager feeding food doth choke the feeder,

or,

> Property was thus appalled,
> That the self was not the same;
> Single nature's double name
> Neither two nor one was called.

We see also that the mechanism we have attempted to describe is like that of the plot in a story, also a magical device for dealing with time as though it were eternity, a way of doing two things—at least two!—at once, a way of handling appearance and reality as mirror images of one another. As Rebecca West says, "I am never sure of the reality of a thing until I have seen it twice." The mechanism we mean is what gives us this power of seeing a thing twice: it is like those striking moves in chess, called generally double attack—the pin, the fork, double check, disclosed check—, which show the contrapuntal effect of getting two moves for one and thus, as it were, making time stand still.

Our examples thus far have been chiefly epigrammatic in nature anyhow, and so the resemblance to jokes has been clear enough. But a poem is, for one thing, more ambitious than a joke; literally, it takes more world into its ambit. So far a conclusion let us look at two somewhat larger instances.

> Glory be to God for dappled things,
> For skies of couple-colour as a brinded cow;
> For rose-moles all in stipple upon trout that swim;
> Fresh firecoal chestnut-falls; finches' wings;
> Landscape plotted and pieced—fold, fallow and plough;
> And all trades, their gear and tackle and trim.
>
> All things counter, original, spare, strange;
> Whatever is fickle, freckled (who knows how?)
> With swift, slow; sweet, sour; adazzle, dim;
> He fathers forth whose beauty is past change:
>   Praise Him.

This poem of Hopkins' seems not only to illustrate the relation we have been discussing, but also to take this relation for its subject: it gives a religious guarantee, which is perhaps the only guarantee available, for the real resemblance between particular and generality, between detail and meaning; it so relates the unique with the universal as to show them the same and not the same; its transaction seems to define metaphor for us as: the exception caught becoming the rule.

And a last example:

The Collar-Bone of a Hare

Would I could cast a sail on the water
Where many a king has gone
And many a king's daughter,
And alight at the comely trees and the lawn,
The playing upon pipes and the dancing,
And learn that the best thing is
To change my loves while dancing
And pay but a kiss for a kiss.

I would find by the edge of that water
The collar-bone of a hare
Worn thin by the lapping of water,
And pierce it through with a gimlet, and stare
At the old bitter world where they marry in churches,
And laugh over the untroubled water
At all who marry in churches,
Through the white, thin bone of a hare.

By the romance of the beginning we are drawn into one sort of world, a belief in one sort of world; of which the decisive emblem at the end offers a sudden and absolute vision. The change could not be more abrupt, but neither could the harmony be more convincing, and one is a function of the other, and both are mysterious. As though to say once more, "It shall be called Bottom's Dream, because it hath no bottom." But now the leaves begin to fall.

On Metaphor

WHILE I am thinking about metaphor, a flock of purple finches arrives on the lawn. Since I haven't seen these birds for some years, I am only fairly sure of their being in fact purple finches, so I get down Peterson's *Field Guide* and read his description: "Male: About size of House Sparrow, rosy-red, brightest on head and rump." That checks quite well, but his next remark—"a sparrow dipped in raspberry juice"—is decisive: it fits. I look out the window again, and now I *know* that I am seeing purple finches.

That's very simple. So simple, indeed, that I hesitate to look any further into the matter, for as soon as I do I shall see that its simplicity is not altogether canny. Why should I be made certain of what a purple finch is by being led to contemplate a sparrow dipped in raspberry juice? Have I ever dipped a sparrow in raspberry juice? Has anyone? And yet there it is, quite certain and quite right. Peterson and I and the finches are in agreement.

It is like being told: If you really want to see something, look at something else. If you want to say what something is, inspect something that it isn't. It might go further, and worse, than that: if you want to see the invisible world, look at the visible one. If you want to know what East really is, look North. If you have a question concerning the sea, look at the mountains. And so on.

I say that is a simple example in part because the finches were visibly there. Even so, the matter is complicated by the presence of language. It is not alone a matter of seeing, but of saying as well, of the power of the word whether in Scripture or Dictionary. I might paraphrase Hamlet's observation: "Nothing is but saying makes it so." Seeing and saying, the dictionary tells me, were perhaps originally related; and "a saw" is still "a saying." As to this power of the word, whose limits are unknown, Erich Heller gives this wise instruction as from teacher to students: "Be careful how you interpret the world, it *is* like that."

In speaking of metaphor, I wish to be free to develop the term as far as I am able, as well as to place it with reference to other words in the series of which it is a part, of which it is perhaps the middle term, standing between the utmost expansion and the utmost compression, between the story or fable at the expanded and the symbol or name at the compressed end.

For this very reason of a proposed freedom, however, it will be well if I apply now to the dictionary to ask about the strict construction of the term metaphor: in Rhetoric, metaphor is one of the four tropes, the others being synecdoche, metonymy, and irony, and is described as "Use of a word or phrase literally denoting one kind of object or idea in place of another by way of suggesting a likeness or analogy between them." Examples: "the ship *plows* the sea; a *volley* of oaths." The examples are suspiciously like those that Pope, in "Peri Bathous," collects under the head of catachresis, or "The Variegating, Confounding, or Reversing Tropes and Figures": Mow the Beard, Shave the Grass, Pin the Plank, Nail my Sleeve. Which is worth remarking only for this reason, that as metaphor depends upon a compound of likeness and difference not always stable in the fashions of thought one man's metaphor may be another man's foolishness. The dictionary, for instance, illustrates catachresis with a rather famous example: "To take arms against a sea of troubles," which some have tried to justify by the example of Cuchullain among many other heroes of fable who tried to fight the sea; if that is fair pleading one may see by it how the metaphor is a highly compressed and allusive rendering of a dramatic episode.

The dictionary goes on about metaphor with a useful distinction: "A metaphor may be regarded as a compressed simile, the comparison implied in the former (a marble brow) being explicit in the latter (a brow white like marble)."

I found that most helpful, for somehow at school I had regularly been taught that the difference between the two terms was that simile used "like" or "as" and metaphor did not, but seemed rather to assert something like identity. I had never been able to understand that distinction very well; to say, as some do, that "he is a lion" is more ferocious or leonine than "he is like a lion" did not impress itself upon my mind as making a real difference. But the dictionary distinction is useful as leading to a further thought: the simile isolates for you the likeness in virtue of which the comparison is made; the metaphor leaves it up to you to isolate the likeness or for that matter not to isolate it. In the given example, I didn't think of "white like marble" at all; the expression "a marble brow" brought into my mind fleeting thoughts of heaviness, coldness, hardness, pallor, a monumental quality associated with the tomb.

Even under the strict construction of a dictionary definition, therefore, the metaphor reveals rather mysterious properties. As though—and these are metaphors—it were a nucleus that held to itself an indeterminate number of particles, a tone to which a not quite random series of overtones responded, a sound that echoed from some surfaces but not from others. Compared with the simile, the metaphor is both more implicit and less selective, less abstract, and more multivalent. It doesn't give itself away, but awaits, if it doesn't indeed demand, the reader's participation for its fulfillment. In this sense, it belongs to leisure, philosophy, and contemplation, rather than action.

Here is an instance, possibly a foolish, and certainly a trivial, instance. If we are at dinner and I say "Please pass the salt," the entire sense of the communication is absorbed at once; you pass the salt, and that finishes our business together. But if we are not at dinner, and neither table nor salt is available, you will think me extremely silly for saying "Please pass the salt." Let us suppose, though, that for some reason you value my good opinion, and that I insist on repeating my silly request. What happens? I think what happens is that your mind begins to play with such symbolic or metaphorical possibilities as learning has acquainted it with on the subject of salt—such things as being the salt of the earth, taking things with a grain of salt, sitting below or above the salt—and that these resonances will come to seem to you expressive of something not necessarily simple about the relations between us: I may be acknowledging our equality, doubting or pretending to doubt something you have just said, or accepting you into my tribe.

But here is, I hope, a better example. At the entrance to the Zoo in Washington, D.C., I read the following notice:

All persons are forbidden to cut, break, injure, remove, or pluck branches, flowers, or plants of any kind, or to have in their possession while in the park any tree, shrub, plant, or any part thereof.

I suppose this message must have a practical use, or it wouldn't be there. All the same, without the message the thought of doing any or all those things would probably not have crossed my mind at all, and I stood there a little amazed, first at the somewhat pedantic detail of the commandment (imagine the dialogue: "I didn't cut it." "Well, you broke it." "No, I did not break it." "Anyhow, you injured it"), but beyond that at the poetical depths and ranges to which the sign invited, or even compelled, anyone who stopped to consider it. The Garden of Eden and man's first disobedience. The wood at Nemi where the challenger plucked the golden bough. Aeneas finding his way to the underworld. Dante in the Wood of the Suicides, where the torn branches screeched at him, "*Perchè mi schianti, perchè mi sterpi?*" What would happen if one had the temerity to cut, break, injure, remove, or pluck . . . ?

So far the relation is not quite metaphorical, merely a parade of harmless educated commonplaces. But that the sign should be at the entrance to a Zoo seemed to add the necessary depening to the complex of resemblance. For surely the Zoo, or Zoological Garden, expresses in imagery something of our feeling for the Earthly Paradise, where Adam gave the beasts their names, where we had nothing to fear from these gorgeous or powerful or merely odd emanations of our as yet undivided nature; even while by its bars and cages and other enclosures it expresses that this feeling is conditioned by the Fall, and that the animal kingdom with its gruntings and brayings and howlings and hissings is a presentation to us of the divisions of our nature, a kind of natural hell externalized.

That leads to something else I want to suggest about metaphor, though quite uncertain of being able to demonstrate it as a law: that one resemblance, insufficient in itself, reveals another. Not that the second is *deeper*, as they say, for one human thought is perhaps no deeper than another; but that there is a gradient between them, shallow or steep, and the revelation of its existence is surprising but somehow just. Another silly example: the words *prenatal* and *parental* are anagrammatic arrangements of one another. That isn't much by itself, but it expresses something of the operation of metaphor to see the mechanical resemblance as it were warranted by another, that the two words belong to the same cluster and have to do with a single subject matter.

One more example here may help. In E. O. James's book *Prehistoric Religion*, I read that with certain exceptions the people of Ancient Mexico "were destined to pass at death to the dreary subterranean region, Mictlan, 'a most obscure land where light cometh not and whence none can ever return.' There they were sunk in deep sleep, but class distinctions were maintained, the lords and nobles being separated from the commoners in the nine divisions into which it was divided. At the end of the fourth year of residence in this cheerless abode the ninth division was reached, and in this its denizens were annihilated."

If I am reading this for information only, to pass a test, say, in a course on the subject of Primitive Religion, I shall probably absorb the "facts" and read on. But if I stop for only a moment, certain mechanical resemblances will very likely make me think of a college or university, and I may try rereading the passage to see how it works when that way regarded. The major mechanical resemblances are, of course, the four years and the class distinctions; the latter might have to do about equally with grades and honors and Dean's Lists, and with fraternities, athletic achievement, popularity, or any other way of becoming a lord instead of remaining a commoner.

But there it will stop, *unless* I happen to be in a mood either viciously critical or sadly despairing of what goes on in universities and colleges. If I am in either condition, I shall go on to develop the allegory suggested by the obvious and mechanical resemblances, and read the passage with the other reference as far as I am able to: "Yes, it's true, there is no light here and once the students arrive they can never go back. They are indeed sunk in deep sleep with reference to the intellect, and aroused only by a perpetual snobbery or squabble over 'class distinction.' But no matter, when they pass through the eight divisions (corresponding to semesters in four years) they will all be annihilated, they will become alumni— which by a foolish etymology would be derived from a (privative) + lumen (light), out of the light."

And so the factual passage has become a metaphor, and far removed from the author's intentions. But for this to happen, I repeat, the factual, mechanical, numerical likenesses were not enough; they had to be reinforced by an attitude, which in this instance I brought to the material. In poetry, most likely, this attitude would in great part be supplied by the context, which would specify the field of application as well as something of the tone of voice.

Resuming what has been said so far about metaphor, I have ascribed to it the following characteristics. 1. The instance of the purple finches suggested there was something uncanny about metaphor, a sleight-of-hand sort of thing wherein the word is quicker than the eye. 2. A metaphor may be a compressed story—much as a joke that appeals to a group of friends need not be told in full whenever some application of it turns up in talk: the last line, or even a single catch-word, will be plenty. 3. The metaphor leaves implicit a complex of resemblances, where the simile will isolate one and make it overt. 4. Metaphor works on a relation of resemblances; one resemblance draws another, or others, after it. 5. Exaggerating, one might say that any piece of language is capable of becoming metaphorical if regarded with other than a literal attention.

The last point most likely has to do also with the circumstance that language is, or seems to be, as Owen Barfield says, nothing but "an unconscionable tissue of dead, or petrified, metaphors." That these metaphors may be not dead but only sleeping, or that they may arise from the grave and walk in our sentences, is something that has troubled everyone who has ever tried to write plain expository prose wherein purely mental relations have to be discussed as though they were physical ones. When I read long ago in college, for example, that Descartes believed the pineal gland to be "the seat of the soul," I heard nothing literal in "seat." Only years later I found out that he supported the belief by identifying two little dents in this gland as the marks of the soul's behind.

Student writing, not unexpectedly, is particularly productive of examples, I suppose because the student is confronting for the first time consciously the fact that mental relations may be quite complex, and because he is often not conscious of the dormant metaphorical life in words that look harmlessly abstract, or safely dead. Thus, "Richard III is impervious to the pitfalls of disappointment because he has no honor to prevent his stooping to find another way out. His wits, sharpened to deadliness on his hump. . . ." This was a hump, indeed, that another writer could not get him over: "His hump is an insurmountable burden." Once in a great while, though, such things become great treasures, they confirm Blake's idea that if a fool persists in his folly he becomes wise, and the plain foolishness of the fact becomes the mysterious truth of metaphor: "Man is descended from the man-eating ape."

It goes with this, and with the complexly associative nature of metaphor, that you cannot reason by means of metaphor or similitude for any length of time without running into trouble. A metaphor in a discourse ought to be like the sudden bursting of a flare, so that you see for an instant not only the road ahead but also its situation in the terrain around. Maybe that is why the best imagist poems are so very short; if the poet

puts himself under the deliberate limitation of never specifying applications, never moralizing or drawing the general conclusion, but proceeds
only by giving illustrations and leaving his auditors the option of saying, if
they can, what the illustrations illustrate, he will do best to stop at that
mysterious place where perception shows signs of turning into thought.
Even in the more traditional discourse of poetry, where argument is not
excluded, there is the danger that if you plant your metaphors too thick
none of them will grow. Dante seems to have been aware of this, by his
way of clearing a space to either side of his formal and extended figures.
But once again the difficulty may be identified by anecdote; this one is
said to have been Einstein's reply to a request for a simple explanation of
relativity:

A blind man was walking with a friend on a hot day; the friend said, "O, for a nice
drink of milk." "Drink I know," said the blind man, "but what is milk?" "A white
liquid." "Liquid I know, but what is white?" "White is the color of a swan's feather."
"Feathers I know, but what is a swan?" "A bird with a crooked neck." "Neck I know,
but what is crooked?" The friend took hold of the blind man's arm and stretched
it out. "That is straight," he said, and then, bending the arm, "That is crooked."
"Aha!" cried the blind man. "Now I understand what milk is!" (after Graves and
Hodge, *The Long Weekend*, p. 88).

II

In what follows I should like to develop the idea of metaphor with a more
particular reference to poetry, saying what I am able to of its uncanniness
on the one hand, and of its relations with meaning on the other. If I find
it next to impossible to talk about what metaphor is and does except in
metaphors, I hope you will take that as a difficulty of the theme itself, and
not as my mere wilfulness; the word itself, after all, is a metaphor, as you
can see from its odd but exact survival in our word "ferry." And when you
look into the derivation of Greek φερειν and Latin *ferre* you find them
associated with our verb *bear*, arousing the wildly metaphorical suspicion
that what is hidden within the word is not only the notion of "carrying
across" or "transferring" something from one place to another, but the
idea of being born, of how thoughts, like children, come out of the nowhere into the here: an ancient and traditional idea concerning the production of thoughts, such as may be seen from Socrates' considering the
philosopher's business as that of the midwife, or from this of Shakespeare's Richard II:

My brain I'll prove the female to my soul;
My soul the father: and these two beget
A generation of still-breeding thoughts,
And these same thoughts people this little world
In humours like the people of this world. . . .

I suppose we shall never be able to distinguish absolutely and with a hard edge the image from the metaphor, any more than anyone has so distinguished prose from poetry or perception from thought (these are instances, not necessarily parallels). We shall very often be able to tell, just as we can very often tell the difference between snow and rain; but there are some weathers which are either-neither, and so here there is an area where our differences will mingle. If the poet says, simply, "The red bird," we shall probably take that as an image. But as soon as we read the rest of the line—"The red bird flies across the golden floor"—there arises obscure thoughts of relationships that lead in the direction of parable: the line alone is not, strictly, a metaphor, but its resonances take it prospectively beyond a pure perception, if perception could ever be quite that. Metaphor stands somewhat as a mediating term squarely between a thing and a thought, which may be why it is so likely to compose itself about a word of sense and a word of thought, as in this example of a common Shakespearean formula: "Even to the teeth and forehead of my fault."

So I assert that the procedures of metaphor resemble the procedures of magic. And if the physical sciences have a relation to magic with respect to the material world, so that men can on their account now do many things that before could only be thought, or dreamed, so I should say that poetry has a relation to magic with respect to the ideal world. Poetry has of course always been associated with magic, though latterly the idea appears as merely sentimental; as people do not "believe" in magic, it may be no more than an honorific way of saying that poetry no longer matters. Yet I wonder if there may not be a more specifiable sense to this metaphor about metaphor.

Speech and light have most commonly been the vehicles of magic art, and it is easy to see why: both share the capacity to act across distances and through an invisible medium. The idea of comparison is like that. And the rhythmical character of poetry, that cosmic and physiologic piety whereby things change while the form remains, is also characteristic of ritual incantations for magical purposes. But it is possible, I think, to go further than this.

In *The Golden Bough* Fraser tells us that magic is based on two principles: "first, that like produces like, or that an effect resembles its cause; and, second, that things which have once been in contact with each other continue to act on each other at a distance after the physical contact has been severed." The first sort he calls Homeopathic, or Imitative, Magic; the second, Contagious Magic. Here is a Malay example that combines both principles: "Take parings of nails, hair, eyebrows, spittle, and so forth of your intended victim, enough to represent every part of his person, and then make them up into his likeness with wax from a deserted bees' comb. Scorch the figure slowly by holding it over a lamp every night for seven nights. . . . After the seventh time burn the figure and the victim will die." The likeness of the victim draws upon the Homeopathic principle, the materials drawn from his body on the Contagious principle.

Transferred to poetry, I imagine that the first principle, of likeness, appears at first glance easy and probable, while the second appears neither easy nor probable. Yet let us try to follow the comparison for a little; if we do, I think we may see mysteries, not merely problems, emerge.

Here is a metaphor from *The Divine Comedy*:

> *Noi siam vermi, nati a formar*
> *L'angelica farfalla.*

> We are caterpillars, born to become
> The angelic butterfly.

Specified in its context, simple in its statement, this figure allows of little if any doubt as to its meaning, though that it should have a meaning doesn't in the least clear up its mysteriousness, which is as much inherent in the metamorphosis of caterpillar into butterfly as it is in the parallel relation of body to soul, or of this life to the next.

Here is a modern example, however, of the same relation: a caterpillar looks at a butterfly and says, "Waal, you'll never catch me in one of those durn things" (Marshall McLuhan, "Understanding Media," p. 34). Though the relation is constant, the applications may be several, though all of them on the lines of Ophelia's "We know what we are, but not what we may become." The figure parodies an old joke about flying machines, the caterpillar's locutions make him out to be a country bumpkin, the story behind the figure may be about growing up, about technological change, or still about the relation of body and soul. In fact, in its context it is used to illustrate "the principle that during the stages of their development all things appear under forms opposite to those that they finally present."

Now both examples are metaphorical: the metamorphosis of an insect illustrates a proposition about human beings. But equally in both the metaphorical relation takes place between two symbols, and at least in the example from Dante the relation is so ancient and widespread in tradition that the symbol of the butterfly alone, in an appropriate context, would carry the sense. So, once again, a metaphor is a kind of condensed myth, and the symbol is its emblem, which conveys sufficient knowledge to those familiar with the story behind it. In the same way, the early Athenians are said to have worn as a badge or totem the golden image of a cicada in sign of their having been autochthonous and self-begotten just as they supposed the cicada to be. So there you have the contagious principle at work: the likeness between an Athenian and a cicada is not self-evident, but requires the knowledge of a tradition behind it, a tradition which must have said that the original Athenians *were* cicadae before the symbol said that Athenians resembled cicadae in virtue of a particular trait held in common.

A metaphor may show signs of being the compact, allusive form of a story or fable; and the symbol, in turn, may be the even more compact precipitate of a metaphor. We might extend these relations in either direction, though I suspect we should come round in a circle by doing so: from story, to metaphor, to symbol, to the name itself. This is not an historical account, for you have to have names for things before you can tell stories about them, and surely the process may work both ways; so that name, or image, might stand equally at either end of the series. The everyday working of such a process of expansion and reduction may be seen in the fact that we have for our convenience *names*, which stand for immensely complex sets of events: your name, my name, the names of Hamlet and Lear, such names as DNA, The Age of Reason, the universe. So do great trees grow from little seeds with the apparent purpose of producing little seeds, and it may be, as I think Samuel Butler was the first to say, that a chicken is but an egg's way of producing another egg.

Something of this may be seen by contemplating for a few moments the mystery of names and naming.

What sort of word is a name? I remember being told in school that a name was a proper noun; an answer chiefly valuable for discouraging a further question. But in later years that word *proper* became a little less empty, and I was able to see that in its curious equivocations lies the traditional answer to my question. A name is a *proper* or correct noun because it belongs to, or is the property of, what it names. The two senses attest to a capitalistically profound respect for possessions (and for being possessed, too, perhaps), and run almost indistinguishably close together: as in the Latin *proprie*, which means both "each for himself, singly," and "correctly, or strictly speaking"; the difference being perhaps no more and no less than that between our verb "appropriate" and our adjective "appropriate."

A name, then, is supposed to be *peculiar* to the thing named (peculiar being also a word of property, *pecunia*, referring to the calculation of wealth in cattle); it is no mere arbitrary label but is felt to bear within itself some real distinguishing essence. If that is so, then naming things will have been the privilege of a very great, even magical, insight or power, such as seems to be ascribed to Adam at the creation: "And out of the ground the Lord God formed every beast of the field, and every fowl of the air; and brought them to Adam to see what he would call them; and whatsoever Adam called every living creature that was the name thereof" (Genesis, 2.19). Nor were these names given by Adam merely arbitrary; on the contrary, it was believed at least as late as the eighteenth century that Adam "came into the world a philosopher, which sufficiently appeared by his writing the nature of things upon their names; he could view essences in themselves, and read forms without the comment of their respective properties" (Robert South, *Sermons Preached Upon Several Occasions*, Oxford, 1742; quoted in Aubrey L. Williams, *Pope's Dunciad* p. 67n.).

So it seems to have been thought that names were essences, that things would reveal their names, which is to say, metaphors about their natures, to the discriminating eye, thereby revealing also, according to the Doctrine of Signatures, their usefulness or menace to man; as the heart-shaped leaves of the fox-glove make apparent that the extract of this plant will be the specific for angina pectoris; concerning which Scott Buchanan observes: "This is a classic illustration and it is usually cited to show the primitive imagination correlating shapes of organs and shapes of herbs by magical impulse. Actually it is the mnemonic distillate of what must have been considerable experience.... Two things should be noted about it: its truth value is not zero: its truth value can be increased by more knowledge" (*Doctrine of Signatures*, pp. xi–xii).

One further consideration will lead us back to metaphor, magic, and our Homeopathic and Contagious principles.

Rabelais tells us, in a passage of most learned fooling with derivations (*Le Tiers Livre, Chapitre* L), that plants get their names in one or another of eight ways:

1. from their first finder, or cultivator, as *"panacea, de Panace, fille d'Aesculapius."*
2. from their country of origin.
3. by ironic antithesis (*"antiphrase et contrariété"*), *"comme absynthe, au contraire de pynthe, car il est fascheux à boire."*
4. from their powers or functions, *"comme aristolochia, qui ayde des femmes en mal d'enfant."*
5. by their distinctive qualities, like heliotrope.
6. after people metamorphosed into them, *"comme daphné, c'est laurier, de Daphné."*
7. metaphorically, *par similitude,"* as *"iris, à l'arc en ciel, en ses fleurs"* (and men reciprocally take their names from plants, as Cicero from *"des poys chices,"* or chick-peas).
8. morphologically, *"de leurs formes,"* *"comme trefeuil, qui ha trois feuilles."*

From this chapter, which is one of the lessons in the great uncompiled handbook of the poetic art, we may learn something of the primacy of the contagious principle of metaphor over the homeopathic principle which at first seemed so much more obvious. In only a very small number of Rabelais' categories do names "make sense," without further knowledge, to present observation and rational reflexion. We can see why a plant with three leaves might be called a trefoil, but no amount of unaided thought will tell us why a plant is called artemisia. In most of the categories, even those based, like antithesis and contrariety, upon formal relations, we cannot understand a name until we understand something else; and that something else is most often a unique and particular something else, something that happened, or is said to have happened, only once, and which therefore does not enter language as a generality; it has to be remembered to be understood, and if it is not remembered it cannot be derived by reason and cannot be known; it is a part of history, or tradition.

Hence, whether names are or are not in the first instance arbitrary, they bring something arbitrary into discourse, something obstinately unyielding: bringing in the individual, they bring in history, or tradition, and the stern idea of a world in which things happen once and for all.

So names are compressed fables, or histories.

And the evocative power of names, whether or not they are recognizable as distorted, combined, or corrupted words, depends upon the strange relation they make between the real world of happening and the ideal world of reason. Names relate to language as human beings relate to possibility, or as, for Dante, Beatrice related to Virgil, and the realm in which Beatrice was the guide related to the realm in which Virgil was the guide.

In general, and without even touching upon, much less trying to solve, the mystery of which came first, we may divide the matter this way, that the Homeopathic principle reflects nature, while the Contagious principle reflects history. And as to what in all this matter of the metaphorical expansion of names or condensation of fables is magical, only this, that although many metaphors propose a relation verifiable to the reader, a relation between objects whose natures are known (the legs of a table, the shoulder of a mountain) another sort of metaphor proposes a relation not verifiable by any living person, between two objects only one of which is known, as for example in "Care-charmer sleep, son of the sable night, Brother to death," and so on, or in the verse of Dante quoted before. There what is known is proposed as a presumptive demonstration of what is not known, what can be seen as a reflexion of what cannot be seen.

Poetry in the hands of the great masters constantly tends to a preoccupation with the second sort of figure, making statements about invisible mysteries by means of things visible; and poems, far from resting in nature as their end, use nature as a point from which they extrapolate darkly the nature of all things not visible or mediately knowable by reason—the soul, society, the gods or god, the mind—to which visible nature is equivocally the reflexion and the mask. Such poetry is magical, then, because it treats the world as a signature, in which all things intimate to us by their sensible properties what and in what way we are. Poetry is an art of naming, and this naming is done by story-telling and by metaphorical approximations and refinements, according to the two principles of magic I have described.

Everything, Preferably All at Once:
Coming to Terms with Kenneth Burke

IN ONE perhaps accidental symbolic act, Burke expressed his essence: he had some of his early books reissued by *Hermes* Publications. Hermes, originally a boundary stone, presently grew a face and a beard and went on to become the Roman god of boundaries, Terminus. Rising still further, he became Hermes Trismegistus, "the fabled author of a large number of works (called Hermetic books) most of which embody Neo-Platonic, Judaic, and Cabalistic ideas, as well as magical, astrological, and alchemical doctrines." In other words, everything, and preferably all at once.

The dictionary from which I drew this description of Burke in his aspect as Hermes identifies him with the Egyptian scribe Thoth, who above all "created by means of words," and "appears sometimes . . . as exercising this function on his own initiative, at other times as acting as the instrument of his creator." That is a doubt one may properly have about any scribe whose *oeuvre* is imposing enough to make one wonder whether he is representing the world or proposing to replace it; Milton, for instance, invoking his heavenly muse, claims to merit the instruction by reason of his "upright heart and pure"; and yet through the intended humility I have always heard a certain obstinacy in "upright," and thought of it as comparable with another Miltonic epithet, "erected." But the doubt may be peculiarly appropriate to Burke, who "above all creates by means of words" in the special sense that he creates words, terms, terminologies—

the business of Hermes. And when you ask whether he does this on his own initiative or as the instrument of his creator, you get the somewhat cryptic though certainly comprehensive reply from his address to the Logos:

> For us
> Thy name a Great Synecdoche,
> Thy works a Grand Tautology.

Schopenhauer once called the world a vast dream dreamed by a single being, but in such a way that all the people in the dream are dreaming too. A lovely figure, and in its logological translation it might do for Burke's world as well: a vast dream dreamed by a single Word, but in such a way that all the words in the dream are dreaming too.

But I have just remembered that part of my title, "preferably all at once," is about Burke intensively: it comes from him. (Somewhat as when you make what seems a good pun you can never be certain it isn't waiting for you in *Finnegans Wake*.) There is a passage late in *A Rhetoric of Motives* that I had been meaning to cite somehow, as an instance of Burke's excessiveness about terms and of one's appreciation of his rightness if one would only think about it (as I. A. Richards said, a book is a machine for thinking with).

The passage is called "Rhetorical Names for God," and after some introductory talk a page-and-a-bit goes to a listing of terms you might use when appealing to the Deity. The range is indeed extensive, as is proper to the All in All, going from "ground of all possibility" around to "nothing" and taking in en route such things as real estate, money, sleep, excrement, and death. But now I especially note: "Center, circumference, apex, base (preferably all at once)."

By this example I mean only that when you speak of the writers you care most for, you not only speak about them—you also speak them.

Here is a sort of monkish metaphor for what Burke does: he illuminates texts. In its application to criticism the figure tells us one of the things we most expect from critics, that they should offer us particular enlightenment about particular works, showing us things we had not seen and that, once seen, compel us to acknowledge their truth and significance. In its more medieval aspect the figure suggests an independent activity integral to the other and, in Burke's criticism, identical with it: as in the illuminations of the *Book of Kells*, Burke is using the text while weaving up his own designs.

Most simply put, he can get more thoughts out of a book than anyone else can, evoking in his reader time after time a mixed attitude of surprise, gratitude, and chagrin—"yes, of course, why couldn't I have seen it for myself?"—while at the same time, in the same gestures, often in the very same sentences, he is developing a method and a terminology which the reader, if he will, can master for application elsewhere.

For this reason, there is very little in Burke's writing of what White-head stigmatized as "inert knowledge." Everything is in movement, in development; everything is always being used for all it's worth, and sometimes maybe more.

There is an enthusiasm in all this that sometimes comes near enough to madness: criticism as rhapsody, or *furor poeticus*. Nor do I mean that in disparagement, though aware that some writers would; for among the most appealing things about Burke, to my mind, is the sense he has, the sense I get from reading him, that thought, if it is to matter at all, must be both obsessive and obsessively thorough, that thinking, if it is to salvage anything worth having from chaos, must adventure into the midst of madness and build its city there. Also that this action never really ends until the thinker does; everything is always to be done again. Also this: that system begins in inspiration, order in improvisation, method in heuristic. Here is one of Burke's own and somewhat breathless descriptions:

> So we must keep trying anything and everything, improvising, borrowing from others, developing from others, dialectically using one text to comment upon another, schematizing; using the incentive to new wanderings, returning from these excursions to schematize again, being oversubtle where the straining seems to promise some further glimpse, and making amends by reduction to very simple anecdotes.

That seems characteristic, even to "we must"—for Burke makes many and difficult demands upon his readers—and even to "make amends"—for he is as magnanimous as he is demanding.

Back in the days when such things mattered more to the literary community at large than perhaps they do just now, there was much debate upon a question, raised I believe by T. S. Eliot, as to whether criticism could be, or should be, "autotelic." Much debate, but relatively little illumination, probably because that forbidding word "autotelic" implied the expected answer, that criticism had better humbly confine itself to the ancillary task of digging nuggets of wisdom, or pure form, or whatever, out of the superior materials provided by the poets and novelists, and not set up in business on its own. And indeed there was much local and practical justification for the expected answer, inasmuch as when criticism did its thing, usually under the formidable name of aesthetics, the results were often of a dullness far beyond the call of duty.

But all the same, the very fact that the question was raised indicated some anxiety about the expected answer; and the massive development of criticism as both an art and an industry around that time suggested the perhaps horrifying thought that if the critics went on as they were going there was some remote chance that some one among them might one day actually learn something about literature *in principle*, and not only about this work and that work in snips and snaps and *aperçus*.

Well, in Burke and some others (among whom I should name especially I. A. Richards and William Empson), I conceive that there began to appear ways in which criticism could be "autotelic" in such a style as not in the least to prevent its traditionally imputed function of praising and damning and qualifying the work of "creative" writers; and it appeared indeed that by its new independence criticism was able to perform its traditional function not merely better than before, producing "insights" at such a rate as for a few years almost made people believe in progress once again, but also at depths and over ranges not previously suspected to exist. Having begun with the usual critical attempt to winkle "meanings" out of literary works, Burke and the others (and a good few more than I have mentioned) were led on into quite new questions—at least for the tradition of criticism in English, and in modern times—about meaning in general, what it is and how it arises and in what ways it relates to language. In fact, the same question that had been asked about criticism now appeared about language: was it ancillary to meaning, instrumental to thoughts that somehow had an independent existence? Or was it autotelic, and capable of generating worlds, or the world, primarily by reason of its own internal arrangements, as the language of mathematics, or, more darkly, of music, seemed to suggest?

Kenneth Burke's researches in this area seem to me venturesome, enchanting, and productive. And I have sometimes thought of them as contributing to the development of a new species of epic poetry, a poetry containing its own criticism much as a dream sometimes contains its own interpretation more or less explicitly; this poetry might be that intellectual comedy which Valéry, himself an anticipator of it, said he would value more highly than either the divine or the human. (The question whether such a poetry would have to come in verse seems entirely secondary; from the "creative" side one might cite *The Magic Mountain, Finnegans Wake,* and *Remembrance of Things Past* as works containing their own critique.) In what follows, rather than trying to describe Burke's "system" or "doctrine," which anyhow is always evolving out of and dissolving into method, I shall try a species of rhapsodic impressionism and imitation.

Putting first things first, in accordance with Burke's principle of "the temporizing of essence," the mind's first move upon the world is to assert something, to be active. The assertion will probably be suggested by the world, yet it will also have in it something both arbitrary and peremptory, and at least prospectively insane. This is what writers commonly call "having an idea," a phrase usually treated as ultimate and unquestionable, but which with Burke's help we may see a bit further into.

The essence of "having an idea" is "giving a name." Its effect is always to say to the phenomenon, "Be other than thou art." It is both prayerful and commanding, it both asks and asserts. It challenges, and upon the challenge it moves into a combat with "the world" which at its best it both wins and loses. Wins, in that a more or less large range of particular appearances is brought into patterned clarity, simultaneously articulated and integrated, by coming under the sway of the idea. Loses, in that the victory is only for a time, and more especially in that the idea of its own nature overextends itself and like a tragic hero perishes in its pride, in its triumph, in the *hubris* brought on by success. This happens from two considerations in particular: every One, in becoming many, attempts to become All and falls abroad into chaos, nothingness, the abyss. Or else: every idea, at the end of the line, loses all content and meaning other than itself; it reaches redundancy, tautology, pleonasm, and at last says, uninformatively enough: I am that I am. These two ways of losing may be regarded as the damned and redeemed forms of one single but unsayable thing.

These two ways, moreover, have to do with simple figurations that may stand for the base of all thought: the line and the circle. Nor is it accidental, I think, that line and circle, and the spiral compounded of their motion, make up our ways of thinking about time—bringing us again to the "temporizing of essence."

We do not ordinarily believe we make progress by going 'round in circles; and yet in a round world we may have no other course. Consider how it is precisely, though mysteriously, the circling of the heavens that creates time, whose even progress along a straight line is among the blandest of our metaphysical assumptions, though possibly surpassed in this respect by the one that claims we don't have metaphysics any more. Or a homelier example: almost any literary critic will affirm, if only as costing him nothing, the assertion that "Finally, what the poem means is what the poem says," a pure yet somehow heartening tautology in that he will as readily affirm from experience that our circular course from what the poem says at first to what it says at last, or as near last as we ever get, improves our knowledge in reckonable ways.

Perhaps both line and circle have damned and redeemed forms, or ways of being thought about. The circle, from antiquity a "perfect" and sacred figure, is complete, hence eternal, simple, and rounding upon itself: the mind of God, in a phrase I've heard attributed to half a dozen writers from Bonaventura to Pascal, is a circle whose center is everywhere and whose circumference is nowhere. Alternatively, the circle may stand for futility and unending repetition and the boredom of a bad eternity. In the same way, the line in its optimistic leaping forth suggests progress; but as the progress is from an unknown (or nonexistent) past to an unknown (or nonexistent or endless) future, it may likewise engender feelings of hopelessness.

Otherwise put: If a storyteller says to us, in effect, "This happened, and then that happened, and then something else happened. . . ." we are bored; no matter how many things happen, we "keep waiting for something to happen." Whereas if a story were limited to the recital of its *idea*, there could be no story; for stories have to be one thing after another. So that a story *is* the compound of line and circle, as Burke indicates in a simple figure:

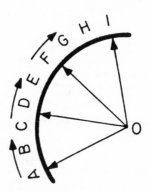

upon which he comments:

Any narrative form . . . in its necessary progression from one episode to the next is like the stages from A to I along the arc. But as regards the principle of internal consistency, *any* point along the arc is as though generated from center O. And the various steps from A to I can be considered as *radiating* from generative principle O, regardless of their *particular* position along the arc of the narrative sequence.*

What is said of stories holds also for philosophies, which arose out of stories and which retain, using terms for persons, the "dramatistic" cooperations and conflicts, mergers and divisions, of stories. It may hold true in a peculiarly poignant way of Burke's philosophy, a corpus of mythology relating how certain heroes or demigods, called by the family name of *terms*, incarnated themselves in the world of action where they overcame the old dragon of chaos, established order, gave laws, and so on, until at last defeated by the dragon's mother, once named by Burke as "material recalcitrance." But, happily, new generations of terms arose ... and the story is always beginning just as it is always ending.

Burke's mind must be a fascinating but terrifying place to live in. So it would seem, anyhow, from the homeopathic experience of it in small doses that one gets from his books. Despite the order imposed by narrative, despite a grand friendliness of manner and a most beguiling disposition to admit mistakes, to begin again, to reveal not only the result of thought but much of its process as well, the chief thing I note about his mind is that it cannot stop exploding. In the early books the footnotes, like large dogs leashed to dwarfish masters, often marched along for pages under a few homeless-looking lines of text; in the later books this habit has been overcome by the expedient of relegating the footnotes into appendices (the dogs get bigger, but are kept in their own kennels); while after *A Grammar of Motives* and *A Rhetoric of Motives* (1945 and 1950 respectively) the completion of the proposed grand design has been deferred by a huge volume called *Language as Symbolic Action*, a smaller though still substantial one called *The Rhetoric of Religion*, and an unpublished though mimeographed *Poetics* of three hundred pages, not to mention numerous uncollected articles, unpublished notes, etc. (the dogs are beginning to wag their kennels?).

Once, when asked to make suggestions about a Burke essay in manuscript, I indicated a few places where it might be cut. Some weeks later a letter announced earnestly that after thoroughly considering my remarks he had rewritten the whole thing and cut it from sixty-five pages to sev-

*Kenneth Burke, "Dramatic Form—And: Tracking Down Implications," *Tulane Drama Review* (T 32), Vol. 10, No. 4 (Summer 1966), pages 59–60.

enty-six. And during the question period after a recent lecture in which he had been talking about the cycle of terms and the generative power of any dialectical term to spawn a terminology, I heard Burke tell the class: "Any term will lead you to the others. There's no place to start." Ah, I thought, that means there's no place to stop, either. And I wondered: which half of Burke's mind will win? The linear, progressive, orderly half that proposes to itself systematic philosophy and sequential argument from beginning to end? or the radical, explosive half, the lyric and rhapsodic philosopher whose entire effort is to make every poor part contain the glorious, impossible whole, as in the Ptolemaic cosmology the Primum Mobile goes racing 'round at enormous speeds only in order that every place may catch up with every place and be at rest in the peace of the Empyrean? For, certainly and a little remarkably, I still have scarcely any idea of what the proposed third canticle, *A Symbolic of Motives*, may contain, no matter what anticipations of it must inevitably have come up in the story so far. Surely a place where any writer might beseech Apollo for both peaks of Parnassus, where either one had served before.

I mention this because it belongs to the figures of line and circle which I seem to have got stuck with, and because it is at the heart of that cooperative conflict between narrative and essence, image and concept, myth and philosophy, that Burke calls "the temporizing of essence."

Language, for Burke, not merely mirrors the world it seems to see, but also generates it. This is the sticking point at which over and over he divides from all philosophies proposing to base on scientific models; and not only divides from, but undercuts and gets beyond, seeing the human hope precisely in the rich polyvalence of terms, the Shakespearean equivocations, which those philosophies propose to exclude.

That language in any sense makes the world is a thought intolerable to those who view the world, implicitly or otherwise, as a solid existent (like Descartes's *res extensa*) which the mind passively records as a camera does in univocal concepts which it may then manipulate as a computer does.

For Burke, language is literally making, constitutive, or *poetic* of "reality." To the extent that its terms are not only positive ones, such as *house*, but dialectic ones, such as *good* or *high* or *sinful*, capable of division into and merger with other terms, it is language itself that makes the symbolic world. This is the distinctively human world in which we struggle along on the guidance of phantasy, the world of human action as over against the world of sheerly physical motion described by physics according to models that positivist philosophers constantly claim to emulate by various "reductionist" schemes according to which human motives are viewed as mechanisms, and according to which "God," "soul," and "spirit" are progressively read out of the act until at last, by a miracle comparable with the stomach's digesting itself and emitting a satisfied belch, "mind" too is read out of the act by the very mind that claims to be doing the reading.

Yet there is an important way in which Burke, while at odds with "scientistic" philosophers if not with science itself, is adventured on somewhat the same quest as that of physics: he would bring the world of human action, as it would the world of physical motion, under the dominion of few, simple, and elegant laws. It is tempting to wonder what would happen if his discoveries in this line educed the kind of cooperation among the learned that routinely goes on in physics; but they do not. And besides, this kind of thought may be peculiarly related to its thinker; as I have heard it observed of another original and self-made philosopher, Rudolf Steiner, that he was everywhere and his disciples nowhere.

The sense in which the internal resources of language themselves generate views of the world formed the subject of *A Grammar of Motives*; whereas *A Rhetoric of Motives* studied the ways in which these same resources might be wilfully manipulated for conflicting purposes. Between the two there was already noticeable a considerable area of overlap, which will perhaps extend also to *A Symbolic of Motives* in its presumable "transcendence" of the area of competitive identifications—the marketplace, the human barnyard, as Burke says—by considering the forms and methods of literature as "timeless" patterns.

So we have a triad, and the progression through it, something like Inferno-Purgatorio-Paradiso, and something like the equally celebrated id-ego-superego. Something like, at least, in the important respect that the outer terms are represented as eternal fixities while the middle one is the scene of conflict, development, and playing-out in time and history of the patterns beneath and above. As if, to adapt one of Burke's analogies, the grammar is a chord which the rhetoric breaks into linear form as an arpeggio, while the symbolic, the chord again and newly understood in relation to its constituent notes, will be but a moment in time, the ear of corn reaped in silence before the initiates at Eleusis, whose trials had brought them to that wordless understanding upon which even Plato and Aristotle agree.

That seems a good place to stop, a high note to sustain so that we know this particular aria is over. Of the much more that might be said, I will bring us down to the ground by only one further reflection.

It was during the normal confusions of sophomore year that a friend

gave me a copy of *Attitudes toward History*—"two mouse-grey volumes,"
he said, "containing all knowledge." And I could see what he meant. The
two things in especial that Burke said to a young man of eighteen were
"Everything is interesting" and "Everything is a language." The sense in
which those two things are one might well take thirty years or more to
put together, but I'll try to put my results into a small anecdote and an
emblem.

Most of one's education in those days was not only liberal education
but self-education, and permissive extremely. The Great Books were the
ones we thought our teachers had never read; at least, they were never
mentioned in lectures. Still, I once confided in an admired professor that
I'd been reading Kenneth Burke. "Ah," he said, and there came upon his
face an expression of solemnity which ever since I've identified with Harvard Square—when you meet it elsewhere it's derivative—as he said:
"Brilliant; brilliant, yes. But hardly solid."

I have sometimes unworthily thought—for that professor was admirable at teaching—that some people found solidity so universal a value
they even wanted it between the ears. But thirty years later I found my
emblem in an invention that was new when the world—the symbolic real
one, of course—was new:

Rounding upon itself, it became a perfect sphere when closed. It was made
mostly of nothing, its critics pointed out that it was full of holes; besides, they said,
it obviously leaks. Philosophers added that it was vain to suppose you could encompass the Void with bits of string, and as a final blow they said it was a tautology.

All the same, it caught fish.

Randall Jarrell
(A Myth about Poetry)

Randall Jarrell, *The Complete Poems.*

L ANGUAGE is a great magic. The young poet turns it on and it begins to
tell him wonderful things, so many wonderful things he can scarcely
believe, at times, that this instrument that the mouth of man has been
playing the tunes of for hundreds of years and for thousands of years
should yet have reserved to himself so many fresh inventions, marvelous
cadences, new sayings of oldest thoughts, and all done by sending out on
the indefinitely accommodating carrier wave of the sentence the huge and
fathomless words of power: night, cold, sky, life, love, water, bread, grief,
fire, death. . . . It is the world over again, the world made new. His favorite
poet has said it: "*Im dunkeln Dichter wiederholt sich still / ein jedes Ding:
ein Stern, ein Haus, ein Wald.*"

A star, a house, a wood, that's how it goes, simple and miraculous. And
to be a poet, a *dark* poet, in whom as in his favorite poet's favorite figure
of pool or lake the world reflects itself again, how fine that is!

The poet works, of course he works; he scribbles and revises and thinks:
There! that's a bit better. But it is not so much like work as it is like watching; he has to be there to watch—that is the condition of its doing itself
under his hand, under his eye; but he has no doubt that it does itself. He
is only the sorcerer's apprentice, who has turned on the broomstick; a
fateful comparison, which we should prefer not to have made, did it not
force itself upon us. For great magic is always dangerous to the magicker.

The language that tells the poet wonderful things is in this way an
embarrassment and then a danger, that it won't stop telling him wonderful

things. More than that, as the wonderful things accumulate they also tend to integrate and form coherencies willy-nilly; they bind up into a story that the poet is not only telling but also being told; they may even insist, finally, on telling him the truth, which is no less true and no less perilous for being true not of some merely objective world but of that peculiar universal, the world with himself in it, or, as literary people like to say, *his* world.

That is something he need not consider at first, for at first what he hears is not *a* story, it is many stories, each one different from the others, and they well up in all their rich particularity and selfness as from a source that ever supplies itself again. Only after many years, maybe, does the outline of the poet's own and unique story begin to emerge among the multitude of stories he has told; a very mysterious course of development, in which his preoccupations, or even his obsessions, go out into the world and shape it slowly in their own image, until by an unreckonable reversal that world returns upon him to flood his consciousness with his own obsessions. It is perhaps this that makes poets, as they grow old, fall silent or else repeat themselves: having made their reality, they have to lie in it.

Something else happens, too. The world goes on, and the poet's life outside the poems goes on, in the inextricably double and mutually concealing motion of its history and his biography, so that change in the one and change in the other, recognition and reversal, increase of anguish in the world and increased consciousness of anguish in the self, can never be quite distinguished one from the other, much less kept separate. And the marvelous sayings that language has said? Language goes on saying them, with an undiminished energy in which there is something impersonal, overpowering, indifferent. Moreover, without the poet's being able to do anything to stop them, the sayings begin to appear as true in application to the world outside the poems that earlier had encompassed them and kept them in their fictive world, the only world in which such sayings may be safely said. The poet had always wanted to reach reality, hadn't he? His elders had always said reality was the object. And there he is at last. His story phases with the world and becomes the world; with its great power of patterning and formulating and recasting every material in its own image, it cannot do otherwise.

In some such ways do poets come into the desolation of reality, or wither into truth. There are many expressions for this condition; many modern artists rather rashly seek it out, optimistically calling it "the breakthrough." Fashionable people a few years ago called it "The Existential Level," unconsciously and not wrongly suggesting it was more like falling through than breaking through. Blake thought of it as dumb Despair always existing beneath "the rough basement" of language. A semanticist called it "the objective unspeakable level," and our poet, in that novel of his where the characters' clichés are wittier than most writers' epigrams, named it "definition by ostentation." How do you do it? "You simply point." And he seems to define it, a few lines later, as the condition in which one sees the world as "one of those stupid riddles whose only point is that they have no point."

That is one side of it, of which Wordsworth said: "We poets in our youth begin in gladness, / But thereof come in the end despondency and madness." And Eliot said:

> That is the way things happen.
> Everything is true in a different sense,
> A sense that would have seemed meaningless before. . . .
>
> And in the end
> That is the completion which at the beginning
> Would have seemed the ruin.

And the other side? The other side is, I think, more personally the poet's own, and to it belong the wit, the charm, the gaiety, the energy, and the courage that for many years and many poems sustain the life, sustain the work, above the gulf—demonic, divine, or void—where all things lose their names.

The foregoing is a myth about poets and poetry. I do not know whether it is true, or whether it is applicable. It came to mind from reading Randall Jarrell's *Complete Poems*, and from reading over also much else that he wrote, and from reading much that was written of him by friends, colleagues, acquaintances, and by his wife in the collection bearing his name edited by Robert Lowell, Peter Taylor, and Robert Penn Warren (1967).

A myth is not a review. Randall Jarrell and I reviewed one another amply during his life—perhaps as many as three times each; we said, both of us, some harsh things, some funny things, some kindly things, and altogether were nothing if not critical. I should feel sorry to write, from ignoble security, literary criticism that is unable to evoke, indeed provoke, his answering voice.

Two Ways of the Imagination: Blake & Wordsworth

THE poetry I wish to talk about may be considered as meditation upon analogy by means of analogy, or as perceptions regarded from the point of view of what they tell us about the nature of perception, or as the making of equations between the inside of things and the outside of things. These are hard sayings, and worse are to follow. Here, for instance, are some sentences of the largest obtainable generality. You need not quite believe them, only entertain them speculatively for a time; and grains of salt will be handed out by the ushers. Anyhow, as Augustine said, "These things are true in a way because they are false in a way."

1. The subject of poetry is the relation of soul and body, mind and world.

2. The poetry in English during the whole of the "modern" period—since Shakespeare—has had increasingly to define itself in relation to the conventional worldly view of this relation, the view named by Alfred North Whitehead as "scientific materialism": "the fixed scientific cosmology which presupposes the ultimate fact of an irreducible brute matter, or material, spread throughout space in a flux of configurations. In itself such a material is senseless, valueless, purposeless."*

---

*Alfred North Whitehead, *Science and the Modern World* (New York: The Macmillan Company, 1925), p. 25.

3. The so-called alienation of poetry from society is a function of this self-definition, and so, too, is an observable tendency for poetry to become the subject of itself.

These are simplicities, and that is what makes them difficult. An appropriate gloss upon the problem they present might be the following passage from Whitehead; he is writing of the same period, roughly from the beginning of the seventeenth century:

The enormous success of the scientific abstractions, yielding on the one hand *matter* with its *simple location* in space and time, on the other hand *mind*, perceiving, suffering, reasoning, but not interfering, has foisted onto philosophy the task of accepting them as the most concrete rendering of fact.

Thereby, modern philosophy has been ruined. It has oscillated in a complex manner between three extremes. There are the dualists, who accept matter and mind as on an equal basis, and the two varieties of monists, those who put mind inside matter, and those who put matter inside mind.*

It is the charm of that last statement, that it gives to the amateur at thought a master's assurance that his problem is simple even while it is also impossible.

I am not to attempt a history of this development as it reveals itself in poetry, but hope rather to elucidate my sentences by means of a comparison between two poets, Blake and Wordsworth, whose major writings offer evidence that a problem exists in the mind's relation with the world, and who represent two approaches to its resolution. First, however, I should like to consider very briefly something about the simplicities of Shakespeare, for whom all this, though a mystery, seems not to have been a problem at all.

Shakespeare's tragedies seem to work on the belief, deep enough to require no justification, that there exist several distinct realms of being, which for all their apparent distinctness respond immediately and decisively to one another. There is the realm of the soul, the mind, the secret wish, or dream, or thought. There is the realm of human community, in itself a complex of several related relations: the lovers, the brothers, the body politic, the nation which is at the same time the family. There is the realm of sublunary nature, ranging, say, from the primrose to the storm at sea. There is the realm of the ancestral dead, shaken from their sleep and appearing ambiguously as portents or symptoms of great mischief. There

---

Ibid., pp. 81–82.

is the realm of the astronomical and astrological heavens, and there is the realm of supernatural solicitings, which in themselves "cannot be ill, cannot be good." And there is the realm of the gods, or of god.

All these mutually reflect one another. You cannot disturb the balance of one mind, or of one king's court, without the seismic registration of that disturbance in the near and remotest regions of the cosmos: an error of judgment will strike flat the thick rotundity of the world; a wicked thought will tumble together the treasure of nature's germens even till destruction sicken. The result is a world of dreadful splendors, but every piece of it is rhythmically articulated with every piece; and the realms which have priority in initiating the great releases of energy are ambiguously psychological and supernatural at once, but unequivocally the realms of spirit, will, mind. All life, and all the scene of life, the not-living around and beneath and above, poise in a trembling balance which is complete, self-moving, extensive in detail through the four elements, from "Let Rome in Tiber melt" and "kingdoms are clay" to "I am fire and air" and "O eastern star!" This, then, is the sublime and terrible treasure which afterwards was lost. Our theme is the attempt of the poets to find it again, and of two poets in particular.

William Blake (1757–1827) and William Wordsworth (1770–1850) are poetically about as unlike one another as they could be. But what makes the unlikeness significant and the comparison possibly illuminating is the fact that it arises out of numerous and rather particular resemblances between them.

Although they are by thirteen years not of an age, the substantial overlap includes for both men the period of their greatest and most significant production. This was the period of the French Revolution and of Napoleon, time of radical hopes, radical despairs, amounting to a dramatically sudden overthrow of ancient ways of looking at the world, and the overthrow, as dramatic and sudden, of the new way which was to have replaced these. Both poets approached the French Revolution as radicals, to a certain extent even as "subversives," "English Jacobins," strongly opposed to the English war with France. For both poets the events of the period had disastrous repercussions on the personal life—for Wordsworth, his immediate experience of revolution and the Terror, and his liaison with Annette Vallon; for Blake, his trial on a false and malicious charge of sedition—and for both the Revolution became the subject of a poetic analysis which made of the political and social events a myth about human motive. Both, in their very different ways, began poetical revolutions against the canons of the eighteenth century, and these revolutions, however they may seem to have begun with technical questions such as the reform of diction, involved their authors in a deeper examination of the premises of perception, the question of the relation between thoughts and things. Out of their poetical inquiries came radically different though related assertions concerning world and mind, or soul.

For both Blake and Wordsworth, poetry has a crucial connection with childhood, and this connection too, however differently they handled it, is revolutionary, a new and independent discovery made by each alone. (Some hints may have been got from Vaughan, but Traherne's work, lost after his death, was not recovered and published till much later.) And both poets, after achieving reckonable success with brief lyrics, turned to the largest possible form of epical and prophetical writings, with the double object of system and vision—oddly as these two traits may appear to go together.

Finally, both Blake and Wordsworth wrote poems which were in a decisive way about writing poems. They attempted, that is, to imagine the imagination, Wordsworth in *The Prelude* especially, and Blake in many places, but especially in *Jerusalem*.

This seems to me a very strange and fascinating circumstance, because the concern of poetry with itself in this decisive way had really not happened before in English, where the self-reference, or reflexive character, of poems had been largely conventional and as it were by the way: assertions of immortality in and by means of verse, invocations to the Muse, or jokes—"I am two fools, I know, / For loving and for saying so / In whining poetry."*

So we may say that in writing works whose subject included and largely was the question of what it means to write works, these two poets introduced into poetry something substantively modern, that is, a doubt which led them to view their own vocations as problematic and subject to investigation. For neither does this mean any diminution of the claims of the imagination; rather the reverse. Imagination now becomes central to the universe and the most important thing to understand about the universe; but becomes this precisely because it has become problematic and doubtful. I should add that this characteristic of the imagination reveals itself no less in Blake's fierce intellectual anger, the appearance he gives of abso-

---

*We must make one grand exception for Alexander Pope, whose *Dunciad* ought ideally—given enough time—to be studied in connection with our theme.

lute intolerant certainty, than in Wordsworth's more hesitant and tentative balancings, his quieter confidence going over occasionally into a religiose smugness.

II

The Prelude, William Wordsworth's creation myth about himself, is in the first place an autobiographical work—it is, said the author, "a thing unprecedented in literary history that a man should talk so much about himself." His observation is in error, for we think at once of Pepys or Evelyn, but the error is a useful one, directing our attention to a striking trait of this autobiography, subtitled "The Growth of a Poet's Mind," which is, that it does not at all consist of the daily life, the record of events such as usually occupies journal or diary. From the very beginning the biography is idealized, mythified, made into fiction, and regarded from a lofty distance, whence it gains its form. Gains, in fact, two forms, both of them perceptible: the intended one, and the one that actually resulted.

The intended form of this early portrait of the artist is a pilgrimage, or journey to salvation. It is a Comedy, in the sense that, although it tells sometimes of lamentable things, it ends happily, with a grave and dedicated happiness. It is also, as I have said, a myth. The stages of the journey are the stages of initiation, wherein the hero, a child especially favored by a divinity, in this instance Nature the Great Mother, enters the world in blessedness, falls into alienation through knowledge, endures certain trials associated with terror, death, the loss of identity, and is reborn "on a higher plane" in such a way as to redeem his early promise and assert more fully the theme of his original divinity.

In this respect *The Prelude* resembles the story told by Dante, the story told by Bunyan; it resembles those modern stories of Stephen Dedalus, Paul Morel, Marcel, Adrian Leverkühn, wherein the young artist, passing through worldliness and suffering, including especially sexual suffering, achieves, or fails to achieve, wholeness, dedication, strength. And the poem is reflexive, like Proust's novel, telling how it came to be, and having for subject that life which prepared the way to its composition.

So much for the form which appears as the intention. A man writes a poem telling how he got to be a poet. Toward the end of this poem, he announces that he is a poet, and offers the poem itself as interim evidence of the fact, to suffice until he does something still greater, or anyhow (as it turned out) still bigger.

But there is something else, amounting toward the end to a quite different form for the poem. For surely many readers of this immense and beautiful work find that somehow it fails of the planned completion, that the promised rebirth, confidently proclaimed to have happened, either did not happen at all, or not to the degree asserted, or else went by us unremarked. Perhaps this has to do with the unwritten but powerful law which forbids a man from describing his own success: even in speaking of one's own humility a tone of pride sneaks in, even in ascribing the victory to God, Nature, or Reason, there may appear a flat noise of self-gratulation:

> Long time in search of knowledge did I range
> The field of human life, in heart and mind
> Benighted; but, the dawn beginning now
> To reappear, it was proved that not in vain
> I had been taught to reverence a Power
> That is the visible quality and shape
> And image of right reason; that matures
> Her processes by steadfast laws; gives birth
> To no impatient or fallacious hopes,
> No heat of passion or excessive zeal,
> No vain conceits; provokes to no quick turns
> Of self-applauding intellect; but trains
> By meekness, and exalts by humble faith. . . .

Yet in somewhat failing thus, if it does, the poem achieves a sort of grandeur other than that intended: not quite a tragedy, perhaps, yet not without elements of the tragic, it has a solemn pathos attendant upon the spectacle of a human failure, which commands sympathy because we all must fail, but it has also a certain grim and moralizing humor because of the poet's resolute refusal to allow for what may have happened, or failed to happen. He goes on proclaiming praise to the end, whereas we might see rather a sad parody of what is claimed in the titles of Books XII and XIII: Imagination and Taste, How Impaired and Not Quite Restored.

A reason for this failure, less personal than the one already suggested, is built into the formal problem of a reflexive poem, a poem about poetry. For poetry may be a subject like time, of which Augustine said, "I understand what it is until I try to tell you." There may be a necessary anticlimax in the poet's announcement that he has just now achieved what we have seen him doing extremely well for a dozen books and more. We may see

from many modern examples that for a poem to be about poetry is no
guarantee of its being a good poem, if only because a poet in doubts or
difficulties about the meaning of what he is doing is always liable to appeal
to this apparently easy way out and end with a vision of himself standing
there with his mouth open, in lines which are the equivalent of the fighter
pilot's "There I was at five thousand feet with no oil pressure."

To put this in another way, I read in the operating instructions for a
sewing machine, "The machine will sew its own thread in crossing from
one piece of material to another, but it is not advisable to let it do this for
long." O well, I thought, that's true of any Singer.

So Wordsworth's problem at the end of *The Prelude* is a vexing one,
and his solution for it is in the main assertion that the miracle has happened, prayerful pleas for belief that it has happened, and explanations of
what it is that is said to have happened. There are, to be sure, several
visions—of the girl on the hill, of the Druids at Stonehenge, the revelation
from the top of Snowdon—yet these revelations are curiously reluctant to
reveal, they do not always reveal exactly what they are announced as revealing, and the insistent work of assertion resumes once more.

Another reason for this failure is more difficult to present because it
demands knowledge not given in the poem—indeed, specifically withheld by the poet. Without the researches of Emile Legouis and George
McLean Harper we should not be able to see that the brief sketch of two
lovers at the end of Book IX was Wordsworth's attempt to deal with—or
avoid dealing with—his love, his illegitimate daughter, his betrayal (whether
or no he could have done otherwise) of Annette Vallon, which amounted
at the same time to a political conversion to a conservative point of view.

Poetically—which is to say, somewhat ruthlessly—this crisis might have
been divinely appointed for the crisis of this poem, for in it the personal
and the political become subject to one decision, a parallel in the true
Shakespearean style, hence the opportunity of a dramatic rather than a
hortatory ending. But the poet was somehow under the necessity of avoiding it. We are not to judge of this necessity, nor to tell that well-known
story again, but rather to make some observations about *The Prelude* which
can now be made independently of the story, even though the story is
what started us thinking about the poem in a new way.

A striking thing about Wordsworth's vision is that it contains almost no
natural evil. Such natural evil as it does contain tends to be majestic and
awesome and soothingly remote; all grandeur and no poison ivy. Aldous
Huxley put the point neatly in an essay called "Wordsworth in the Trop-
ics," saying that the Nature Wordsworth wrote about was already human-

ized, civilized, not to say Anglicanized, and that a few weeks in the equatorial rain forests might have cured the poet of "the cozy sublimities of the Lake District." Of course, Huxley saw quite well that the problem is not to be solved by a simple change of venue, for it is a problem of imagination, or primary belief, without which no "Nature" is thinkable. We may confirm this by noticing that Blake, at about the same time and also from England's green and pleasant land, was viewing Nature as "a devouring worm" as

> a wat'ry flame revolving every way,
> And as dark roots and stems, a Forest of afflictions, growing
> In seas of sorrow.

The difference is accountable to the fact that Blake reads Nature as illusion (Vala, the veil) resulting from the shrunken senses of the divided man; resulting, that is, from the Fall. But for Wordsworth Nature is herself divine, and the Fall a rather limited, almost parochial phenomenon having to do with his fastidious or even fearful reprehension of cities, human beings, love, and accordingly he approaches the crisis of his poem, the second journey to France, by seeing himself Miltonically as Adam

> yet in Paradise
> Though fallen from bliss, when in the East he saw
> Darkness ere day's midcourse, and morning light
> More orient in the western cloud, that drew
> O'er blue firmament a radiant white,
> Descending slow with something heavenly fraught.

If I pursue the question a little further, asking what is the evil which is missing from the Wordsworthian Nature, I remember the definitions offered by the psychoanalyst Ella Freeman Sharpe, to the effect that, for the superego, good is whatever has nothing to do with sex, and evil is whatever has anything to do with sex. It is true, and rather remarkable, that *The Prelude*'s great meditation on how things come to be and on the sources of our being is just about entirely silent on the subject of carnal generation. Even in the lines about the two lovers, Wordsworth contrives to avoid the mention of sex and birth entirely by referring the reader to his poem about Vaudracour and Julia (originally composed for this place in *The Prelude*, but withdrawn) instead of telling their story.

Amateur psychoanalysis is not to the purpose, even though an autobiographical poem might be supposed to be self-revealing. But, continuing to speak only of the poem, the absence of any account of natural generation suggests another observation, on what might be thought of as the absolute segregation of the sexes in Wordsworth's view of life. It is a very slight exaggeration to say that Wordsworth, like some primitive people, does not know about the role played by the father in the getting of children. Certainly he never acknowledges it. The world of *The Prelude* is very largely the world of mother and child in the first place; and it is right, I think, to say that every male figure entering the poem is a solitary: the veteran met on the road at night, the Bedouin of the dream who is also Don Quixote, the Blind Beggar seen in London, the Shepherd (portrait of the poet's ideal type among men), the French officer modeled on his friend Beaupuy ("A patriot, thence rejected by the rest"), and finally, of course, more than the rest, Wordworth himself. His mother receives an elegy of some fifty lines—beginning, I am afraid, "Behold the parent hen amid her brood!"—but his father is mentioned only once, to say that he died, and that certain related circumstances made the event appear "a chastisement."

It is perhaps not this avoidance alone which impairs the poem as an account of creative mind, but certain parallel avoidances implied in it and made necessary by it. The omission of fatherhood in the natural sense somewhat weakens and limits the account of a process which may be not so natural as to a thoughtless eye it may at first appear, the process of the imagination's dealing with the world, and this poet cannot say, as Shakespeare does, "My brain I'll prove the female to my soul, / My soul the father," or speak so energetically as Shakespeare does of "the quick forge and working-house of thought." His "wise passivity" seems sometimes a touch too passive, too receptive, and of his attempt to hold, as at his best he does, a monist and interpenetrating balance between the mind and nature, we might say, as I suspect Blake is saying in certain passages we shall soon consider—if you don't beat nature, nature will beat you; there is no middle ground.

How this works in *The Prelude* may be seen from the poet's unconscious use of that tradition of natural symbolism, the initiatory ascent from earth through water and air to fire, which all poets come into some relation with whether knowing or unknowing. Seen in one way, *The Prelude* is a series of mountain climbs, with visions at the top of each mountain, climaxed by the grand vision from Mount Snowdon; that is, each time he attains the Earthly Paradise, the most refined earthly element of air, traditionally feminine (Blake calls it the region of Beulah) and traditionally representing the achievement of a purified natural reason. Further than this, the point at which Dante takes leave of Virgil and flies beyond the sun and stars, Wordsworth does not go: the sun, the fire, the father, remain unknown to him; his poem belongs to earth, water, air, to Nature, as protecting mother, it is written under the auspices of the powers of the air, and its highest moment of vision—universal mind, "a majestic intellect" imaged by clouds imitating the forms of earth and sea—takes place not in the fiery sun but by the light of the full moon.

One excerpt may serve to sum up the poet's approach to and withdrawal from the complex of feeling I have tried to outline. It comes in Book XII, just before the mention of his father's death, to which in scene-setting it is explicitly a parallel.

He remembers how as a child he strayed into a valley "where in former times / A murderer had been hung in iron chains." Though gibbet and bones were gone, there remained on the turf the murderer's name, carved in "monumental letters" annually cleared of grass "by superstition of the neighborhood." Fleeing in fear from this gloomy scene he climbed a hill and saw

> A naked pool that lay beneath the hills,
> The beacon on the summit, and, more near,
> A girl, who bore a pitcher on her head,
> And seemed with difficult steps to force her way
> Against the blowing wind.

It is for him an "ordinary sight," yet full of "visionary dreariness," and fascinating enough for him to speak again of

> moorland waste and naked pool,
> The beacon crowning the lone eminence,
> The female and her garments vexed and tossed
> By the strong wind,

and to remember that the same scene, when he was in love, appeared pleasurable.

This is his closest and clearest approach to the mystery of generation, composed in the sign of crime, punishment, and superstition, the murderer's name spoken as by the earth itself. He views the landscape exclusively in genital and sexual terms: hill and naked pool its natural symbols, beacon and pitcher its emblems in the realm of human artifice. The girl with the pitcher walking against the wind, her garments "vexed and tossed,"

glancingly allusive to legends of virgins impregnated by the wind—he
sees that all this is somehow about love. But it puzzles him, and he retires
on a somewhat general moral, which the passage itself only in very general terms will support, and delivers a sadly accurate prophecy of the future as a falling back, a return to the past:

> So feeling comes in aid
> Of feeling, and diversity of strength
> Attends us, if but once we have been strong.
> Oh! mystery of man, from what a depth
> Proceed thy honours. I am lost, but see
> In simple childhood something of the base
> On which thy greatness stands; but this I feel,
> That from thyself it comes, that thou must give,
> Else never canst receive. The days gone by
> Return upon me almost from the dawn
> Of life: the hiding places of man's power
> Open; I would approach them, but they close.
> I see by glimpses now; when age comes on,
> May scarcely see at all. . . .

Those hiding places of man's power are indeed associated with vision,
though sometimes negatively and dreadfully, as in Edgar's saying to Edmund about their father, "The dark and vicious place where thee he got /
Cost him his eyes." But for Wordsworth, what Nature generates, over and
over again, is thought, and thought alone.

Much might be said in defense of the poet; for surely the times were
out of joint, they always are. But after it is said there will remain something
about this wonderful poem sad, guilty, and unachieved. There is a marvelous moment just about at the middle of *The Prelude*, when the poet
sees something about the human condition, and sees it clearly. In a London street, "lost Amid the moving pageant," he sees a blind Beggar,

> who, with upright face,
> Stood, propped against a wall, upon his chest
> Wearing a written paper, to explain
> His story, whence he came, and who he was.
> Caught by the spectacle my mind turned round
> As with the might of waters; an apt type
> This label seemed of the utmost we can know,

> Both of ourselves and of the universe;
> And, on the shape of that unmoving man,
> His steadfast face and sightless eyes, I gazed,
> As if admonished from another world.

"My mind turned round as with the might of waters." Or, as Blake says, "in Time's ocean falling drown'd." For that written paper includes all the poems ever written or to be written. But from this dire vision of blindness Wordsworth retreats, as we all do every day, as only the very greatest now and then do not.

Wordsworth and Blake were not acquainted, though Wordsworth read some Blake poems in manuscript sent for his inspection by Henry Crabb Robinson, and was "interested"—as well he might be, writes Robinson, for there is an affinity between them "as there is between the regulated imagination of a wise poet and the incoherent outpourings of a dreamer."* Blake, on the other hand, thought Wordsworth the greatest poet of the age, but sometimes feared he might be an Atheist. For Blake, as Robinson correctly reports, "Atheism consists in worshipping the natural world, which same natural world, properly speaking, is nothing real, but a mere illusion produced by Satan." Robinson also preserved for us Blake's marginal annotations in a copy of Wordsworth's poems, and some of these may exhibit strikingly the difference which is our subject.

For Wordsworth at his best the mind's relation with Nature is mutual, a matter of the finest, most hypnotic transactions flowing between substance and sense, whereby the world becomes what Yeats calls "a superhuman mirror-resembling dream." But for Blake the point of art becomes increasingly as he goes on the rejection of nature altogether as a wicked enchantment. Of Wordsworth's famous "natural piety"—epithet as celebrated in its time as "artifice of eternity" in ours—Blake writes in the most unequivocal manner: "There is no such Thing as Natural Piety because the Natural Man is at Enmity with God." Similarly, if Wordsworth regards Natural Objects as strengthening the imagination, Blake's response has the sound of immediate violence: "Natural Objects always did and now do weaken, deaden and obliterate imagination in Me. Wordsworth must know that what he Writes Valuable is not to be found in Nature." And, later on, "Imagination is the Divine Vision. . . . Imagination has nothing to do with Memory." Wordsworth writes in *The Excursion* of how exquisitely the

* George McLean Harper, *William Wordsworth, His Life, Works, and Influence*, II (New York: C. Scribner's Sons, 1916), p. 342.

mind is fitted to the external world, and how exquisitely, too, the external world is fitted to the mind; Blake writes in the margin: "You shall not bring me down to believe such fitting and fitted. I know better and please your Lordship."

These too are hard sayings, and it should go with them that Blake said, about a proposed meeting with Wordsworth: "You do me honour. Mr. Wordsworth is a great man. Besides, he may convince me I am wrong about him; I have been wrong before now."

Blake's views of Nature and the Imagination are not easy for us to understand or give a full assent to. Yet it remains true at the very least, as Professor Harper writes, that "the convictions, however singular, of this rare spirit demand our entire respect, and are of value to us in proportion as they conflict with all our ways of thinking."

Jerusalem is a huge poem, in many details extremely obscure, and in any event scarcely compassable in only part of one essay. But it is also a very reckonable poem, whose incoherencies are largely peripheral (I sometimes think that some of its incidental impossibilities, such as huge compounds of geographical, historical, and mythical names, are there *because* similar things happen in the Bible). At its center the poem is coherent for all its strangeness, and our difficulties with it might well be resistances masquerading as criticism. Blake is really writing prophecy, that is to say, a very ancient thought lost sight of by his contemporaries yet about to become, in part by his instrumentality, a very modern thought; no wonder if the expression of it was full of difficulty.

Jerusalem is a vision of the Fall of Man—of the giant Albion, who is like the primal man of light, the Adam Qadmon, of The Cabbalah—and its consequence in his enslavement to Space, or Nature, and Time, or History. The piece ends with the redemption of Albion by the fiery work of Los (Sol?), the poet, poetry being seen as the type of man's proper work; but the plot moves rather by repetition and development than in linear sequence, and might be thought of as having the form of a theme, variations, and finale. It views the events as *always happening*; one of the substantive claims of the poem is that the process described in it is psychological and metaphysical in a primary way, and historical only secondarily:

> All things acted on Earth are seen in the bright Sculptures of
> Los's Halls, & every Age renews its powers from these Works
> With every pathetic story possible to happen from Hate or
> Wayward Love; & every sorrow & distress is carved here,
> Every affinity of Parents, Marriages & Friendships are here

> In all their various combinations wrought with wondrous Art,
> All that can happen to Man in his pilgrimage of seventy years.

The key to this poem, its metaphorical or mythical or religious premise, is that the spiritual is primary and substantive, the material world its phantasied derivative. The failure to see this *is* the Fall, dividing man against himself and creating the world of Nature, that is, of sexual generation and death. For because imagination is primary, the universe is in the first place human, its truth a human truth. Imagination, Blake says, is Jesus Christ, meaning at the very least that imaginative sympathy is the power of forgiveness of sin.

What initiates Albion's fall we are not told at once; in the very beginning of the poem he is already the "perturb'd Man" who turns away down "valleys dark," and the overwhelming of the imagination is signified by a Flood:

> In all the dark Atlantic vale down from the hills of Surrey
> A black water accumulates.

In successive episodes this fall is related variously with Pride, Fear, & Lust, and held responsible for creating the body, the world, extension in time and space. But its primary form is the separation of the abstract reasoning power from the rest of man's faculties, and its attempt to create and impose on the creation the tyranny of an abstract, rational, and ultimately punitive world whose God is both invisible and merciless. This is the world of human institutions, religious, political, educational, and scientific equally, an insane, meaningless mechanism devoted to suffering, repression, and death:

> I turn my eyes to the Schools & Universities of Europe
> And there behold the Loom of Locke, whose Woof rages dire,
> Wash'd by the Water-wheels of Newton: black the cloth
> In heavy wreathes folds over every Nation: cruel Works
> Of many Wheels I view, wheel without wheel, with cogs tyrannic
> Moving by compulsion each other. . . .

These wheels are the cold wheels also of the astronomical heavens, with their inhuman order, and they relate to Whitehead's vision of the "irreducible brute matter," which "just does what it does do, following a fixed routine imposed by external relations which do not spring from the nature of its being."

The Fall of Albion creates the vegetative world of generation, suffering, and human sacrifice:

> Hertfordshire glows with fierce Vegetation; in the Forests
> The Oak frowns terrible, the Beech & Ash & Elm enroot
> Among the Spiritual fires; loud the Corn-fields thunder along,
> The Soldier's fife, the Harlot's shriek, the Virgin's dismal groan,
> The Parent's fear, the Brother's jealousy, the Sister's curse. . . .

It is strange to consider that such a phrase as "the Corn-fields thunder along" will be regarded as wild, meaningless excess by people who view the statement that "an army marches on its stomach" as the plainest sense.

Now this fall consists for Blake in the false perception of this world as another, as other than human: this false perception is what at every moment creates an unreckonably large part, perhaps all, of the world of sin, pain, and death, at least all death inflicted by human beings on human beings. Since, in the refrain of the poem, you become what you behold, the consequence of man's viewing the world as other, as over against, is that he imitates in his history and institutions this phantasy of a something other, an external something mighty and imposing and ultimately immortal because inhuman: the State, and the State Religion, deemed by Reason to be the right true and deserved consequence of an alienated Nature to be appeased by Moral Virtue, punishment, human sacrifice, according to the "demonstrations" of a materialist science. Art itself, under the domination of this phantasy, becomes Memory, the mere copying from nature, and it is this that Blake means when he says that Imagination has nothing to do with Memory. Mathematic form, machines, warfare are all seen as consequences of man's pursuing an ideal other than his own being. This tyranny, under which we all live, is regarded as feminine, not because Blake is a misogynist—"the lust of the goat is the bounty of God . . . the nakedness of woman is the work of God"—but because Nature considered as thing-in-itself, rather than as an Emanation of the divine-human, is traditionally thought of as a woman (Mother Nature, Mother Earth), and the bondage to this Nature is a sexual, generative, and mortal bondage:

> If Perceptive Organs vary, Objects of Perception seem to vary:
> If the Perceptive Organs close, their Objects seem to close also.
> "Consider this, O Mortal Man, O worm of sixty winters," said Los,
> "Consider Sexual Organization & hide thee in the dust."

In *Jerusalem*, as elsewhere in Blake, this woman is called Vala, her name is sometimes associated with the word "veil" because in her separation from Albion she is Maya, the veil of illusion, and in this character she invites Albion to sexual knowledge:

> "Know me now Albion: look upon me. I alone am Beauty.
> "The Imaginative Human Form is but a breathing of Vala:
> "I breathe him forth into the Heaven from my secret Cave,
> "Born of the Woman, to obey the Woman, O Albion the mighty,
> "For the Divine appearance is Brotherhood, but I am Love
> "Elevate into the Region of Brotherhood with my red fires."

Albion's answer is sublime poetry; perhaps no poet has ever been more terrifying and majestic than Blake here in the simple statement of these relations, the devastating identification of sexuality, under the traditional image of the plow, with plowing the earth for food and plowing men under in war:

> "Art thou Vala?" replied Albion, "image of my repose!
> "O how I tremble! how my members pour down milky fear!
> "A dewy garment covers me all over, all manhood is gone!
> "At thy word & at thy look, death enrobes me about
> "From head to feet, a garment of death & eternal fear.
> "Is not that Sun thy husband & that Moon thy glimmering Veil?
> "Are not the Stars of heaven thy children? art thou not Babylon?
> "Art thou Nature, Mother of all? Is Jerusalem thy Daughter?
> "Why have thou elevate inward, O dweller of outward chambers,
> "From grot & cave beneath the Moon, dim region of death
> "Where I laid my Plow in the hot noon, where my hot team fed,
> "Where implements of War are forged, the Plow to go over the Nations
> "In pain girding me round like a rib of iron in heaven?"

Blake's poem is, as he says elsewhere, "Allegory addressed to the Intellectual powers, while it is altogether hidden from the Corporeal Understanding." Its language therefore is often strange to us, because in order to address the intellectual powers rather than the corporeal understanding it is convenient and perhaps necessary to speak of relations by giving strange and not traditional names to what things are to be related. It was in just this sense that Aristotle said human actions could not be depicted except by the use of human actors; and Blake's way of putting this, in the preface to *Jerusalem*, is to say: "We who dwell on Earth can do nothing of our-selves; everything is conducted by Spirits, no less than digestion or sleep."

That is a hard saying, too. And yet I think we have come to understand it quite well. In the seventeenth century, according to Molière's mockery, sleep was said to be produced by *virtus dormitiva*. Another two centuries, according to D'Arcy Wentworth Thompson, saw a great advance in knowl-edge, so that sleep was said to be produced by a substance of unknown properties called "dormitin." We may translate generally thus: in abstract discourse, in discourse having to do with invisible things, or relations, every substantive is a Spirit, and only by becoming a Spirit gains the po-tential of becoming allegory addressed to the intellectual powers. So when Blake proclaims the fourfold wholeness of the truly human, and names its divisions as Urizen, Lur vah, Tharmas, & Urthona, the sense of these names may be teasing to us (though not without the possibility of being inter-preted even so), but we are merely deluded if we think that the abstract names given to forces and influences in ordinary discourse are less myth-ological on account of their supposed familiarity, when in fact these nouns exist only to stopper up the abyss which opens at both ends of a sentence. Here for example is a contemporary account of something like what Blake is talking of when he describes the Fall: "Possessive mastery over nature and rigorously economical thinking are partial elements in the human being (the human body) which in modern civilization have become tyrant organizers of the whole of human life; abstraction from the reality of the whole body and substitution of the abstracted impulse for the whole re-ality are inherent in *Homo economicus*."*

In effect, one thing that Blake is saying is that when the intellect breaks up any wholeness into parts for "purposes of discussion" (to discuss = to break apart) the separate parts may become imbued with lives and pur-poses of their own, inimical to the wholeness from which they came. Naïve believers will always be found who will take these names as realities, or gods, and defend their mysterious purposes with fire and the sword. The contemporary I have quoted is telling a very similar story: "possessive mastery over nature" and "rigorously economical thinking" regarded as "tyrant organizers" come close to being, and are no less mythological than, Blake's "Urizen," his "priestcraft" and "Druids," his skygod whom he calls "Nobodaddy."

It will be fair, by way of summary, to translate rather freely. The Fall,

---

*Norman O. Brown, *Life Against Death* (Middletown, Conn.: Wesleyan University Press, 1960), p. 236.

for Blake, begins when man, identifying his humanity with his power of abstract reasoning, turns against his bodily or animal self, the way he had of being at home in the world, and creates abstract time and space out of his new feeling of being lost; having rejected himself, he experiences himself as an other, and this other both loves and hates him. Unable to accept himself, then, he cannot accept the other human beings for whom he himself is an other; he cannot believe in the community without giving it the phantasied form of a most powerful other coming over against him from outside, a father, a mother, an abstract god who in the name of forgiveness of sins exacts obedience in the form of religious, moral, and legal codes, human sacrifice in the form of slavery, punishment, and war.

The key word in Blake's account is "division." Two divisions are especially to be remarked. Man's reasoning power divides from the rest of him and holds in subjection the other qualities which might roughly be thought of as passion, sense, and spirit; and man divides from woman, rejecting the feminine in himself (as Freud said, every love affair takes place between four people). Hence sexuality is viewed as domination and submission. For the male, it becomes a military exploit to "invade" and "possess"—setting up in this way a dialectical relation wherein the female, precisely because viewed as an other, an enemy, is by definition eternally unpossessable, the image of a cruelly smiling Nature who beckons to destruction by love and war. It is thus that Nature herself divides: Vala in eternity, in time she becomes ambiguously Rahab and Tirzah, Tirzah being prudery and sexual hypocrisy, Rahab—the harlot who saved her life by betraying the city—whoredom and sexual license. The separation of the Spectre, or reasoning power, on one side, and the Emanation, or sexual love, on the other, leaves Los "the victim of their love & hate," and the Spectre, mocking, says of Man and Woman, "I will make their places of joy and love excrementitious."

Blake sees these and other, consequent divisions as responsible also for the mad dream called History, that record of the relation of suffering and knowledge which, speaking plainly, appears very often to have the purpose of propitiating the god of any given time, whatever his name, with human sacrifices. In the following passage Luvah, one of the four Zoas, or primary qualities of the human, may be thought of roughly as Passion, set free from the original balance and growing cancerously in freedom:

> Luvah tore forth from Albion's loins in fibrous veins, in rivers
> Of blood over Europe: a Vegetating Root, in grinding pain
> Animating the Dragon Temples, soon to become that Holy Fiend

> The Wicker Man of Scandinavia, in which, cruelly consumed,
> The Captives rear'd to heaven howl in flames among the stars.
> Loud the cries of War on the Rhine & Danube with Albion's Sons:
> Away from Beulah's hills & vales break forth the Souls of the Dead,
> With cymbal, trumpet, clarion & the scythed chariots of Britain.
>
> And the Veil of Vala is composed of the Spectres of the Dead.

Wordsworth too has a vision of that Wicker Man, a sort of cage in which victims were hung over the flames, and a comparison of the two passages is of interest.

In one of the greatest moments of *The Prelude*, the poet, on Salisbury Plain at night, sees "Our dim ancestral Past in vision clear." It is a vision of dark horror, warfare, death, and "barbaric majesty," and chief among its elements is

> the sacrificial altar, fed
> With living men—how deep the groans! the voice
> Of those that crowd the giant wicker thrills
> The monumental hillocks, and the pomp
> Is for both worlds, the living and the dead.

But this contemplation leads him on to consider the Druids and their astronomical knowledge, until he is charmed to see, "with believing eyes,"

> long-bearded teachers, with white wands
> Uplifted, pointing to the starry sky,
> Alternately, and plain below, while breath
> Of music swayed their motions, and the waste
> Rejoiced with them and me in their sweet sounds.

Here we may see one more extension of the theme, which says that the imagination of nature is an imagination of history also. Wordsworth sees human history as somehow reconciling despite its cruelty: the pomp, he says touchingly, is for both worlds, the living and the dead. In that marvelous line he sees something of the tragic relation between suffering and civilization, and the fearful fascination with death on which both are based; so that the poetry of human sacrifice is somehow at one with "geometric truth," though at a terrible price. In this, perhaps, he sees more deeply than Blake, who, abominating geometric truth as an example of the reasoning power abstracted from the human, intransigently holds to it that human history is evil and an offense against imagination and, finally, not necessary.

So the question of the two natures, that independent nature which is perceived and that other which is created by the imagination of man, may be seen as having to do with the question of how to handle the past; one's own and that of the race. For it may be said, and perhaps ought to be said, that poetry has always lived on wickedness, great cruelty, man's inhumanity to man, and, moreover, been richly at home in that realm; so that, morally speaking, poetry may be accused of cosmeticizing the cosmos, and bringing most reprehensible things under the dominion of beauty.

It seems to me that I am not in this to settle the rights of the matter, deciding for one poet and against the other; life is hard enough without that. But here are what might paradoxically be called some final balancings.

Wordsworth, who began by viewing nature and imagination as in fruitful tension, seems to have finished with reason: there was the world, the mind was somehow in it, and so, consequently, were the mind's institutions, state and church, the laws, modes, manners of the society of which he was a most distinguished ornament; it is true however that the imagination closed down on him.

Blake remained all his life a radical who held the imagination to be primary, and took literally its one instruction: forgiveness of sins. He held that intellectual fight could and ought to be substituted for warfare. To him, nature was a dream, history its aggravation into nightmare, and the institutions of human society could not be tolerated on the foolish, insubstantial ground that they appeared to exist. Regarded as at best a dreamer, at worst as mad, he persisted in his folly, and even some of the wise who thought him insane also thought him a saint.

But, alas, this clear division is also mythological, for we cannot say that either man was as he was because he wrote as he did. In any event, it is perhaps fortunate that the choice offered is offered in poetry, for it is an impossible choice, between a grimly reasonable despair and an exuberant, gay madness. But what is poetry if it is not the place where the impossible, and perhaps the impossible alone, is true?

It will be well to allow, here at the end, that what we have is a comparison, not a competition. *The Prelude* and *Jerusalem* are individual expressions, they are not methods or recipes. In one way *The Prelude* has had a great advantage: it seems to belong to the tradition of English poetry as *Jerusalem* does not, hence it appears technically more accomplished. But such an advantage can turn into its equivalent disadvantage almost

overnight, and a "tradition" of a hundred and fifty years' solid dominance
come to seem a mere parochial divagation from the true or real tradition.
So subject are we to the rule of fashion, our modern name for the goddess
Fortuna.

In a considerable degree, the rightness of a poem depends on our
familiarity with it. That statement initiates, or takes up, a circular argument,
for becoming familiar with a poem depends on interest, or love, which
presumes a certain rightness even to what we do not perfectly understand.
Yet within limits not clearly to be discerned the phrases of a poem gain a
magic by many repetitions in many minds; and by the same means lose
this magic betimes. So in the present age some few poems widely understood and agreed upon twenty years ago as sacred books now begin to
appear to some of us who are older though not wiser as, to say the least
of it, mistakes. We shed certain of our symbolic illusions not necessarily
to reach reality, but, far more often, to pick up other symbolic illusions.

The recent renewal of scholarly and critical interest in these great lost
books of Blake is probably not a mere momentary upset in a stable situation. More likely it is the symptom of a deep change in the mind of the
world. If so, it is probable that Blake's prophetic phantasies will progressively lose some of their strangeness, some of their obstinacy of phrasing,
and assimilate with the general character of thought, responding to intelligence, so it will seem, in the measure that intelligence has responded to
them. Our symbolic world will then reverberate to Blake's language more
than to Wordsworth's, and that language, or the language we derive from
it, will by ironic paradox come to seem "natural" to us. For language,
which Blake calls "the rough basement," is the symbolic intervention of
imaginative mercy between ourselves and a further Fall into a dark and
silent abyss; it was on this account, he says, that

> Los built the stubborn structure of the Language, acting against
> Albion's melancholy, who must else have been a Dumb despair.

Figures of Thought

THOUGHT is the strangest game of all. The players are the Nominalists vs. the Realists. Realists wear colorless jerseys and are numbered One, Many, & All. Nominalists wear crazy quilts instead of uniforms, and their numerals tend to be such things as the square root of minus one. This figure conceals two important circumstances: that there are not in truth Nominalists and Realists, but only the nominalism and realism of each player, who happens to be alone on the field where he plays himself; and that by the tacit pregame move of dividing into Nominalist and Realist he has made it impossible to win or even finish the game, although—and it is not a little—he has made it possible to play.

Thought proceeds to create the world by dividing it—what? the world, of course—into opposites, as in the initial Yin and Yang of the *Tao Te Ching*, the series of divisions in the first chapter of *Genesis*, the Love and Strife that Yeats took from Empedocles to be the base for the sequent complications of *A Vision*, and so on. Once there are the opposites, a mere two tricks make game. The first is that the opposites will have to bear on one and the other hand the whole weight of the much and many of the world as experienced: every leaf and every star must join one team or the other. The second is that, as a world of opposites is impossible, intolerable, the opposites must be mediated and shown to be one; because, of course, in the world as experienced they *are* one. That was where we began.

A productive model for the enterprise is map-making. Projecting a spherical world on a plane surface involves the cartographer in several distortions for every accuracy, beginning with the creative and mythological decree that there shall be two opposites named East and West; not quite truth, not quite fiction, this prevents any absolute or metaphysical arrivals, or even destinations; on the other hand, it makes—and nor is this a little—navigation possible.

The opposites at first embody themselves in stories. How stories got started is as unknown and like to remain so as how language did (they got together and talked it over among themselves?). With interpretation, whether exegesis or eisegesis, we are in a little better case: Edwin Honig tells us in his lovely book *Dark Conceit*, that the behavior of the gods in Homer and in Hesiod was so scandalous it couldn't possibly mean what it plainly said it meant and had to be allegorized; hence scholiast, who begat rhapsode (like Ion) who begat exegete who begat theologian who begat literary critic who so far has begat nothing but more literary critic; an entire and respectable industry raised upon the strange mythological ordinance that things, in addition to being themselves, hence uninformative enough, had to mean something . . . else.

A splendid instance of how all this works except when it doesn't is Lord Bacon's procedure in dealing with the Wisdom of the Ancients. Having first decreed that the figures of Greek myth *meant* something esoteric and wise and open only to initiates but dark to all the rest of the world, and having then decided, or decreed, that the Sphinx *meant*, of all things, Science, he goes about with equal enthusiasm and ingenuity to translate term for term out of story and into thought, and is able to tell you why Science should have talons, why Science should appropriately be thought of as carried to Thebes on the back of an ass, and so on and so on, not at all indefinitely.

A main consideration to emerge is this: there is a plenty of ways to be wrong in our interpretations, and no way at all to be sure of being right. It is in this respect that the story—the novel, play, poem—is, as Northrop Frye said, silent; and it is in this respect that the story resembles Nature. That is, I may identify a certain tree by as many characteristics as the handbook affords me, but it will never up and say 'You guessed it. I am indeed a box elder.' What we know is never the object, but only our knowledge. Though Milton might well have wanted to condemn Dr. Johnson and approve John Crowe Ransom for what they wrote about *Lycidas*, the poem itself will never do either. What we know is not it, but only our knowledge of it. That may be sad, but it does, as beforesaid, make navigation possible.

How then do we, even tentatively and provisionally, approve one interpretation above another? One possible answer, a humble one concealing, as so often happens, titanic pride: We just like one interpretation better than another, and as soon as we do that we find reasons plentiful as blackberries, just as Lord Bacon did in demonstrating that the Sphinx was, or meant, or represented, Science. We may, and often do, try to recommend ourselves, our interpretations, and the reasons for them to some not quite identifiable community of our fellows, involving ourselves in some risk of tautology, not to mention snobbery—this is the sort of thing you'll like if you're the sort that likes things of this sort, as I do—and an infinite regress, which will probably, however, be put a stop to by a change in Fashion, that last and most pervasive and secret of mythologies.

Harold Bloom's *The Anxiety of Influence* (New York: Oxford University Press, 1973) is offered as A Theory of Poetry. It is praised by no less sufficient an authority than Morris Dickstein, as "The most provocative and original piece of literary theory in English since Frye's *Anatomy of Criticism*." I can agree to provocative; I was provoked. And to original as well, but only in the sense of Dr. Johnson's saying that when the cow ran dry you could always milk the bull. But my trouble with the book may merely have been that it was too difficult for me, as I am afraid my brief description of its contents must inevitably show.

Bloom begins with the beguiling simplicity—but it is the last one we are to meet—of his premise: poets are influenced by the poets who have gone before them. His figurative way of describing the situation also looks simple at first: the problems of poets in dealing with the influence of past poets, or with the anxiety attendant upon it, are comparable with the problems people have in growing up, or dealing with the influence of the parents (though to Bloom the Father alone seems important), so that the model in both instances is what Freud called, "with grandly desperate wit," the family romance. Upon this base the author quickly erects a large rhapsodic apparatus of specialized terms and perhaps somewhat too many characters.

The ways in which the new poet (ephebe) copes with the old poet (precursor) are six in number, and their names are: Clinamen, Tessera, Kenosis, Daemonization, Askesis, and Apophrades. These Six Revisionary Ratios, as Bloom calls them, are summarized in an Introduction. One example will be fair to give, and as it must stand for all I rolled a die and came up with:

5. *Askesis*, or a movement of self-purgation which intends the attainment of a state of solitude; I take the term, general as it is, particularly from the practice of pre-Socratic shamans like Empedocles. The later poet does not, as in *Kenosis*, undergo a revisionary movement of emptying, but of curtailing; he yields up part of his own human and imaginative endowment, so as to separate himself from others, including the precursor, and he does this in his poem by so stationing it in regard to the parent-poem as to make that poem undergo an *askesis* too; the precursor's endowment is also truncated. (*The Anxiety of Influence*, Introduction)

Rating the above for difficulty, I should say it is harder than Clinamen, much easier than Apophrades, and about the same as the other three.

These titles head up the six main chapters, to which are added a Prologue, an Interchapter called A Manifesto for Antithetical Criticism, and an Epilogue. Prologue and Epilogue are about the Fullness, the Father, the Path, and sound enough like a statement of faith that I may excuse myself from dealing with them; the Manifesto, however, is criticism, and I cite a few provocative and original sayings from it:

Every poem is a misinterpretation of a parent poem.
There are no interpretations, but only misinterpretations, and so all criticism is prose poetry.
The best critics of our time remain Empson and Wilson Knight, for they have misinterpreted more antithetically than all others.
Criticism is the discourse of the deep tautology . . . the art of knowing the hidden roads that go from poem to poem.

Alas, I do not know whether these things are so or no. If I too admire Empson and Wilson Knight I have evidently been doing so for thirty years for the wrong reasons. Bloom is unflinching about accepting the consequences of his axioms: he really does believe that his book is a poem, "A theory of poetry that presents itself as a severe poem . . ." It doesn't *look* like a poem. And it doesn't *sound* like a poem. But if he says it's a poem? He ought to know, he wrote it, didn't he?

While he limits himself to assertion, Bloom is on privileged ground. But the two brief appearances of reasoned argument in what I have quoted— "and so" in the second sentence and "for" in the third—don't at all appear to me to connect, and I am tempted to think of Bloom that his form is logic but his essence is confusion. Nor is it at all easy to improve one's opinion as to whether these things are so or no by applying to the six main chapters, for Bloom's explanations routinely seem to make things worse, as in, e.g., a paragraph about "Binswangerian *Versteigenheit* (or 'Extravagance,' as Jacob Needleman wittily translates it)," about which my bewilderment is not resolved by being told that "Binswanger's summary is useful if we read it backwards." Maybe my problems with Bloom's thoughts are problems merely of style; but what's so mere about that?

One minor nuisance. Bloom improves his quotations from the masters by adding their intentions, tones of voice, and even probable facial expressions, as in "Freud, with grandly desperate wit," above, and "Kierkegaard ... announces, with magnificently but absurdly apocalyptic confidence...." And he can go further along this line, not only reading Binswanger backwards but telling us what Nietzsche might have thought had he lived to read Freud. But there are greater difficulties than that.

Bloom writes a literary and allusive shorthand which is, moreover, almost entirely associative; one thing reminds him of another and he can't stop, so that he is sometimes nothing but ellipsis, all beads and no string. On a single page he names, not merely in a catalogue but in what is proposed as a series of related relations, Goethe, Nietzsche, Mann, Emerson, Thoreau, Blake, Lawrence, Pascal, Rousseau, Hugo, Montaigne, Johnson, Aristotle, Homer, Arnold, Keats, Kierkegaard, several of them more than once. Not counting the repetitions, this amounts to one name every two lines, and is very hard to understand. No doubt that to the formidably learned author each use of each of these names stands for something he could identify far more precisely; but to the reader the game becomes merely bewildering in a short while. Finally I thought to recognize the source of this idiom as the graduate seminar; just to have done the required reading is not enough, you have to have done it in the last twenty minutes.

Bloom has too many hypostases, too many nonce characters, more terms than he has work for them to do. The principal ones are the Six Revisionary Ratios, which are held to be *the* ways in which poets may handle—or fail to—the anxiety of influence. After being summarily described, these terms are treated throughout as unquestionably distinct clinical entities, as real as if each one had been abstracted from hundreds or thousands of cases, when in fact the whole field of observation contains not many more than half a dozen major instances from Milton on, and maybe a dozen more fleetingly alluded to.

In addition to the six principal terms and the anxiety of influence itself there are ephebe and precursor (he doesn't always capitalize his characters), The Covering Cherub (by Blake out of Genesis and Ezekiel), The Idiot Questioner (Blake, in *Milton*), a bald gnome called Error and his two little cousins, Swerve and Completion (the feeling of having strayed into a comic book grows stronger here), and as many more as you can or care to identify by the mode of their generation and decay, of which the following gives an instance:

Chomsky remarks that when one speaks a language, one knows a great deal that was never learned. The effort of criticism is to teach a language, for what is never learned but comes as the gift of a language is a poetry already written—an insight I derive from Shelley's remark that every language is the relic of an abandoned cyclic poem. I mean that criticism teaches not a language of criticism (a formalist view still held in common by archetypalists, structuralists, and phenomenologists) but a language in which poetry is already written, the language of influence, of the dialectic that governs the relations between poets *as poets*. The poet *in every reader* does not experience the same disjunction from what he reads that the critic in every reader necessarily feels. What gives pleasure to the critic in a reader may give anxiety to the poet in him, an anxiety we have learned, as readers, to neglect, to our own loss and peril. This anxiety, this mode of melancholy, is the anxiety of influence, the dark and daemonic ground upon which we now enter. (p. 25; italics in original)

Chomsky's remark *is* an illuminating one; indeed, it is a key to his work. But what save rhapsodic association governs its relation with the ensuing sentences? Unless Bloom has some other source of Shelley's remark than the celebrated place in the *Defence*, the remark is really quite different: "Every original language near to its source is in itself the chaos of a cyclic poem." I don't know that the difference makes much difference to the argument, for I'm not at all certain what the argument is, though Bloom's misremembering suits his theme of melancholy declension, influence, and anxiety, better than Shelley's Romantic fervor about origin and source. Further, I am aware that there are these three ways of reading, as reader, as poet, as critic. But the hypostasis of them as three distinct persons together with the permutations mentioned—and those not mentioned but which the reader trying to negotiate the sentence to its end may already be fearfully anticipating—makes hash of what sense may be intended.

If you took the key sentence beginning with what he means ("I mean ...") and removed that parenthesis during which you spent three weeks in the stacks, you would still not be quite out of the woods:

I mean that criticism teaches not a language of criticism ... but a language in which poetry is already written, the language of influence ... (p. 25)

Reader, this statement is made by the same fellow who has just handed out his half-dozen Revisionist Ratios, Kenosis . . . Apophrades, holding them to be the nub of the matter, and now declares that criticism does not teach a language of criticism. My ho head halls. What criticism teaches, he says, is a language in which poetry is already written, e.g., finding the Emerson in Stevens, the Milton in practically everyone? No doubt this is a rich territory for scholarship; but criticism? When I dreamed long ago about an art critic who went to the museum to measure the distance between paintings I thought it was hyperbole, but now it turns out to be Bloom.

He does admit at least once to a doubt about the enterprise, ascribing it to his own Idiot Questioner: "What is the use of such a principle, whether the argument it informs be true or not?"

Is it useful to be told that poets are not common readers, and particularly are not critics, in the true sense of critics, common readers raised to the highest power? And what *is* Poetic Influence anyway? Can the study of it really be anything more than the wearisome industry of source-hunting, of allusion-counting . . . ? (p. 31)

And he develops the doubt for another ten lines citing Eliot, Emerson, Frye, and Arnold. But he overcomes it.

Such doubts as may occur to a reader, however, or as did occur to a poet, Wallace Stevens, get the usual short Freudian shrift. There are two devices which may be appropriate to the analytic session, as from doctor to patient, but which, when used in discourse between supposed equals, turn brutal and vulgar. One is to say that if the reader is not conscious of the problem then he must be *unconscious* of it. Bloom's example is Stevens. The other is to say that if the reader thinks an idea inapplicable, inaccurate, or plain not true, he has a *resistance* to it. Bloom's example is Stevens. And the final flip is to say that one's denial is an example of what one is denying; thus Bloom, after quoting Stevens (including "I am not conscious of having been influenced by anybody"):

This view, that poetic influence scarcely exists, except in furiously active pedants, is itself an illustration of one way in which poetic influence is a variety of melancholy or anxiety-principle. (p. 7)

As for the Six Revisionary Ratios themselves, I cannot tell the reader whether they are so or no, whether they exist or not. Kenneth Burke once quoted C. S. Peirce on the usefulness of "words so unattractive that loose thinkers are not tempted to use them," with this sequel:

It is vital for science that he who introduces a new conception should be held to have a *duty* imposed upon him to invent a sufficiently disagreeable series of words to express it.—*Attitudes Toward History* (New York: *The New Republic*, 1937), Vol. I, p. 10)

Peirce called this "the moral aspect of terminology," and surely Bloom has done his moral duty. But though the terms are sufficiently disagreeable, are they science? These ways of being influenced, or of showing it, exist only for so long as enough of us agree with Bloom that they do; built into the nature of things they are not. Even in science, alas, if the new conception you introduced happened to be phlogiston or dormitive virtue or the luminiferous ether, you would no doubt do well to distinguish a half-dozen varieties of each by wonderful names.

I've a good few more quarrels with Bloom, both style and substance. But sufficient unto the day. I guess the main one is that though I agree to influence as a fact, and agree that the project of Coriolanus ("as if a man were author of himself, and knew no other kin") is unlikely to work for any of us, I hold to the belief that you do at last grow up and stand there on your own, as what Philip Rieff called "the healthy hypochondriac who rightly expects to survive all interpretation" (*The Triumph of The Therapeutic* [New York, 1966], p. 40). When you begin, you write: "The grass is green," and everyone says "Aha! Wallace Stevens." Twenty years later you write: "The grass is green," and it sounds just like you. This is a mystery, with which relation durst never meddle. But Bloom, as far as I make him out, doesn't believe it. Even his "strong poets" (he's very high on poets being *strong*), the ones whose poems "most move me"—the only statement made independently of apparatus that I found in the whole book, a touching moment indeed—, even those poets, A. R. Ammons and John Ashbery, are much diminished in comparison of the former times:

> And as in lasting, so in length is man
> Contracted to an inch, who was a span. . . .
> (John Donne, *The First Anniversary*)

The world just is degenerate from Milton's day, that's all. The myth latent in Bloom's book is perhaps the oldest one of all, an inheritance already aeons old in the Hindu tradition when the anxiety of its influence affected Daniel and Hesiod, Ovid, Dante, Peacock . . . and Bloom. It is the Myth of the Four Ages, of which the first three range from paradisal to endurable but happen to be mythological, while the fourth miserable one is perfectly real and happens to be home to us. Bloom doesn't appear to notice this, but he states the sequence plainly enough. Shakespeare is out of it; he "belongs to the giant age before the flood" (and Marlowe his precursor just wasn't big enough to matter). So the four ages are: Milton, the Enlightenment, Romanticism, and "a further decline in its Modernist and post-Modernist heirs."

From Bloom's book I derive three melancholy lessons, or laws.

1. That the life of the institutionalized intelligence, as by its own sort of entropy, grows ever more difficult and never less so.
2. That intelligence itself, which is responsible for so much of the small freedom we have or can use, is intrinsically committed to determinism. That is one way of expressing the curse on knowledge.
3. That the effort to render English unintelligible is proceeding vigorously at the highest levels of learning.

It is the more reassuring, then, to have Denis Donoghue's *Thieves of Fire* (New York: Oxford University Press, 1973) as a moving demonstration that none of the three is necessarily true.

There are a few ways in which the two books are alike, and the comparison is illuminating as to the differences as well. Both are short, both are about interpretation, the principle of action in both is the application of a myth to several writers, Milton being the one they have in common and the one they begin with in principle as well as in time. Beyond this, though, they resemble one another mainly as opposites might be thought to do; in the terms of Pascal's famous antithesis Bloom is geometry and Donoghue is finesse.

Donoghue's myth is that of Prometheus, and because his book began as the T. S. Eliot Memorial Lectures for 1972 at the University of Kent the author must have faced a pretty problem in manners right at the start, for not only was Eliot himself the least Promethean of poets, he also had the most serious and grave reservations, however now and again qualified, about all Donoghue'sIum Prometheans: Milton, Blake, Melville, Lawrence. I am glad to say Donoghue's solution is as elegantly courteous as his problem may have been shrewd, as time after time Eliot is brought in to have his say from the shades, reminding the author and his readers that the Promethean is not the only kind of literature, and certainly not the only one worth having.

Thieves of Fire seems to me a beautiful example of thought at its work of creating by dividing; of the use of myth as an instrument or figure of thought: "The myth of Prometheus begins as a story, an anecdote of transgression, but because many generations have found it significant it has become a category, one of the available forms of feeling" (p. 18). In Donoghue's deep and sensitive reading, the story of the theft of fire, with the associated stories of cheating Zeus out of the sacrifice and of Epimetheus and Pandora, becomes the story of the Fall which is also the Rise: the fire is not only what broils the flesh and forges the sword, it is also thought, consciousness, conscience, guilt; our first benefactor being also the first great thief, and we ourselves uneasy with the gift because we are connivers and receivers of stolen goods. "Prometheus provided men with consciousness as the transformational grammar of experience" (p. 26).

From the story, too, comes the figure and character of Prometheus as an identifiable type of mind, or imagination:

There is no evidence that Zeus thought any the better of men for their new skills. The imagination has always been a contentious power, as a result, so far as men are concerned in their relations with the gods. A typology of the imagination would be an explication of the several ways in which men have risen above themselves by the possession of consciousness. The Promethean imagination is only the most extreme gesture in that account, and it is not alone in featuring arbitrary defiance in men, a show of force in the gods answered by a show of blasphemy in men. The predicament remains: imagination, the divine power in men, falsely acquired, stolen from the gods in the first of many similar outrages. Since then, the Promethean imagination has always been defiant: it starts with an incorrigible sense of its own power, and seeks in nature only the means of its fulfilment. (pp. 26–27)

Thought of this kind delights me by its clarity and serviceableness; and an integral part of the delight is Donoghue's modesty, tact, and sense of limits: simplification is a necessity of thought, but all simplification is oversimplification: "There is no thought which embraces all our thought," he says, quoting Merleau-Ponty and going on to his own equally engaging formula for the tragedy of mind: "One of the deficiencies of anything is that it is not also something else."

Out of this balanced good sense emerges not only the Promethean imagination with its titanic powers and devastations, its sense of destiny's being, as Rilke said, *always against*, but its antitype, the imagination receptive and obedient; "content with ready procedures and with the range of feeling which they allow . . . he hands his feeling over to the language, and is happy to abide by its determination." That is said in description of Herbert's "Decay" as over against Milton's sonnet "On the Late Massacre in Piedmont," and a similar balance obtains between Wordsworth and Blake.

Donoghue is especially convincing about the consistency of his related relations as to their characterizing presence in attitudes to language, nature, and God or the gods: his poets are compared as "prescriptive" or "descriptive," as modelers imposing their own thought upon the material and even upon its recalcitrance, or as carvers concerned to release from the material significance felt to be already present in it.

The feeling I got over and over from *Thieves of Fire* is that its author is making his cuts through reality just at the joints, and that is why it looks so easy. I am sadly conscious of having given much more time to saying why I don't like Harold Bloom's book than I am able to give to saying why I do like Denis Donoghue's book; a matter of the squeaky axle getting the grease. And I suppose it may be said that my likes and dislikes are, after all, arbitrary. But I would add one criterion for "liking" that may be thought to relieve it at least somewhat of its absolute subjectivity, willfulness, or capriciousness, though it too must, I suppose, depend ultimately on my feeling that it is so. That criterion is the production of insight, the power conferred on the author by his metaphor, or myth, of producing one after another observation about literary works and about the imagination that impress his reader as fresh, useful, true (remembering always that interpretation *is* misinterpretation, or, as Augustine put it, "What I am telling you is true in a way *because* it is false in a way.") I think Donoghue has had great and merited good luck in this respect; time after time I find him making remarks, whether he is interpreting the story of Prometheus itself or using it to illuminate certain traits in his authors and their books, that arouse my warmest admiration—together with, of course, that bare edge of envy that along guarantees my feeling that he is getting things right: "Yes, of course, why couldn't I have thought of that myself?" Donoghue's interpretations, in detail as in the large, bring conviction because they illuminate. I can't bring the two sides of criticism's tautological equation any closer together than that, and had best stop right there.

Poetry and Meaning

WHAT I have to say to you is very simple; so simple that I find it hard to say. It is that poetry is getting something right in language, that this idea of rightness in language is in the first place a feeling, which does not in the least prevent it from existing; if it is subjective, which I doubt, it is not "merely subjective" (as students say, and o dear how often they say it); that this feeling of rightness has largely been lost, if not eagerly assaulted with destructive intent, by people who if they ever wake up are going to find it extremely hard to recapture or even to remember what that feeling was.

One possible, and to me likely, consequence of these simplicities will have to be contemplated; it is that poetry in English is coming to an end. I have hesitated fearfully for a long time before that statement, realizing that coming from a middle-aged poet it will helplessly be heard as one more variant of the common cry of middle-aged poets, "I had talent once, where did it go?" And yet it seems as though the evidence is massive that not poetry alone but a great deal to do with language in relation to mind is fast approaching an end where it will be transformed into something unrecognizably other. To some of this evidence I shall return later on; meanwhile I can at least show that the thought of such an end or such a transformation is not one I hold all by myself.

To show that the question has been seriously entertained I may cite the instance of H. G. Wells and his last work, a little pamphlet called *Mind at the End of Its Tether* (London, Toronto: W. Heinemann, Ltd., 1945). It was written just after the Second World War and in the last year of the author's life, and in it this great progressive, humanitarian, scientifically-minded, and positivist intelligence—who had predicted in one work after another so much that has come literally true—turned right round to the opposite and declared that intelligence and world, which had for the length of history run on parallel courses, were now separating, like two ships whose paths diverge in the night, or like two celestial bodies that approach one another only to fall away into illimitable dark. Admitted that Wells was old, tired, mortally ill, we have still to inquire whether he was saying something true, or at least probable enough to be given the steadiest consideration, or whether he was merely expressing one more symptom of his malady.

A. M. Turing once said that the question "Can machines think?" was too meaningless to deserve discussion, and suggested that the proper short answer was "Can people?" But he added this: "Nevertheless, I believe that at the end of the century the use of words and general opinion will have altered so much that one will be able to speak of machines thinking without expecting to be contradicted." You will observe that to this scientist the point is not that superior machines will be invented, though they almost undoubtedly will be; it is that we will have changed our ways of using words, so that thinking will no longer mean what it did. Indeed, this change may in large measure already have taken place. Hannah Arendt says of this, "If we compare the modern world with that of the past, the loss of human experience ... is extraordinarily striking. It is not only and not even primarily contemplation which has become an entirely meaningless experience. Thought itself, when it became 'reckoning with consequences,' became a function of the brain, with the result that electronic instruments are found to fulfill these functions much better than we ever could."

And Owen Barfield, possibly the clearest and most searching thinker of the present time, says—though he calls it a provocative heterodoxy— "I have been coming to feel for some time that imagination, *as an end in itself*, is a vein that has been, or very soon will be, worked out. I am in doubt whether much more that is really significant can be done with it" (*The Rediscovery of Meaning*, Middletown, Connecticut: Wesleyan University Press, 1977, p. 125).

There is at least a funnier way of viewing the matter. Otto Rank says somewhere that it took long ages for soul, or spirit, or what we call mind, to work its way up into the head. In some cultures this vital principle inhabited the soles of the feet—the Buddha's footprint is holy—and in others the genitals, the stomach, bowels, heart, liver, and solar plexus were its abode. But among us for a couple of centuries or more thought is commonly believed to be something done in the head, and its sacred function is protected from contamination by the lower parts of the body by collar and tie; compare the expression "white-collar worker" for someone whose business is mental.

Considering this progression we might reasonably ask by way of extrapolation where this principle of life has left to go. And the student of such matters might look long and hard at the sudden efflorescence of hair styles, including beards and wigs, among the young in late years. It suggests sadly enough people's coming to the dismayed realization that the only thing about yourself you have the power to change, until you go bald, is hair; and it irresistibly reminds me of that species of scientific thought, becoming every day more common, which observes that hair grows out of the head and goes on to infer that the head is full of hair. We are already assured by science that the head does not contain thoughts or words, but only neurons—to which I suppose the teacherly response would be, "Which of you neurons said that?"

Turning from this topic for the present, I remark that the spectacle, now some centuries long, of western man patiently endeavoring to reason himself out of thought and read himself out of the universe, would be as fit a subject for a comic poet as for a tragic one, were its consequences not so brutal and so lamentable.

I return now to my first assertion: poetry is a way of getting something right in language, poetry is language doing itself right. This idea came first, as ideas have a way of doing, as a thoughtless phrase. I am a most inefficient teacher of verse-writing—but imagine what a monster an efficient one would be!—and term after term, no matter what resolutions of patience and goodwill I began with, three weeks later I found myself saying to the students about their productions such things as: But it's not right, it just simply isn't right ... and even more cruelly on occasion: if there's nothing right what's the use of trying to say what's wrong with it? And sometimes I would rhapsodize to my poor class about how poetry was simply language doing itself right, language as it ought to be, language as it was in the few hours between Adam's naming the creation and his fall. The whole art of poetry, I would say, consists in getting back that paradisal condition of the understanding, the condition that says simply "yes" and "I see" and "it is so." Naturally enough, it doesn't happen often. But it does happen.

My students, accustomed to classes in which their instructors explained themselves, explained literature, and in fact left nothing unexplained that could possibly be explained, and now confronting a teacher who apparently couldn't or wouldn't explain one blessed thing, and especially not the one blessed thing they were there to have explained to them, were understandably puzzled. All the same, they behaved very kindly about it. At most, the ones inclined to philosophize would point out to me that my criterion of rightness could never be defined and in any event was merely subjective.

Meaning I could never *prove* anything was right.

I do have a reply to that objection, though unfortunately it is a rather unwieldy one because it has to include some consideration of our intellectual habits with respect to subjects and objects, or, as Coleridge used to say when drinking, sumjects and omjects.

It was Coleridge, I am told, who introduced the words subjective and objective into our language. Ruskin, who was very funny on the theme, hated the words and said they were foisted on us by a combination of German dullness and English affectation. However that may be, I call it to your attention as significant that whole populations which had formerly been able to express their thoughts without resort to the words subjective and objective—whole populations, by the way, including Chaucer and Shakespeare and Milton—now, less than two centuries after their entrance into the language, can scarcely get through a classroom hour without leaning heavily on them. Students, in particular, appear to experience from their use some kind of magical resolution of any difficulty of thought.

I am not trying to take away these terms, which seem to stand to our intellectual astronauts as spacecraft and space respectively. But I would point out first that though Coleridge introduced the words into philosophizing in English he was far indeed from denigrating thought, feeling, or belief by calling them "merely" subjective. In fact I came by chance on a place where he does just the opposite and refers to the natural world as "all that is merely objective."

The great dictionary is pretty funny, as well as illuminating, on *subjective* as a philosophic word, now obsolete, "Pertaining to the real or essential being of that which supports qualities, attributes, or relations; substantial; real," for it adds, after what might be a thoughtful pause, "objective in the modern sense." Funny, as the sight of great learning trapped in its words may often be, and illuminating about the great change in the mind of the world from a time when true subjectivity could strictly be attributed only to God, to the present, when saying that something or someone is being subjective means a considerable variety of things, all pejorative, e.g., you think it's so but it's not; maybe, but it's not important; you're being emotional when you ought to be reasonable.

It is by some such process as is represented in the changed meaning of such a word as *subjective* that the mind has reached its present most familiar predicament, ludicrous and pathetic by turns, whereby a learned discipline begins its course of studies by excluding as far as possible all feeling, including especially the feeling of interest, curiosity, pleasure, delight that prompted the study itself, and winds up several years and thousands of pages later plaintively asking itself about human values and wondering where they are to be found. The entire development is of the greatest historical interest, but in the result, it is rather like the man found by a policeman searching under a streetlight for his lost watch. Did you lose it here? asks the policeman, one would have thought unnecessarily. No, I lost it over there, but I'm looking here because the light's better.

This distinction of the whole world into subjective and objective probably began with Galileo's, and then Locke's, division of the qualities into primary and secondary. The dictionary gives the former as bulk, figure, number, situation, and motion or rest, "which are in the object as in our perception of it," while the secondary qualities, tastes, sounds, colors, and so on, "are modes of our perception induced by some character in the object which does not coincide with the perception itself." One notices immediately that the primary qualities have the air already of being what are called "hard facts," while the secondary ones are already a touch sentimental and unmanly. And the scientific way of developing this distinction had the effect of progressively reducing even the primary qualities to quantity, or number, alone, so that only what is enumerable is effectively regarded as real. With this fateful distinction, which indeed did not rest as a distinction but became a division, much else separated that had formerly been one and the object of a single attention; poetry, for example, in the eyes of most of the world, became "only poetry." I shan't pause to drop a tear for "only poetry," but would suggest that poetry, and literature generally, may be the last remaining place where that about subjective and objective does not apply; and that an appropriate emblem for this characteristic of literature is the situation you have in *Hamlet*, where the Ghost is neither subjective, for the soldiers can see it just as well as Hamlet, nor objective, for when it next appears Hamlet alone can see it, while his mother can see "Nothing at all; yet all that is I see." I've a sense that we all incline by training and study to be like Gertrude about our ghosts. Wallace

Stevens poignantly varies Gertrude's line, speaking of "a mind of winter" and of

> the listener, who listens in the snow,
> And, nothing himself, beholds
> Nothing that is not there and the nothing that is.
> ("The Snow Man," *Collected Poems*
> [New York: Knopf, 1955])

Now there is one great trouble with the intellectual and learned school of approach to the art of poetry; it is a trouble that secretly afflicts, I am convinced, a great part of our thoughts about a good many things, and it is this: we are much too concerned to turn our experience into a result, something tangible, and in the course of doing this we forget what the experience felt like in the first place, and, still more important, how through all our studies we remain related to time in two ways, biographical and historical. This is a simple enough thought, and that may be why it is almost always forgotten, though sometimes I've the feeling of its being deliberately excluded. But it bears importantly on this business of poetry as getting things right in language. For the lover of poetry would never have become a lover of poetry, much less a student of poetry, had he not at first had this feeling of rightness and certainty about some piece of language. That came before all question of study, of English courses, of why it was so; enough that it simply was so. James Dickey writes in an essay that he remembers what first attracted him to poetry; it was the rightness of the expression "to sweat it out," in relation to the soldier's experience of war.

That brings me to another point about the experience of the rightness of language, and to another thing that is dreadfully wrong about the idea of poetry as a subject to be studied in schools.

It is most important to any inquiry into this idea of rightness in poetry that we be as candid as possible about our actual relation, of feeling and thought, to the phenomena; and with respect to this problem I begin by observing that neither teaching nor criticism is very often quite candid about this relation. For there is always present a temptation, which we almost always yield to, to make our experience of poetry both more intellectual and more pretentious than it is or ought to be. There is a somewhat comic, somewhat vulgar and mercantile, aspect to our serious and no doubt well-meaning endeavors to convince others and even possibly ourselves that the experience we are getting from poetry is certifiably profound, lofty, sublime, organic, harmonious . . . even pleasurable. You may supply other adjectives, from whatever schools of criticism, as you care to.

Without denying that our experience of poetry is sometimes one or more of those things, I think it proper to acknowledge that it is not always like that, and may not often be like that. A primary pleasure in poetry is surely something low enough to be beneath the notice of teacher or critic— the pleasure of saying something over for its own sweet sake and because it sounds just right. For myself, certainly, and for you if you will remember how it truly was, the thing said over will not necessarily be A Great Thought, though great thoughts are not necessarily excluded either; it may be as near as not to meaningless, especially if one says it without much attention to its context. For instance, a riddling song has the refrain: Sing ninety-nine and ninety. I can remember being charmed enough with that to say it over and over to myself for days, without ever having a single thought about its meaning except for a certain bemused wonder about how different it was from singing a hundred and eighty-nine.

Or else it may be something proverbially helpful, that you say to yourself when things are going wrong: "Time and the hour runs through the roughest day." Perhaps this would not have meant so much to me without the little grammatical oddity of "runs" instead of "run." And here are a couple of lines from the *Comedy* that delight me as much now as they did when I first came across them so many years ago:

> *Cosi di ponte in ponte, altro parlando*
> *Che la mia commedia cantar non cura*
> (*Inferno*, XXI, 1–2)

No deep insight here, nor lofty wisdom; he is talking in effect about what he is not going to talk about, though it is wonderfully appealing to be told that Dante and Virgil said things to one another in Hell that we are never going to know, that is not the whole charm of the lines:

> So from bridge to bridge, talking of other things
> That my comedy cares not to sing.
> (my translation)

It loses much of its delightsomeness in English; loses that lovely, off-handed strolling lilt that makes the Italian, especially of the second line, so wonderful to say. There's a clue in that, maybe, in that *ambulando* rhythm that imitates the two poets walking along; for Paul Valéry gave perhaps the shortest definition of poetry recorded: it is what it says.

One more example. I sang to my children a nursery rhyme I must have missed in childhood:

> Fiddle dee dee, fiddle dee dee,
> The fly has married the bumble bee.
>
> Said the fly said he, will you marry me
> And live with me sweet bumble bee?
> Said the bumble bee, I'll laugh and sing
> And you'll never know I carry a sting.
>
> Fiddle dee dee, fiddle dee dee,
> The fly has married the bumble bee.

I don't know in the least what there is about this that made me so happy I went about the house chanting it for days on end, in all sorts of situations . . . until I observed that when I did my wife was beginning to look sideways at me, as though this little verse was turning into A Dark Thought About Marriage.

Which suggests a further step. It is part of the power of a poem to generate meanings from what may originally be meaningless. Perhaps what I am thinking of as rightness in language is this abstract power, or power gained from being very abstract (as Stevens said a supreme fiction had to be)—the power to handle a great many situations at once, the power of poetry to be somewhat more like a mind than a thought. These apparently trivial examples of things that one repeats to oneself rather as though they were talismans, are they not after all the stuff and substance itself of poetry, and more visibly so for not being so cluttered with meanings that we can't see the things themselves? After all, delight itself may mean nothing. Love may mean nothing. The world appears to have every prospect of never meaning anything again. But love and delight and, so far, the world remain.

In an earlier essay I made a detailed comparison between the mechanisms visible in certain sorts of poetry and the mechanisms of jokes. I found the comparison illuminating even if it would not hold equally for all kinds of poetry (I never claimed it would). But in connection with the question of rightness in language as over against the claim that such rightness is "merely subjective" it is appropriate to draw on that earlier essay for a moment, in order to say as follows.

1. When you understand a joke, you laugh. In fact, your laughter quite simply *is* your understanding, which doesn't express itself in a separate verbal form.

2. When you fail to understand a joke, in a company where every one else seems to understand it and laughs, you either say "I don't get it," or you give one of those fake and feeble laughs which you know everyone else will see through at once. What do you not do?

3. I submit that what you never do in this situation is say that the joke is subjective or merely subjective.

4. If someone explains or interprets the joke to you, your difficulty will perhaps be cleared up, but too late; you won't laugh as hard as you would have, had you understood immediately, that is, without the mediation of more words.

5. Therefore a joke is a way of getting something right in language.

6. A poem too is a way of getting something right in language, save that the proper response will be not laughter but silence, or the acknowledgment that it is so, it is as it is; that the miracle has happened once again: "something understood," as Herbert says finally and ever so quietly about prayer.

7. It is in this sense that poems ought to be approached as sacred objects. One expects not so much to learn them as to learn from them. They give a certain definition to experience, and it may be that it is to experience we should refer them, rather than to exegesis. By contrast, definitions given in dictionaries break up experiences into units in order to make them—the units, unhappily, not the experiences—easier to understand; but dictionary definitions will at last be found to be circular, hence not definitive, while a poem is "the burning bow that once could shoot an arrow out of the up and down" (Yeats).

You will no doubt have been thinking for some time that this is all very well, but when are we to have an example? other than, of course, those agreeable trivialities he quoted a few minutes back. But I have deliberately withheld examples because I want the idea of rightness to be as open, contentless, empty if you like, as may be. For I am not at all certain it is so important for each of us to have the same ideas about the same things, even if it is that particular species of what Lovejoy called "metaphysical pathos" that more than anything else informs and sustains the university and the culture. What is important to each of us is to have the idea of rightness, to grasp it feelingly. If we do not have it, perhaps poetry is not for us; music goes on though many are tone-deaf and few have absolute pitch; absolute pitch has never been accused of being subjective on that account. If you are in the presence of a greater vision than your own—Shakespeare's for instance—and do not see what he is talking about, you don't say he sees nothing, for that would be like telling a microscope that it exaggerated.

In keeping with a somewhat oriental style of going at a subject, a style that abstains from saying what the subject is directly, but hopes to produce an immediate vision of it by indirect means and dark hints—this negative approach is usually translated as "no-knowledge," and commentators warn us not to confuse it with "no knowledge"—I shall present, instead of examples of rightness in poetry, a couple of examples in which, as far as I am able to see, nothing went right at all.

The first is by a student, who has generously allowed me to make use of his effort. In fact it was this student who kindly put me straight by telling me that my idea of rightness was purely subjective.

OPUS 125

The hall of deafness still had heaped
a confusion of memories,
a pile awaiting craftsman's wit;
but he wished he could hear his sobs
when pain forced and hacked into tears,
or, the huge laugh like a giant's
that knew that after all it was
hard work setting sounds in order. . . .

I forbear to quote the remainder. I don't want to make fun of it either. It's sad. You can see it's about Beethoven writing the Ninth Symphony, and you can feel that it is very sincere, but it's awful. I said to the student, who by the way is a very intelligent one, "Here you are, you've read and probably understood half the literature of the past four hundred years—but you've never heard anything." Maybe the motto of the English Department could be this line varied from Eliot:

We missed the experience, but we had the meaning.

My second example of getting it wrong is professional work, so far as poets may be said to be professionals. Anyhow, it appeared in *Poetry Magazine*, a title in which, I have often thought, the word *poetry* has exactly the force that the word *beauty* does in the title "beauty shoppe." Beyond

that, not wishing to be invidious, I shall not identify the author; the following is how he begins a piece of some sixty lines:

> A small voice is fretting my house in the night
> A small heart is there . . . Listen,
> I who have dwelt at the root of a scream forever,
> I who have read my heart like a man with no hands
> reading a book whose pages turn in the wind,
> I say listen, listen, hear me
> in our dreamless dark, my dear.

If I read that in a sufficiently sonorous and reverential tone, some of
you will doubtless have thought it beautiful, but you are wrong. (It is best,
I think, for me to say such things plainly and without qualification.) That
is one of the unmentioned and possibly unmentionable dangers to poetry
recitations, that any old garbage will go down all right if it's read with
conviction.

About that passage I shall comment briefly. For if silence is the appropriate response to rightness, it may be that the real use of talk is about
wrongness.

To read the book of the heart is an ancient, conventional expression,
hence not good enough for our poet, who wishes to be simultaneously
intense, complex, rhapsodic, and desperate, not to mention modern. Still,
he is unable to resist this honorable old figure, the heart as a book to be
read. So he fancies it up a bit. The speaker is reading the book of the
heart? well, chop off his hands at the wrists to show that this is no easy
matter; now, to clinch the point home, spring up a wind and start the
pages of the book flapping; compared to the speaker's problems here, it
would be a cinch for him to dwell at the root of a scream forever. This
poetry is intense, indeed, with the grim intensity of someone trying to
masturbate too soon after having masturbated.

Maybe from examples such as these we can see the beauty even of
wrongness, that from it we infer that a right way of doing things does exist,
even that many right ways of doing things must exist, even as from the
idea of getting lost we infer the existence of roads and destinations.

I began by saying that I thought this idea of rightness had largely been
lost, or destroyed, and that on that account we might have to contemplate
the end of poetry as we have known it. And I promised to return to that
thought and the evidence for it, knowing that everyone likes a bit of an
apocalypse to finish on.

It is a sound maxim for a prophet to hold before him, that when he is about to peer into the future and say that something awful is going to happen, he might well turn around and ask himself if it hasn't happened already. Blake said of this, that prophecy meant simply, If you go on doing thus, the result will be thus. And I add that my favorite prophet is Jonah both for being short-winded and for being wrong about the destruction of Nineveh, that great city wherein, says the Lord in one of his infrequent jokes, are more than sixscore thousand persons that cannot discern between their right hand and their left hand; and also much cattle. Which a poet once brought up to date as follows:

> The Lord might have spared us the harsh joke;
> Many that live in Nineveh these days
> Cannot discern their ass from a hot rock.
> Maybe the word 'cattle' refers to these.

I hope that I, like Jonah, am wrong; though if I should be I too might be displeased exceedingly.

There is a sense, utterly true but not very helpful, in which everything is always ending and always beginning. The fabric of the generations simply is woven that way, seamlessly, and only the work of the historical intellect divides it up. Imagine someone living through the fall of the Roman Empire in a provincial town, in Marseille say, or London; he would live his life day by day, as we all do, and never know that he had lived through the fall of the Roman Empire. He would notice, perhaps, certain signs of neglect; the garrison might go slovenly and unshaven, the roads might not be so well kept up, proclamations would be fewer than they used to be . . . and when people began to notice the absence of something called The Roman Empire they nostalgically replaced it with a Holy Roman Empire and pretended it was the same thing, sort of. So it may be with my subject. I will present my evidences as best I can.

For one thing, the posture of the literary mind seems these days to be dry, angry, smart, jeering, cynical; as though once people had discovered the sneaky joys of irreverence they were quite unable to stop. This is one typical process of Shakespeare's tragedies, where the intelligent and crafty young destroy the stupid old and, with them, the sacred something that these complacent dodos by some accident had in their charge, and the intelligent and crafty young at last, as Ulysses says, eat up themselves.

This symptom in itself is perhaps not much. Literary quarrels have usually been acrimonious, indeed are less personally spiteful now than in the Age of Pope. The world has always been as full of people plugging their friends as of people unplugging their enemies. Yet the public discussion, the criticism, that attends on poetry, has appeared to me as coming close to the point at which a smart shallowness and verbal facility will jettison meaning altogether; the same thing has been happening in poetry itself. I shall not now give examples, but I ask you to consider whether it is not as I have said. Not only the terms of abuse, but more importantly the terms of praise, appear in a language whose vagueness of sense is closely related to the extravagance of its claims.

This kind of shrillness may be the sign of considerable unacknowledged anguish of spirit. As though everyone felt some big thing was breaking up, and made bigger and louder noises to pretend that all is as it was. For it ought now to be possible to turn and look back over the modern period, as it foolishly goes on being called, and see how some one thing—I should date it perhaps from the middle of the last century, from Baudelaire and Swinburne, say—was gathering momentum in a direction and was assembling armies of adherents, but that not so long ago this momentum, giant as it was, divided itself among the members of the armies, diminished, and may now be flickering out in brief contingencies.

I don't know just what name would be right for this momentum. It had to do with a slow collapse in the idea of meaning which progressed simultaneously with an imposing acceleration of the rate at which knowledge was accumulated. Everyone who thinks much about poetry will have observed how in the early years of this century it abruptly became much harder to understand. Not all of it, by any means, but I need mention only Eliot, Pound, Hart Crane, as instances. By heroical efforts of criticism and exegesis Eliot's poems, which seem to have impressed many of their first readers as being written in Linear B, were made part of the common language, so that even ball games now may end not with a bang but a whimper. The same process has not happened to the *Cantos* of Ezra Pound, and I incline to doubt it will happen.

What I am calling the slow collapse in the idea of meaning, which made poetry so very hard to understand and consequently conferred on English Departments a large part of both their real and spurious importance, evidently did not happen in poetry alone. It happened even more conspicuously and at about the same time in physics, in painting, in music; the whole world suddenly became frightfully hard to understand. And there is a corollary to this that I find most interesting: the mind responded magnificently to the challenge of all this difficulty in ever so many ways . . . and from asking concerning the meaning of this poem or that went on to ask concerning meaning itself. Again, I need mention only a few names: Kenneth Burke, William Empson, I. A. Richards, all seem to have begun by inquiring about the meaning of poems and then to have felt themselves irresistibly drawn to the question beyond: what is meaning, and how does it happen to arise? And the new science of linguistics here enters the picture. Men are now beginning to understand, doubtless as yet in a fumbling and vague sort of way compared to what may be coming, what sort of entity a language is and what relations, of possibility and of limitation, it has to thought. Realizing that language is an abstract and utterly arbitrary but totally articulated system of relations, men now begin to see that they may invent other languages for other purposes—indeed, they do so already.

Anthropology too, with its close relations, folklore and comparative religion and mythology, gets into the act, and for the first time men begin to have a clear and coherent understanding of how literature arose, and what it is, and even a little what it does.

Now these are very real and reckonable advances. I am not antiscience, though I do think that our ways of thinking about what science does and is doing are inadequate and even stupid, and I am not against the accumulation and coordination of knowledge. But I think it is clear that to understand a given matter will have its effect on doing. Students of what is called nowadays The Creative Process do not observably turn into artists. And when the depths of things are exposed to the dry light of reasoned explanation, they may well dry up. For it is paradoxical, and therefore in a round world true, that a great deal of knowledge may come to resemble a great insanity. That may be why I am forced to contend that a vast increase in knowledge was simultaneous with a slow collapse in the idea of meaning.

It is commonplace to observe that we today are the beneficiaries and victims of more language than any people has ever been subjected to in the history of the world. Even going for a walk or drive in the country, we see that the landscape more and more carries written messages—signs. Two strange and related consequences come from this circumstance.

For one, the public language of press and the other media imposes upon us a public dream, a phantasy written in a language that is neither right nor wrong but, say, serviceable. Not so much that it tells us what to think, though it tries to do that as well, but it makes of no avail our freedom of thought by telling us what we must have these thoughts about, and by progressively and insensibly filling us with a low, dull language for thinking them.

The second consequence seems to be that the languages of art and of learning grow ever more recondite, as if they were the distorted mirror images of the public language, which they relate to, more or less as a dream relates to a newspaper.

Yet here too the opposites coincide, for the public dream that is the daily dream of all appears as no less insane, and no less under the threat of an ultimate meaninglessness, than the private dream that is the nightly dream of each alone. And if the languages of the arts and sciences grow progressively harder to understand, the matching phenomenon on the other side is that in the public language it is getting progressively harder to say anything that refers to reality.

I think I can now give a name to the period that is over. I shall assert that it lasted from the middle of the last century to the middle of this one, and I shall call it The Age of Art, or The Aesthetic Age. Its dominant characteristic was the claim that salvation was by art alone. What that salvation would be, or would be like, was specified in ever so many different ways by different artists, but it scarcely ever failed to be asserted that the way and the truth and the life was by art.

Matthew Arnold has often been rebuked for suggesting that art would be the religion of the future, but if you take his statement not as a slogan to wave but as a statement of what was going to happen, it would seem that he was historically accurate, or prophetic.

And if you ask why I hazard a guess that the great period of art may now be over, I can but suggest that, while holding that idea firmly in mind, you look around you. And I would remind you that even if I am somewhat right about what is happening, it may not be altogether a disaster. The world is a very deep place, no matter how much of it we explain, and explain away, and the end of a particular form of experience does not mean the end of experience. Forms are there to be transformed, and of all this something kind and good may come one day. Or so I hope.

The Dream of Dante

THE dream nowhere says it's about Dante, it doesn't even mention his name, nevertheless I woke up knowing it was. It came at a time when I was desperate over an essay about the *Comedy* that wasn't going at all well, and I was saying such things to myself as "If we go on like this right to the deadline we'll have a hundred and fifty single-spaced pages and no essay on Dante." It is true, however, that I go through these agonies with any and every piece of writing that cannot be completed in a day; so maybe this dream, which I apply to the piece on the *Comedy*, means to be paradigmatic about my troubles in this line generally.

We are having, it seems, an emergency, but one which ought to be handled with great ease, for we have a stretcher and ambulance (the scene is a garage), and the hospital itself is visible just across the street. (Who is the patient? That remains undisclosed.)

Instead of the obvious and easy solution, however, I find myself upstairs with two or three other people confronting a big, shabby truck, which, moreover, carries atop its cab a sort of thick rug or mattress about the size of a tennis court. We get this latter object down and folded, then it seems we have to strip the truck into parts small enough to carry downstairs so that we can assemble it again elsewhere. And this we do, under the supervision of a bald, squat German who is understood to be a professional mover. We have to pass through a second floor which is evidently the warehouse of a museum or antique shop, crowded with junk from the ages, chiefly furniture, pedestals for statues, and so on.

Outside at last, we are on a football field. More people keep arriving to help put the truck together, and when at last this is done everybody gets in and I am obscurely aware that now there will be no room for whoever the patient was, but this doesn't bother me much at all. What does bother me, though, and bothers everyone else, is that the radiator cap won't stay on. I fiddle with it and discover it is so dilapidated it has no thread on the screw. But I hold it precariously in place with my finger.

Dearly beloved, the patient who never appears and eventually gets forgotten altogether is Dante Alighieri, and I very much fear that the name of the German professional mover is Scholarship, while the truck, of course, is Scholarly Apparatus, a theme reiterated in the warehouse of museum or antique shop. The dream as a whole reflects my nervousness about tackling the great work head on—is that why a football field appears?—as well as, perhaps, a certain sense that the world does not stand in dire need of one more essay on the *Divine Comedy*. My defense, and this is not the first time the thing has happened, is to pretend earnestly to be a scholar, which I am not, and try to sound learned throughout perhaps a dozen false starts, before getting down to being my mere self again, and simply saying what I think. All that is figured by the business of taking apart the truck—and that damn mattress—carrying the pieces downstairs through a collection of antique dreck which perhaps stands for foot-notes—there are four editions of the poem on my office desk and two more, different ones, at home—and putting it all back together elsewhere, with the help of a growing throng of scholars; while the concluding image, of the damaged radiator cap which I hold down with my finger, merely shadows forth my sorry-cynical belief as to the probable result of all my efforts.

Even the assertion that "I go through these agonies with any and every piece of writing that cannot be completed in a day," though appearing above, belongs to the dream-thoughts, for one of the things which chiefly amazes me about Dante is his successful determination to complete a huge design, a true life task lasting many years:

> *il poema sacro*
> *al quale ha posto mano e cielo e terra,*
> *si che m' ha fatto per piu anni macro....*
> (*Paradiso* xxv. 1–3)

as he says with a kind of divine chutzpah redeemed only by his being quite right.

This is a power of poetry, a power of mind itself, far beyond what I could have imagined without having the proof of the poem to hand. As if he had said to the Muse—dared to say to Polyhymnia, Muse of Sacred Song—"Lady, you show up at nine every morning for a decade and more, and I'll let you know when we're finished."

Struggling with the thoughts that were to make this essay, which had been giving me a bad time for a couple of weeks, it happened that I took the children to a night game. But Dante's poem, for anyone working with it closely, has the power of infecting a good many thoughts about things that would seem quite remote from it, so that when on some occasion of local triumph I saw on the electric scoreboard a bright red cardinal swooping madly up and down and across, I thought: O dear, that's the trouble, isn't it? I mean, that Cross in the heaven of Mars, the imperial Eagle in the heaven of Jove, the ladder in the heaven of Saturn, all made up of spirits who are lights (after you get up past Justinian in Canto vii they no longer have human faces)—we can actually do, or show, these things. That scoreboard could as readily flash out to us glowing crosses and ladders and eagles as it can that cardinal or the pitcher of pouring golden beer which will likely come next ... and what a vulgar reduction it is. Surely poesy rules in the realm of the impossible just because it *is* the impossible; realization is ruin.

But a few nights after, taking the children to the Fourth of July fireworks, and seeing those truly wonderful sprayings and flowerings, those glowing showers of embers slowly going out—they actually do make people say ohh! and ah!—I thought, with a kind of stupid relief, Ah, well, that's more like it, the spirits on cross and ladder come and go swiftly, like the fireworks, brilliant with heat as well as light, and with the continuousness of a musical phrase, *legato* ... only they don't go out. And I felt better, heaven knows why. For both these comparisons, scoreboard and fireworks, had merely obtruded themselves on my vision of the poem because I saw them while preoccupied with the poem. The poem, however, is to be read with the mind's eye, not the body's eyes, which are the necessary but not sufficient receivers of its words or of its visions.

Still, the poem is near seven hundred years old, and if much has remained the same—including death, cruelty, stupidity, and smiles—ever so much has changed. And, still thinking of cross and eagle and Jacob's ladder, I remembered two quotations bearing on this matter, though written three centuries apart. I'd had them about for some years, and here seemed to be an occasion for putting them together.

What a beautiful hemisphere the stars would have made, if they had been placed in rank and order; if they had all been disposed of in regular figures ... all finished, and made up into one fair piece, of great composition, according to the rules of art and symmetry.

That is Bishop Burnet, as it were introducing the eighteenth century. But here is how the same thought occurs to George Santayana, introducing the twentieth:

... imagine the stars, undiminished in number, without losing any of their astronomical significance and divine immutability, marshalled in geometrical patterns; say in a Latin cross, with the words *In hoc signo vinces* in a scroll around them. The beauty of the illumination would be perhaps increased, and its import, practical, religious, cosmic, would surely be a little plainer; but where would be the sublimity of the spectacle? [And he answers] Irretrievably lost.—*The Sense of Beauty* (New York: C. Scribners Sons, 1896)

It's a matter of your—or your century's, perhaps—taste in universes. Dante's cosmology is as absurd to us as—well, as ours would be to Dante. In effect, he might claim with reason, in spite of all our chains of zeroes hiding behind the exponents, we don't have a cosmology at all, any more than the ancient Maya, who kept accurate calendars extending many thousands of years into a future in which there would not happen to be ancient Maya, could be said to have a cosmology.

Much has changed, yes. On this point, an anecdote.

A student came to his teacher just after commencement, and paid him what at first looked to be, and certainly was intended to be, a tremendous compliment. "Sir," he breathlessly said, "there was one thing I learned in your course that is of greater significance than anything else I have been taught in my four years at this university." Teacher, bridling prettily, inquired what this wonderful one thing might be. "Why, that right during John Milton's lifetime the sun stopped going around the earth, and"—he made a twisting motion with his arms—"the earth began going around the sun!"

As a testimonial to effective teaching, that's as pathetic as it's funny. But if that teacher had happened to take his motto from Leibniz—"there's nothing so stupid I can't learn from it"—he might have gone on to consider thus.

A silly error, yes. But also a convincingly surrealist metaphor about how it might have felt mentally if not physically, that violent wrenching of the frame of things begun by Copernicus and Kepler, Brahe and Galileo. And if you continue along the lines it indicates about the relations of mind and world, you might wonder at other of the great changes since Dante's time, changes having to do with the age of the universe, of the earth, of life, of human life; and changes having to do with the size of the universe, which has grown so exponentially from the little local affair it was to something of a size so unimaginable that it has to be expressed in light years—to give one figure only, our sun and its system lie on the rim of our galaxy 26,000 light years distant from the center, which is to say, being interpreted, the distance covered by light traveling 6,000 billion miles a year multiplied 26,000 times.... Can you say with utter confidence whether changes of such quality and magnitude take place in the world or in the mind, whether Aristotle himself would be quite clear as to whether they are recognitions or reversals? So it might be with the Copernican Revolution just as that student said: the sun stopped going around the earth and the earth started going around the sun, with consequences, including the demythologizing of knowledge, the dissociation of cosmos and consciousness, physics and faith, which I am sure you are as much and as little familiar with as I. Much has changed.

But when I look up into the night sky—and no matter how much science insists that the direction of my gaze is out, not up, my neck tells me I am looking up—I see not Dante's neat Ptolemaic universe, nor the elegant Copernican universe that replaced it, still less the vast universe more recently offered us by Harlow Shapley and others; I see, as men always have seen, the appearances which were to be accounted for by these universes; indeed, I don't see very many of them, owing to the smog, which seems to be one of the conditions under which it becomes possible for men in windowless buildings watching television monitors to send travelers to the Moon and Mariners out past Mars. So that although the size of the Milky Way has increased to include an unimaginable and indeed incredible 200 billion stars, it is among the effects of the scientific and technological civilization which makes this and the like assertions that I was unable, at last look—Fourth of July again—to see any Milky Way at all. That's a bit more of the much that has changed.

So Dante's cosmos does indeed look silly, but only until I try to contemplate my own and learn that I don't effectively have one. Not only the smog that prevents me from seeing the stars, but the electric light so effective in demythologizing the world that it shields me from demon and angel alike, and insures that save for the Fourth of July I will not worry enough about the stars to go outdoors and see whether I can see them or not. And not only that, but this: Increased knowledge increases ignorance exponentially, and every triumphant advance in knowing means that millions of us won't know it.

That, perhaps, is poetically the point. Dante has a small universe, but a full one, and he knows it thoroughly. I have, if I can in any sensible way be said to have it, a vast universe, but it is empty and dark, and compared with what is to be known I do not know it at all.

Away from the *Comedy*, I may have my doubts. But while I am reading, the illusion of plenitude is complete; I am convinced. I don't know whether to be more amazed at his faith or at his knowledge, at his humility or at his pride, but when I read the poem I am kept constantly under an enchantment that says, "Everything you need to know is here." So much is this so, that when I hear at the opening of *Inferno* xii:

> *Cosi di ponte in ponte, altro parlando*
> *che la mia commedia cantar non cura,*
> *venimmo . . .*

> So from bridge to bridge, talking of other things
> which my comedy cares not to sing,
> we went along . . .

(my translation)

I am amazed all over again to learn that Dante and Virgil said things to one another in Hell that we are never going to be told.

This must be, I think, the supreme illusion possible to poetry, perhaps to any power of the mind, and it makes me think of the *Comedy* as a kind of holography, in which everything is always present at every point. Or of Borges's Aleph; or of a famous remark of Whitehead's, that "In a certain sense, everything is everywhere at all times, for every location involves an aspect of itself in every other location. Thus every spatio-temporal standpoint mirrors the world." Or of this that happened between Juliana of Norwich and her Saviour: "He shewed me," she says, "a little thing, the quantity of an hazel-nut, in the palm of my hand; and it was round as a ball. I looked thereupon with the eye of my understanding, and thought: 'What may this be?' And it was generally answered thus: 'It is all that is made.'"*

Revelations of Divine Love, Ch. 5. See the point in the *Paradiso* (xxvii. 41–2) of which Beatrice says:

> *Da quel punto*
> *depende il cielo e tutta la natura.*

This illusion of plenitude has to do in the first place with an exact fit between inside and outside in the poet's arrangements. There are in the main two sorts of outside, the articulation of the poem and the articulation of the universe, and they too coincide to give the impression that everything is contained within them and that nothing remains outside them. But then there is the inside, the human action that expands so as to fit exactly with its ordained outward.

The briefest reminder of these articulations ought to. do, as they are well known to every reader of the poem. First, the arithmetic, built chiefly upon three and ten. Three canticles of thirty-three cantos each, with one canto for general prologue to the whole, bringing the total to one hundred. The cantos are of varying lengths, but average out so as to make each canticle about the same number of lines, and the poet keeps a strict awareness that this is so, warning himself at the end of the *Purgatorio* that all the pages ordained are filled up, so that the curb of art allows him to go no further; and being similarly warned toward the end of the *Paradiso* that it is time to stop, like the careful tailor who cuts the garment according to the cloth at hand, he stops.

To these purely arithmetical or numerological dispositions the physical and moral natures of the universe conform themselves. Corresponding to the three canticles, the three realms of Hell, Purgatory, Heaven. Each of these is again divided into three main stages of the moral life imaged forth in the architectural arrangements of circles, terraces, and spheres. In Hell these divisions descend in the order of incontinence, violence, and fraud; in Purgatory they ascend in the order of perverse, defective, and excessive love; in Heaven they are represented as raying outward according as the blessed were affected by worldliness (and are accordingly seen within the cone of the earth's shadow) or lived lives of action or of contemplation. Outside of these schemes is another realm of a different order, bringing the total in each canticle to ten: Limbo, the Antepurgatory, the Empyrean.

The marvelous thing, poetically, is that this scheme is not set forth complete but built up for us by stages of description and reminder until it stands forth in memory with its symmetries and balancings and intricate cross-relations, all deriving ultimately from the mind of God but all, the one and the many, experienced serially as an adventure of the pilgrim through the types of the adventures of mankind generally—*exemplorum positivus*, as he says elsewhere—driven home by examples. And in the mystery of the many examples we are gradually to perceive the mystery of the link between human freedom and the workings of divine necessity, the link between individual and type. It is as Blake described it in a famous passage of *Jerusalem*:

> All things acted on Earth are seen in the bright Sculptures of
> Los's Halls, & every Age renews its powers from these Works
> With every pathetic story possible to happen from Hate or
> Wayward Love; & every sorrow & distress is carved here,
> Every affinity of Parents, Marriages & Friendships are here
> In all their various combinations wrought with wondrous Art,
> All that can happen to Man in his pilgrimage of seventy years.

Indeed, Blake, who illustrated the *Comedy*, may even have been thinking of it in these lines, and perhaps especially of the marvelously carved illustrations on the cornices of Purgatory.

So, in a fanciful comparison, the poet is like Theseus, led by the thread of love in such a way that in the journey to the Minotaur he also learns the labyrinth as a whole.

So far we have stressed the architecture, in its correspondence to the articulation of the divine plan, or Necessity. Through this web of geometry, geography, and cosmology, all the creatures move, as Beatrice says, to diverse ports over the great sea of being. But at the very fulcrum of the poem, the middle of the fiftieth canto, Marco Lombardo makes it clear that human beings have freedom from stellar or other necessity; they have mind, which the heavens have not in their charge; hence their salvation or damnation is not under the doom of Necessity, though it will indeed illustrate Necessity.

This is the mystery of individuality itself, and in it the problem of universals is not so much solved as set forth and assumed poetically to be solved.* Against the background of the circles of Hell, the terraces of purgation, the starry wheels of Heaven—all that insane arithmetical regularity as circular as a Kandinsky, which in my moods of disaffection with the poem make me think of it as *The Rube Goldberg Variations*—is placed the wild richness and unpredictable particularity of people on their ways through the dark wood or their moving over the great sea of being.

Here perhaps is where the illusion of plenitude is most convincing, or is totally convincing. Dante knows so many people; he knows so many

---

*As, in experience, it is always presented as solved; if no solution, perhaps no problem?

stories! He seems never at a loss for a story striking in its individuation, epigrammatic in its allusive concision, and pointed as to its illustrative quality with respect to salvation or damnation and exact moral type. This quality chiefly is what led me to say that Dante's universe, though small in both space and time compared to ours, and more especially *closed* in both space and time, is a full universe, and one which he knows thoroughly, is utterly at home in—as one could be only in a universe which, at whatever size, is closed. The inside exactly fills up the outside. Hence my impression while reading the poem that everything is in it.

This impression is reinforced by the multitude of symbolic resonances and redundancies that echo through the work and are the other side of his striking power of individualizing his figures. Dante's habit of mind is deeply, almost involuntarily, typological, not only with respect to the correspondences between the Old and New Testaments but with respect also to the correspondences between scriptural history and pagan myth and history, and the continuity between both of these and the history of contemporary Europe. It is in this poetic power of com-position, literally of putting together, that he is supreme.

He is also the most learned of poets, or the one who, among the greatest poets, relies the most upon learning and allusion. Side by side with his magnificent attentiveness to the visual, the power of putting before us with the utmost plainness what he is seeing, so that we see it too, there is this other power of riddling diction that is constantly making us supply more information than the words themselves convey, and infer whole stories from an image or a line. Consider, in this light, such things as the sketches of the images of Pride carved on the pavement of Purgatory, where in thirty-odd lines of paralleled tercets he swiftly reviews a succession of paired examples from Scripture and Greek myth: Satan and Briareus, the Titans and Nimrod, Niobe and Saul, Arachne and Rehoboam, Alcmaeon and Sennacherib, Cyrus and Holofernes, finishing with the ruins of Troy. Or consider the arrogant virtuosity of Justinian's history of Rome under the figure of the imperial Eagle, sweeping *cito et velociter* back and forth across Europe so as to summarize the span from Aeneas to Charlemagne, about a millennium and a half from the founding of the city, and on to the disputes of Ghibelline and Guelf of Dante's own time, all in eighty lines or less, only for the poet to balance all this gorgeous speed and strength against the story of the humble pilgrim Romeo, a spectacular contrast of pride, power, scope, and speed with a quiet tale of a faithful servant misprized and exiled to beg his way through the world in poverty and age (in which respect he may be, as so many others are throughout the poem, a type of Dante himself). The passage about Rome is thick with famous names to which the reader's memory must supply the stories, and includes even the crucifixion and the destruction of the Temple under Titus, given in a sentence so riddling that its full elucidation by Beatrice takes up the whole of the next Canto.

One last illustration of what I have been calling the illusion of plenitude returns us to that idea of the presence of everything in something, which is of the essence of the art of poetry and which is imaged forth in such stories as that of Juliana and the hazel-nut.

The scheme of the poem is in a certain sense anecdotal and picaresque. Our hero, alone alive among a host of the dead, alone moves on through all the three realms, and there is consequently a temptation to read each episode as entirely separate from all the others, if only because the persons in it will never reappear.

But there is, owing to Dante's power of composition, a further dimension, of resonance, of symbol, of mysteriously allusive interconnection, between this example and that, between the examples and Dante himself, and so on.

Dante sees his poem as a sea voyage, as is well-known; the chief places are the beginning of the *Purgatorio*—

> *Per correr miglior acqua alza le vele*
> *omai la navicella del mio ingegno*

—and near the beginning of the *Paradiso*, with its ominous warning to the reader not to put forth on a sea never sailed before unless he is one of the few who have stretched forth their necks to the bread of angels, a passage followed by an odd comparison to Jason and the Argonauts.*

Human life, too, is a sea voyage, says Beatrice, over the great sea of being.

Later on, Beatrice mentions, as a warning against believing one has seen deeply into the divine will, having seen a ship complete a long voyage only to be wrecked on coming into harbor; whereupon one can't help hearing a faint echo of the mad voyage of Ulysses, shipwrecked within uncomprehending sight of salvation, the mountain of Purgatory.

Now Ulysses' voyage, very likely invented by Dante, was characterized not only as the *folle volo*, the mad flight in pursuit of knowledge, but also as the *alto passo*, the deep passage, the high adventure, which is the term already applied by the poet to his own pilgrimage.

---

* See also *Paradiso* xxiii. 67.

Such dark prophecy as Lewis Mumford has seen in the technological schemes of Leonardo, as Loren Eiseley in Bacon's summons to the study of nature, as Eiseley and Richard M. Weaver in the apparition of the witches to Macbeth, I seem to see in Dante's story of Ulysses: a story of heartbreaking brightness on the way to doom.

Ulysses wants knowledge, and for knowledge he will break his ties with Telemachus, Laertes, even Penelope, to sail westward through the Mediterranean after escaping the enchantments of Circe, who turns men into beasts. The object of this knowledge? It is at first to become expert in the world, learned in human vice and human worth; but this knowledge is dismissed in three lines of tourism: he and his men saw Spain, Africa, Morocco, Sardinia and some other islands; then, old and slow with age, they come to the straits of Gibraltar where Hercules had set down his pillars as signs to men of limits, that they should go no further. Here worldly knowledge can no longer be the goal, because there is nothing out there, nothing but water. Ulysses exhorts his fellows, in the name of the dangers they have shared in reaching the westernmost limit of the world, to continue in the name of knowledge (*esperienza*) even though, or just because, the knowledge is of nothing, of the unpeopled world behind the setting sun. As if the journey were to begin with what indeed it presently becomes, a journey into death. And again, as if remembering Circe, he concludes what he calls "this little speech" by reminding them that they were not made to live as beasts but to pursue *virtute e conoscenza*. One of my editors says tersely of *virtute* that it means *il bene*, but perhaps we may see in anticipation here the Baconian coupling of knowledge and power. What knowledge and power may be expected of the void, however, we are never told. Instead, Ulysses conveys rather backhandedly his opinion of his fellow men by saying that the "little speech" so fired them up that he could not have held them back from what he knows (now, or even at the time?; the text will tell us nothing on this point) to be "the mad flight."

So they turn the poop toward the rising sun—given the consistency of the symbolism of the sun throughout the poem, even this navigational detail is a tellng one—and row out into vacancy, always bending leftward, to the sinister side; indeed, to the sinister, for this is forsaking the *via diritta* in its bodily form.

And out of all this, after five months, they do achieve a distant view of Purgatory mountain—dark with distance—and are peremptorily struck down by the whirlwind of the divine displeasure, though even now Ulysses knows the will behind the storm only as "what pleased Another."

That is the strange story told in dark Hell out of a tongue of fire, a story full of the freshness of sea, wind, and sky, a story of courage, nobility, and strength, and, as it happens, madness. The voyage of Ulysses is a mad flight, yes, but it is also the *alto passo* (the deep passage? the high adventure?) which is the term the poet has already applied to his own journey proposed by Virgil (*Inferno* ii, 12). It is like a fleeting glimpse, from the closed and closing universe of the high middle ages, of the coming of the Voyages of Discovery, which themselves were associated in men's minds with the chance of finding the way back to the earthly paradise from which their first parents had, being driven out, driven out all.

But it is more than that. It is also, I think, an account of the *terribilita*, nobility and pathos of the drive toward knowledge that has with an increasing acceleration obsessed the world since Dante's time. Not, obviously, that the men of the Middle Ages were not themselves obsessed with knowledge; if we had Dante's poem for the only evidence of that, it would be enough. But this seems an intuition of the practical knowledge—*esperienza*, our poet calls it—that Bacon would associate with power: the knowledge that imposes upon the knower an ultimate compulsion to know, to experience, to find out, even if the object of the knowledge be nothingness, even if the result of the finding be death and hell.

And when, from high in heaven, the poet turns at Beatrice's command for one of his two marvelous looks back and down at the *aiuola che ci fa tanto feroci*, the little threshing floor of earth that makes us so ferocious, he remembers just in passing that voyage of Ulysses—as though, one feels, it formed some sort of doomed counterpart to his own fortunate and blessed voyage.

Ulysses and the fall of man both relate to knowledge and lust. Whenever Ulysses turns up, three times in all, it is in the company of some sort of sexual enchantment. When he tells his story, he begins with leaving Circe, who had kept him for over a year, and his exhortation to his crew includes a denunciation of bestiality. In Purgatory, Dante dreams of a siren who mentions having enchanted Ulysses just before she is revealed by Virgil as a creature of falsehood and filth. The last memory of Ulysses and his *varco folle*, high in heaven, is companioned in the next line by a reminiscence of Europa's rape. So sexuality, bestiality, and the voyage are brought together in these fleeting and riddling allusions, which echo over great spaces of the poem. And, remembering these things well enough to put them together as a dream might do, we remember that Dante began his journey somewhat as Ulysses did—threatened by bestiality in the form of three beasts, previously guilty of allowing himself to be seduced by both sexuality and knowledge (in the form of philosophy, his own Circe), for which in the Earthly Paradise he will suffer the scornful rebuke of Beatrice—with the sole redeeming difference that Dante is under the protection of faith, the protection of a Lady who is not Circe or the Siren or Europa.

And the vision of the voyage returns once more, with all these various voyages, to form its overtones in a figure of the strangest harmony in all poetry:

> *Un punto solo m'è maggior letargo*
> *che venticinque secoli alla 'mpresa,*
> *che fè Nettuno ammirar l'ombra d'Argo.*

This one moment in the presence of God is both a moment, a timeless Now, and the moving Now of all of human time, and both are made equivalent: It is a greater *letargo*—the word includes both fatigue and oblivion—than all the five and twenty centuries since the enterprise that made Neptune marvel at the shadow of the Argo, the first ship, hence the beginning of the enterprise of history. In this strangely displaced figure the unitive experience of the divine compounds the consciousness of the long fatigue of history with unconsciousness itself, the moment as part of duration with the moment as timeless and already in eternity, and—poetically, at least—the Christian revelation and promise with the ancient pagan god of the sea and with Jason on another of those doomed and damned voyages like that of Ulysses . . . for one remembers already, long ago, having seen Jason, stalking so proudly through Hell that even Virgil admires his royal port; and to have heard of him once again, intruding figuratively into the warning to the reader near the beginning of the *Paradiso*, where the furrow ploughed by the poet's keel reminds him of Jason ploughing at Colchis in the presence of his marveling crew.

Such resonances, whatever they mean—and of their nature, perhaps, our idea of their meaning will be flickering and mysterious as is the meaning of coincidence and relation in life itself—seem to touch upon an essence of the purest poetry in their strange power of balancing, blending, harmonizing many diversities across great and sounding distances, giving a riddling hint of a oneness in the world that for a moment shines through the manifold appearances—the moment, as it were, just before metaphor is born and explanations—such as these helpless ones of mine—begin.

The Winter Addresses
of Kenneth Burke

with some Thoughts about Interpretation

F IRST off, it will be convenient to have the text before us:

> *College Garden Apartments*
> *5831 Walnut Street,*
> *3 Apt. 24*
> *Pittsburgh, PA 15232*
>
> *University of Pittsburgh*
> *6 Department of English*
> *526 Cathedral of Learning*
> *Oakland*
> *9 Pittsburgh, PA 15260*

One imagines that even a superficial reader will respond immediately to the appeal of this muted little lyric, so full as it is of verbal play, subtle variation, and incremental repetition. But to the reader steeped in the Judaeo-Christian tradition, the reader whose delight is response, interpretation, the unfolding of what is infolded, there is much more here to meet the mind than at first meets the eye: Compacted into nine short lines we find the speaker's cryptic parable of his religious history and of that of a larger part of mankind, of which he is the type.

The method is threefold: Paratactic, elliptical, and allusive. Paratactic, in that the items, as of a catalogue, are given without syntactical or causal relation—*post hoc*, with the reader left to infer the *propter hoc*. Elliptical, in that what is omitted may be of as great import as what is said. And allusive, of course, chiefly to the scriptures and their sacred history.

Our interpretative method, correspondingly, will demand much tact. For as there is no overt, coherent narrative, we shall have to proceed by comparing and contrasting elements that appear in both stanzas and testing these for their precise degree of likeness and difference, or likeness-in-difference. For convenience we prefer to go from the more obvious to the more recondite; hence we shall leave number symbolism until the end. And, one last preliminary point: the two stanzas may be related indifferently as either a drama developing in time or as an arrangement in space; we shall try to show how both readings harmonize.

We begin in a *garden* with two trees in it. The *walnut*, bearing edible fruit, is mentioned at once; the *oak*, not bearing edible fruit, is withheld till line eight, almost the end of the poem, and partly concealed as *Oakland*. The reference to Genesis 3 is of course obvious, and we anticipate being told a version of the Fall of Man, though with certain highly individual features; Eve, for instance, does not appear, nor does the Serpent; anticipating further, we hazard a guess at the significance of these omissions, that this story of the Fall is being told with a peculiarly exclusive emphasis on knowledge, or *learning* (line seven), hence perhaps—but this is inference—with an exclusively masculine and even onanistic emphasis on a certain pride, balanced by a certain sterility, in the human project of mastering the world by knowing.

So. We begin in the Garden, alone. Considering a little more closely the first line, "College Garden Apartments," we compare the innocence of "college" in the first stanza with the somewhat lofty, not to say pretentious, claim implicit in "university" in the second, noting as a couple of corresponsive changes that we also go from *garden* to *cathedral*, from *walnut* to *oak*, and from *apartment* with its idea of being set *apart* whether for good or ill to *department* with its ominous hint of *departure*, or being sent forth. It goes with this that the idea behind *college*, if this be not to consider too curiously, comes from L. *legare*, to be chosen or sent as deputy. This will give a clue to one more significant omission as we note that we have been taken from *garden* to *cathedral* with no mention whatever of the incarnation, crucifixion, and resurrection of Christ as the savior of mankind; the inference, of course, is that the speaker views himself as a secular son of God exiled from the garden with the purpose of redeeming mankind by knowledge alone, by building not Jerusalem but the *Cathedral of Learning*, which, evidently, is the eulogistic name for what the Bible names dyslogistically the Tower of Babel. (There may nevertheless be a kind of grotesque or parodied kind of crucifixion concealed in *English*, if, joycing the word as other writers have done before this, we hear "the anguish languish;" but we shall not insist on this.)

The story told in time is complemented by the relation set forth in space, where the two stanzas, or *addresses*, relate as *home* and *office*, or *work* ("in the sweat of thy face shalt thou eat bread"—Genesis 3:19), so that as temporally we proceed from innocence to experience, spatially we endure a tension between innocence and experience, though it is well to note that both, according to the refrain of lines four and nine, come equivocally under the power of the Devil and the Father, as is clearly made to appear in *Pittsburgh*, or City of the Pit, and PA, or the fatherland (whose Jupiterian emblem is also the *oak* of *Oakland*). A plaintive communication from the poet will confirm this reading, as well as serving to introduce the difficult subject of number symbolism: "The difference betwixt thirty-two and sixty makes me wonder whether I may be housed farther from headquarters"—sc. heaven,—"than I had hoped."

The poet's propensity to lisp in numbers is not, for me, the happiest aspect of his production. For example, does "Apt. 24" refer to his eager setting-forth on the road to knowledge at that age, to his aptitude? I do not know. But I can see some reason for the submergence of part of the underthoughts in cipher, for that part is about relations of orthodoxy and heresy.

Very briefly, then, 5831 breaks into five plus eight equal thirteen, and the reversed thirteen, or three in one, of the Trinity. Bad luck and the sacred. 15232 also adds up to thirteen, as does 526 in line seven; while the last number, concluding the whole, totals fourteen, with a hint of the one in four, the quaternity, opposed to the Trinity in some Gnostic and Manichaean beliefs, or religions with an exclusive emphasis on *knowledge*. What to make of that last despairing zero, I confess, I do not know, but the rest of the last line seems to me to acknowledge the reality of evil in the City of the Pit, while stoically or minimally affirming the presiding presence of PA the Father.

That joke, which perhaps went on a touch too long as it is, might have been even longer had it not been interrupted by the visit of a student from Porlock in distress about a term paper. I am not at all sure just now what lessons if any may be drawn from it concerning poems and interpretations, but on the principle that he goes farthest who knows not where he is going, I am ready to launch out more or less at random. First, then, with some observations about how the foregoing happened to happen.

Kenneth Burke and I have exchanged, I guess, about a letter a week for a good many years now, and in the course of these letters it sometimes happens that one will include a new verse, on which the other is expected to comment and sometimes does. So when I opened a letter from Kenneth and saw that the reverse of the page bore a couple of groups of indented lines, I suppose I was already anticipating a poem while I read the beginning of the letter, following the hard-nosed definition laid down by Jeremy Bentham, that when the lines run all the way to the right margin it is prose; when this fails to happen, it is poetry. So that when I turned the page and saw that the indented lines were really giving me my friend's addresses in Pittsburgh where he was to spend the winter months, it seems that my rhapsode's interpreting mood was still strong enough to override the plain fact of the matter. Obviously, though, it could not have done anything of the sort without some help from the matter itself.

Then a strange thing happened. I knew instantly that I could, and would, interpret these addresses as though they constituted a poem. Not only that, but I knew instantly the main lines of the interpretation, and that I would certainly write them out on the morrow; and so in fact it went. Confirming something I had frequently observed about interpretation, whether in the classroom or when writing: that interpretation is rapid, rhapsodic, sudden, unexpected, having all the signs of being inspired—a distant, impersonal, yet excited seeing, or *realizing*, such as goes with the composition of a poem you *know* is going to work, is going to come clear. (It need not affect the argument that this feeling of inspiration and immediacy of knowledge, whether in composing or interpreting, may turn out to have been mistaken; it nevertheless exists and is a happiness while it lasts.)

So that is more or less how it happened. Now I wonder if it is possible to say at all what happened, or anything about this kind of happening in general.

The objections I want from the reader just now, the ones I feel confident of being able to deal with, are two:

1. But it isn't a poem.
2. You are reading things into it.

As to the first, I should reply that one is not so certain these days as formerly what is a poem and what isn't a poem. And I point out that your confident assertion as to what it *isn't*, a poem, is predicated upon your knowing what it really *is*, a couple of addresses. If you didn't know that, you would certainly sound less assured, and might find no identifiable ground at all for saying it is not a poem. Maybe its so looking exactly not like a poem is exactly what confers its poetic character and title? No, this isn't spinning paradoxes, or not altogether. The poet's task has generally been conceded to be hard, but it may be so described as to make it logically impossible: Make an object recognizable as an individual of the class *p* for poem, but make it in such a way that it resembles no other individual of that class. It's not really that bad, for in fact poems come in waves of kind, not to mention in imitation of other poems; but with a sufficient emphasis on individuality it might be that bad.

Now as to the second objection: All right, it's a poem, if you like but you're reading things into it. Well, I should be very happy to have someone bring up that old crux, for it's where I want to be, where I want us to start.

In literary criticism the charge that you're reading things into the poem—things, it is understood, that aren't there—and defining the word *there* in that context might give some bother—is so automatically accepted as the sin against the holy ghost that I have never heard anyone say what needs to be said: Why yes, of course I am, what else would you do with a poem? (On this, a student with whom I had been reading, not a whole book, but two or three sentences with conversation about these, gave me this surprised definition: "I see what reading is; it's putting together what it says with what you've got." And surely this is the right place for a motto by Wallace Stevens: "The poem must resist the intelligence / Almost successfully.")

I shall go further now, and assert that the two addresses have become a poem, though they weren't one before, largely in virtue of my having read things into them; things that are now there even if they weren't there before. And I shall go much too far, as well, and assert that you can no longer read those two addresses together purely as addresses, without taking into account the sort of syntax of elements I have made explicit, such as for instance that between garden and cathedral. It's a joke, if you like, but it's a pretty dirty joke. This is so for a reason that is rarely if ever said aloud, maybe because when said aloud it becomes self-evident: that interpretation, of its nature, is or at least overlaps with misinterpretation; were that not so, it would be either fact or revelation. To go with that, here is a definition to deal with: a poem is a dream containing its own interpretation. Which means you have to tease the interpretation out of the dream, but in awareness that while doing so you are dreaming too. Concerning this, Claude Lévi-Strauss said something thoughtful to this effect: it matters little, he said, whether I am interpreting certain myths, or whether in truth they are interpreting my mind to me; what matters, he added, is to get a view of "the mind imitating itself as object" (paraphrased from *The Raw and the Cooked* [New York: Harber & Row, 1969]). On this point I too have thought that in general I do not much care for myths, which before they have been treated by a great poet are so often dull, confused, rambling, repetitive—but I do care ever so much for the myths we are sometimes able to make up about what they mean. For it is there that you get a glimpse of a theme that must surely be of the greatest interest to teachers: how meaning gets into the world at all.

It is time for an illustration of how this works, if it does work, to set against my two addresses, and by good luck I've remembered one short enough to fit in here, and clear enough, if not to convince, at any rate to make the position clear in turn.

THE JEWEL STAIRS GRIEVANCE

The jewelled steps are already quite white with dew,
It is so late that the dew soaks my gauze stockings,
And I let down the crystal curtain
And watch the moon through the clear autumn.

To any untaught reader, I daresay, this is transparently a visual (and tactile) poem of the generically "oriental" kind that has been fashionable quite often in recent times; it is an "imagist" poem, we might say, even down to its "jeweled" quality, a clear little moment demanding no interpretation but only, perhaps, a connoisseurish appreciation of its delicacy: interpretation would be not only far-fetched and uncertain, we think, but vulgar as well.

The poem is in fact a translation, or imitation, by Ezra Pound from Rihaku (which I've been told is the Japanese name for Li Po), and Pound adds the following Note:

Jewel stairs, therefore a palace. Grievance, therefore there is something to complain of. Gauze stockings, therefore a court lady, not a servant, who complains. Clear autumn, therefore he has no excuse on account of weather. Also she has come early, for the dew has not merely whitened the stairs, but has soaked her stockings. The poem is especially prized because she utters no direct reproach.— Ezra Pound, *Selected Poems*, edited by T. S. Eliot (London: Faber & Faber, 1928), p. 111.

This is the sort of thing that separates sheep from goat and Nominalist from Realist, though even when you have the two parties sorted out it remains hard enough to tell t'other from which. But, putting it as crudely as possible: Does the meaning, the reiterated inference "therefore" from the facts, improve the poem? Or were you happier with just the text of the poem alone? Or—the tricky third thing—could you remain happy with just the words of the poem after someone had told you it had a hidden meaning but refused to tell you what it was? Pound's answer seems to me decisive at least for the tradition out of which the poem emerged: it is "especially prized because she utters no direct reproach."

And some generalized corollary of that answer is also the answer honorably given by teachers of literature on our professional occasions. Mr. MacLeish's celebrated slogan to the contrary, a poem must be and mean at once. Doing that is a tricky thing, too, and I propose to give the last part and instance of this essay to the mystery of it.

Although the "intentional fallacy" is also numbered among our deadly sins, we do all the same believe that poems are intentional, and that the intentions of them do belong "somehow" to their makers, even if we are prepared to concede that the makers were not thinking about intention, or meaning, during the course of composition. One part of the mystery of poetry is that it does not clearly distinguish the plan from its fulfillment. There is in general no blueprint to be followed in other materials; the blueprint, in poetry, is the bulding. That is because, say, the poet makes an image, in which meanings somehow inhere, and which it is the honorable work of interpretation to distinguish in the poem, without dividing them from the poem.

Two brief instances. Shakespeare's 107th Sonnet, "Not mine owne feares not the prophetick soule . . ." is a mysterious poem which has evoked and provoked comment about its meaning in just the degree, perhaps, that it has resisted the same. The poem must resist the intelligence almost successfully. Its fifth line, "The mortall Moone hath her eclipse indur'de," has received more attention than most, possibly because it is more uncertain than most. Some propose it as a means of dating the Sonnets by literal lunar eclipses visible from the Greenwich Meridian (unhappily, there were a good many of those), and at least one writer, Leslie Hotson, has argued for a date on the ground that "the mortall Moone" represents the Armada, which was at least believed to have approached the English shore in a crescent formation. While others, arguing that the Moone is conventional poetic talk for Elizabeth, propose to date the Sonnets that way. Unhappily, the line contains an equivocation fatal to the argument, for it could mean either "Elizabeth has recovered from a serious head cold which might well have been fatal" or that she had died. Needless to say, all these interpretations are such as divide the meaning from the poem, rather than distinguishing the meaning in the poem.

The following exchange between Robert Frost and myself took place only in a dream of mine, but may be illustrative all the same. I, the eager interpreter, said of "Spring Pools" that it was "obviously" about one's growth from young to old, from potency to act, and the pathos, or even tragedy, attendant upon even the most successful completion of the process. To which, in my dream, the poet smiled and said that he rather thought he was writing about capillary action in trees. Of course, I should contend, at least in waking hours, we were both right, he about fact and I about inference from fact. It is always the poet's privilege to retire upon what the poem says, for that is his business; while the interpreter, so long as he knows the fact of the poem and does not contradict it, has the liberty, and indeed the duty, of ranging widely indeed in the drawing of inferences from the fact. On this account I have devised and tried to obey the following instruction about writing: The saying as clear as you can make it—for that is your duty and your gift—; the meaning as mysterious as may be. For the universe is so.

My first instance was a pair of addresses treated as a poem. The illustration was a pure and perfect one because in the first place it had no author, so could have no intention other than what I supplied and made coherent by interpretation. My last instance seems to me somewhat the same and yet reversed. It has to be a poem of my own, both because about a poem of my own I can assure you that I did not know of any abstract intention, or blueprint, while writing it, and also because for some reason I can remember and tell you, by a kind of biographical archaeology, about the source of practically everything in it; in fact, because it is "the same and yet reversed," I will give you the heap of elements first, and the poem only afterward.

In chronological succession as nearly as I can remember, here are the elements.

1938 or so. A friend told me of having seen the terse inscription "to die is gain" on a young girl's tombstone in a New Haven graveyard. That the phrase is from Philippians I is something I didn't know for many years, and doesn't seem to matter anyhow.

At about the same time I was first studying Dante, and reading of the leaves of Sybil's prophecies scattered by wind and right afterward, also in the last canto of the *Paradiso*, the famous vision of the volume of the universe whose leaves appear to us on earth as scattered.

1950 or so. Driving among the mountains of Vermont in Fall, my wife said that the varicolored forests resembled the reverse side of a tapestry. An unconsidered trifle I naturally snapped up and saved for some fifteen years.

From the fifties also. One observed that there began to be Fall Foliage Tours, with people coming to Vermont from as far as New York and Boston, in buses, to take pictures of the brilliant spectrum of the leaves, which, incidentally, they did through tinted windows.

1960 or so. I came to know Robert Frost one summer toward the last of his life, and somewhat against the odds we got to be friends, though we did not meet often. No anecdotes, but it may have been the sympathetic vibration of two misanthropes; and the poem was written in the autumn after his death. As though in slight defiance, its last line, about a pair of maples I had walked under every autumn for many years, was ready and waiting to fulfill its poem; Frost held that it couldn't be done that way. In a well-known discussion called "The Figure a Poem Makes," he described that figure as beginning in delight and ending in wisdom, insisted that its outcome be unforeseen but predestined from the first image of the original mood, and added with perhaps a touch of petulance, "It is but a trick poem and no poem at all if the best of it was thought first and saved for the last." I incline generally to agree, but may say in extenuation that if that line was thought of first and saved for the last, that included the fact that I had tried it in other poems over several years and always destroyed them for exactly the reason that though it was obviously a last line it was not *their* last line, being so far and away too good for them.

So. There are the elements. Here is the poem.

FOR ROBERT FROST, IN THE AUTUMN, IN VERMONT

All on the mountains, as on tapestries
Reversed, their threads unreadable though clear,
The leaves turn in the volume of the year.
Your land becomes more brilliant as it dies.
The puzzled pilgrims come, car after car,
With cameras loaded for epiphanies;
For views of failure to take home and prize,
The dying tourists ride through realms of fire.

"To die is gain," a virgin's tombstone said.
That was New England, too, another age
That put a higher price on maidenhead
If brought in dead; now on your turning page
The lines blaze with a constant light, displayed
As in the maples' cold and fiery shade.

About a decade after writing that, I think I've some idea how its elements fit together, and even why. But perhaps after being so very voluble an explicator of both a nonpoem and the poetry of other poets, I should properly fall silent about this one, taking to heart the instruction I paraphrased for you earlier:

As with a dream interpreted by one still sleeping,
The interpretation is only the next room of the dream.

Quidnunc the Poet
and Mr. Gigadibs

A BAD thing happened to me recently, bringing with it the humiliating conviction of my age and obsolescence: I read *The New York Times Book Review*, and found it too avant-garde.

Not all of it, not for example the lead review where Muriel Spark is praised for having composed the simile "a mind like a blade," and for having a character in a story think, "There is no health, she thought, for me, outside of honesty." That much originality and that much psychological penetration, even that many commas, I am still able to keep up with.

Nor do I have any trouble understanding my being somewhat *démodé* when it is explained to me in plain language by a reviewer who says: "The forties and fifties were a bad time, isolated and provincial ... a time of teaching English literature for very little money at some hideous little college in the woods." Yep, that's me, I say as the reviewer continues, "The new scene is urban and 'anti-academic.'" That too I can accept, though I wonder about the quotation marks; does he believe the new scene is really urban but only sort of pretending to be anti-academic? A note about this reviewer says that he has just completed a novel. He writes criticism and teaches at The State University of New York at Stony Brook.

But the real revelation of how far I had fallen behind came from a reading of Mr. Gigadibs's review of Quidnunc's book of poems. It happened that I had been reading this book during the past week, and finding it a comfortably familiar sort of composition, openly acknowledging such influences as Blake, Whitman, Pound. It is very earnest and high-minded and rather religiose in tone; the poet gives a sermon against President Johnson, grieves for the victims of a very wicked war, excoriates Clark Kerr and Chancellor Strong (who he thinks of as a dragon, possibly because Blake would have viewed him that way), writes a great deal of poetry about the writing of poetry, and so on. I thought I was getting on famously, understanding fine—save for a line in Greek, which a friend skilled in such matters tells me has an error in every word—and now comes Mr. Gigadibs with the humbling news that begins "Quidnunc must certainly be our most difficult active poet." Suppressing a shudder at the thought of all those inactive poets who must be more difficult still—otherwise why the precaution? or does he mean passive poets?—I read on, and learn that to read "with any immediate grace" what I had foolishly thought I was reading "would require Norman O. Brown's knowledge of the arcane mixed with Ezra Pound's grasp of poetics." Well, I certainly don't have those. Mr. Gigadibs goes on:

Though Quidnunc avows himself a purely derivative poet, his capacities are monstrous and have taken a singular direction: . . . in Quidnunc the range of affection is great and nothing is barred entrance from the "field" of composition.

There are those quotation marks again. Does Mr. Gigadibs believe in the existence of a field of composition or not? It is surely a notion familiar enough by now not to need so gingerly a pair of tongs to pick it up with. Mr. Gigadibs too teaches English at Stony Brook.

"Though Quidnunc avows himself a purely derivative poet. . . ." Back in the bad forties and fifties, poets used to be called derivative by critics; they never *avowed* it of themselves, and even critics were rarely so rude as to say a derivative poet was *purely* so; for it was possible that something of his own had got in maybe by accident. But that red herring must not be allowed to divert us from the true postmodernism of the sentence, which is in its construction: instead of the antithesis we might expect—"he says he's derivative, but I say he's not"—Mr. Gigadibs springs the planned surprise of an irrelevance:

Though Quidnunc avows himself a purely derivative poet, his capacities are monstrous and have taken a singular direction: . . .

Can this mean that when capacities are monstrous enough to move in a direction at all they might be expected—if one didn't watch out—to move in more than one direction at once? Singular indeed. As to the last clause, the one after the colon which characterizes the direction:

... in Quidnunc the range of affection is great and nothing is barred entrance from the "field" of composition.

—does this, can it, mean that he likes a good many different things and doesn't refuse to put them in his poems? Mr. Gigadibs's next two sentences do not altogether remove the difficulties already raised:

The structure of (these poems) is the "grand collage." It is for this reason that his poetry has been called cluttered and self-defeating, even swollen and diversive by his admirers.

Divisive? diversified? (or even, considering the poems, de-versified?) It is curious that a dictionary so careful as to give things like "diversipe-date" and "diversisporous" should fail of "diversive." What could the admirers have meant? that the poetry was diverting? And isn't there a comma missing, as though the strain of inventing "diversive" had been so great that something had to give immediately after it? Even the placement of "even" is odd; for surely the force of the thought is that these nasty things are said about Quidnunc's poetry even by his admirers, making us wonder what stronger terms his detractors could find, if he has any. But in Mr. Gigadibs's prose it is the admirers that thus intensify from one epithet to the next their hostility against the work they are said to be admiring.

Now Mr. Gigadibs himself is one of the admirers, and he begins the next paragraph by telling us that we shall think these nasty thoughts only if we persist in our stupid old habit of reading the poems from beginning to end; that at least is the sense I take from his sentence: "These qualifications are only relevant [his word order] if we are unable to transcend our purely linear sense of what a poem should be." If we achieve this transcendence, and read properly—not in a purely linear sense—the poems which make up the largest part of the book, we shall be able to share with Mr. Gigadibs the following revelations:

Form in (these poems) is a four-dimensional process, constantly active, never passive, moving through time with the poet. The poems are music-based rather than ideational, the rhythms concentrated in time, avoiding any strict sense of measure. . . .

This is impressive stuff indeed, but I have questions. The dictionary says that "ideational" means "consisting in, or referring to, thought of objects not immediately present to the senses"; is Quidnunc then like the philosophers in Swift who carried with them the things they wished to speak about? Or does it mean that he never thinks? Another question: when one writes or reads a poem, does one expect its rhythms, whether concentrated or diffuse, to be elsewhere than in time? Leaving aside whether an object-in-language, either lying flat on the page or spoken aloud, can possibly be four-dimensional, if it moves with the poet where else than in time could it possibly do so? And another: You can avoid strict measure, but how do you avoid a strict sense of measure? In any event, what about the measure of these lines?

> Slowly the toiling images will arise,
> Shake off, as if it were debris,
>   the unnecessary pleasures of our lives
> And all times and intents of peaceful men
> Reduce to an interim, a passing play. . . .

It is true that Quidnunc doesn't often do this, though in the same passage he has extended quotations from Spenser and Shakespeare that do it for him; what Mr. Gigadibs means may be illustrated also from the same passage:

In the carved panel of the sarcophagus from Golgoi (The Metropolitan Museum of Art, *Handbook of The Cesnoa Collection of Antiquities from Cyprus*. As given in Cook, *Zeus*, vol. two, part one, p. 718).

Finally—or not finally at all, but as far as I am going with him just now—Mr. Gigadibs, somewhat in the voice of Eliot introducing schoolchildren to the *Cantos* of Pound, sees clearly and says sadly and a little wearily that if we don't understand Quidnunc the trouble is that we just plain don't know enough:

Another more obvious stumbling point for the reader is Quidnunc's aggressive syncretism: he is personal rather than confessional and writes within a continuity of tradition. It simply helps to be familiar with Dante, Blake, mythography, medieval history, H. D., William Carlos Williams, Pound, Stein, Zukofsky, Olson, Creeley, and Levertov.

No doubt a continuity of tradition containing ten or twelve items and beginning with Dante and Blake will have to trail off a little toward the end; but a continuity of tradition having one representative around 1300, another around 1800, and all the rest in the last ten minutes may appear as somewhat failing of tradition and continuousness together. As for the difference between being personal and being confessional, I'm no more certain of it than of other of Mr. Gigadibs's 112° antitheses, but after long thought I was able to produce a possible illustration:

> I have bad breath. I am being confessional.
> You have bad breath. I am being personal.

Some Minute Particulars

O N this otherwise happy occasion of the *Post-Dispatch*'s making its century—and long may its pages flap—the editor's mandate to his contributors is formidable, severe, and forbidding: we are to "search for ways to identify a new set of ideals and principles shared by most Americans to form the fabric of a firm social order, while retaining the underpinnings essential in the struggle for democracy and the fullest possible realization of freedom for the individual." The premise for our mission is the agreement of many observers "that the American Dream has been shattered, that many Americans have discarded the old structure but have yet to agree on a new one to guide this country in the future." My own part in all this is indicated by two questions: "Are new directions needed in what our writers are saying or how society receives what they have to say? Does the structure by which the arts are organized and supported need to be changed?"

This is a mighty big order. We are being positively invited, if not indeed firmly instructed, to do some Viewing With Alarm before winding up with positive, practicable recommendations such as "Go thou and do otherwise." As a respectable minor poet not accustomed to seeing a whole civilization change its ways at his bidding, I am a touch bemused as well as bewildered, grateful for being invited to join so distinguished a company but uncertain how to behave in its midst. Sort of typical of poets, I think, not to begin with "What do I think about all this?" but with the more technical question of "What sort of style, tone, voice, is best for dealing with these great and vital, but also vague and general, issues of the time?" But then, as one of my teachers was fond of saying, "How do I know what I think till I see what I say?"

The premise that things is bad all over, that the country is going to hell in a bucket, is very hard to beat, ancient, traditional, honorable as it is. For one thing, if a contributor to a symposium of single voices in individual broom closets were to say, "Well, taking a quick view of western civilization since, say, Easter Week of 1300, which Dante spent in hell, purgatory and heaven, and taking no bets on what may be going to happen tomorrow, I'd say we weren't getting on badly, no, not badly at all," he would surely lay himself open to accusations of wilful blindness, optimism, and above all hardheartedness. For look at all the suffering, the misery, starvation, unemployment, anxiety, inflation, taxes, illness . . . the list could be endless. It would be no defense, either, for such a contributor to point out that, just at the moment at any rate, we are not in The Black Death, the Thirty Years War, that ever so many maladies formerly fatal have been overcome, that our lives, those of ordinary citizens, are comfortable in ways and to a degree beyond what the Sun-King Louis the Fourteenth could have imagined or commanded had he had the imagination. No, all this would not do, and quite properly not. The trouble about evil, whether natural or humanly contrived, is that a very little of it goes such a long way, and the answers to our many and difficult problems will differ extremely depending on whether they are given by people who are going on to dinner at the Ritz or by people who are kept in tiger cages and fed on catfood when fed at all. Nor would it avail for such a contributor to point out that for all the many predictions of doom unless we mend our ways, much wickedness, great tribulations, and maybe even greater inadequacies, are still with us; Chicken-Licken would continue patiently pointing out that the heavens, after all, were really falling this time, and would probably adduce incomprehensible statistical curves to prove it. Alas, it is not only our sins that resulted from the Fall, so did their remedies; so do our virtues.

The first rule for taking an exam is not, as some pupils seem to believe, "Bullshit your way through," which rarely works. It is, "When you don't know the answer, dispute the question." Question the question, argue about its legitimacy, criticize every term in which it is phrased, and finally deny the questioner's right to ask it *in those terms*. It'll get you a C+ almost every time. As I certainly don't know the answers to the editor's questions, that is what I shall have to do, or at any rate try to do.

For one thing, do I know what this American Dream that has been shattered is, or was? Three martinis in every lunchbox? That the rich should be able to lie down on the poor in perfect safety as well as comfort? Liberty and justice for all, and now leave me alone while I go pursue some happiness the way the Declaration says? These do not strike me as responsive, yet they have the minimal virtue of acknowledging my ignorance of what this Dream may really be.

Another of my questions has to do with "a new set of ideals and principles," which comes very close to being a contradiction. Ideals and principles are of all things the ones most firmly identified with the past, the archaic, the springtime of a people. The mere mention of them is almost bound to be followed by reference to Socrates, Jesus, the Buddha, Confucius, followed by a glance at the Hebrew prophets, Magna Carta, the Declaration and the Constitution; even the beginning of all things, in Genesis, is given in the Vulgate as "In principio," meaning that not only in the beginning but also in principle God created the heaven and earth. The sole exception I know of to the above list of venerable notables is Lao-Tse, who was too funny to be included, his view being that wickedness entered the world with the advent of benevolence and right thinking. No, ideals and principles are not all that easy to fashion anew, they are difficult or impossible even by definition: like inventing a new platitude (difficult), or girlwatching in the Men's Room (can't be done).

There follows the appalling question of our adherence in conduct and thought to whatever ideals we do now have or profess. For it does seem as though, while the religious rebuke us for our failure to live up to our ideals, writers, beginning perhaps with Blake and continuing through Ibsen, say, and Shaw, and growing in fervor if not in diagnostic power through the present, have rebuked us for the ideals themselves as containing vast and secret capacities not only for cruelty and injustice but for justifying cruelty and injustice as the greatest virtues, without which civilization must inevitably go to pieces; a sort of moral equivalent of the Second Thermodynamical Law, according to which without a steep gradient between rich and poor, powerful and feeble, no work could get done. The argument, too long to take up here, might best be expressed in a sorry aphorism attributable, say, to a team of anthropologists looking at our lives: "We thought they were sinning against their religion, but no, they were only practicing it."

My last and hardest question is, how do you get a clear overview of something so vast as a civilization? How do you get a handle on so complex a set of variations in order to find their theme? After all, we use in a

single day more printed-upon paper than all Europe used during the whole
of the eighteenth century (I made up that statistic some years ago, to sound
impressive, and no one has ever contradicted it; it must be true), so that
any opinion whatsoever can count on massive and flabbergasting support
from pictures, charts, graphs, percentages of persons polled, and so on.
About this, the poet William Blake instructs us with characteristic vigor
and certainty:—

> He who would do good to another must do it in Minute Particulars:
> General good is the plea of the scoundrel, hypocrite and flatterer,
> For Art & Science cannot exist but in minutely organized Particulars
> And not in generalizing Demonstrations of the Rational Power.
> —*Jerusalem*, plate 55, lines 60–63

Oliver Wendell Holmes took a slightly different slant on the same
question when he announced that the whole business of man upon the
earth is the framing of general propositions, and no general proposition
was ever worth a damn.

But here we touch on some pretty high matters having to do with the
power of language to talk about itself, and therefore to contradict itself,
quesitons associated with mathematics and with such names as Gödel,
Tarski and Russell; all of whom I so perfectly don't understand that I should
get right away from the subject after only one instance: The Barber of
Seville says he shaves every man who does not shave himself. Does he
shave himself?

Retreating from all that in fair order, here is a particular sufficiently
minute drawn from my own business of fooling around with language to
see what turns up; it is an old New England rime ascribed by Bartlett's
Familiar Quotations to that prolific poet Anon:—

> Use it up
> Wear it out
> Make it do
> Do without

I have long liked it for its terseness. But the reason for bringing it up
in this discussion is that it does seem to offer some kind of handle to the
national character with its ideals and principles. Its intention is evidently
to recommend to us as a model for conduct the Puritan virtues of thrift,
frugality, industry, as exemplified in the lives of our forefathers and their

moremothers in building up the country out of their stern and rockbound souls as well as shores; and the tight-lipped, give-nothing-away quality of its diction excellently illustrates the moral instruction offered. Of course, a moment's reflection upon humankind will tell us that our forebears (and moremeres?) must have had among them as many lazy, profligate, lecherous slobs per thousand head of the population as we have among ourselves, so that the little rime reflects not the truth, but only what people a bit later on would like to believe was the truth. Once again, ideals and principles are invariably referred to the past, and the past referred to is always a mythical past.

Now it's a funny thing that if you look again at that little rime, thinking about the present instead of the past, and apply it not to individual behavior but to the nation and the world, you can see a quite different, indeed opposite, reading from what we suppose was its original intention. If you were concerned about ecology and pollution, you might say that far from being a moral instruction to thrift, &c., it is a devastatingly accurate pithy description of what advanced technological civilizations are in fact doing to the earth and its resources, its last line being a plain prophecy of the probable result:—

> Use it up
> Wear it out
> Make it do
> Do without

Drawing on William Blake again, we may use his notion that any honest man is a prophet, because prophecy is nothing but saying, "If you go on thus, the result will be thus." And on Bertrand Russell, who said that for us to have an entirely unambiguous language would be extremely inconvenient, and therefore, thank God, we do not have one. Just imagine, I add, what would happen if we all took a Stop sign to mean unambiguously and exclusively what it said.

One way or another, I was enough taken with the old New England maxim that while driving through Massachusetts and seeing how many towns ended in "ham" (pronounced "em" and meaning a pasture beside water), I answered up as follows:—

> If you can't Wareham
> And don't Needham
> Stoneham
> And Dedham

which I imagine to be another aspect of the national character, as real and as mythological as the first.

Now viewing with alarm and looking into the future are more than national pastimes, they are huge industries appealing to our fears and to our desire for spectacle. Because we all are fated to die, apocalyptic scenarios have a considerable power to thrill and chill at once, and consequently we have a large class of apocalypticians paid handsomely enough for imagining alternative disasters; not only in movies, where burning buildings, sinking ships, and giant sharks are presented as allegories of our predicament, but also in think tanks where serious scholars are said to consider for our good the relative probabilities of (a) nuclear annihilation, (b) overpopulation so severe we shall have to sleep in shifts, and (c) our extinction by boredom owing to immensely increased leisure. On those terms, you not only can't win, you also wouldn't want to.

There is even a new art, with pretensions to science, called Futurism, or Futurology, and I have on my desk (and have but briefly looked into) one of its latest manifestations, called *Handbook of Futures Research*, edited by Jib Fowles (Westport, CT, and London, 1978), from which I learn, first, that the whole business has come into being only during the last decade (which might have mightily surprised the Roman augurs and haruspices, had they been around to know it), and, second, that one chapter, called "The Optimistic Outlook," is followed by another called "The Pessimistic Outlook," offering us a choice of futures to suit—what? our temperaments, perhaps? being in this way like the Letters to the Editor column, often the best and the worst written parts of a newspaper on the same day, where we are offered a balanced sample showing that what is good is bad, and vice versa, and leaving us hopelessly confused in the middle, or muddle.

Of all this looking into the future—which may be what "new ideals and principles" come down to—I imagine a large part to be composed of serious thought and study, another and unfortunately large part to be seriously intended but based on pseudoscientific or at least inapplicable and misunderstood scientific methodology—ever so often the idea appears to be that if you quantify your doubts, uncertainties, or plain ignorance, they will magically turn into knowledge—and a third large part, composed of nuts. We may wish them all well, these thinkers, while keeping to ourselves a little irreverent skepticism just short of the cynical.

For ever since I became conscious, a little, of this great country and this great world, we have been hit by about one major catastrophe a decade (at least), and I should like to look at a couple of these in order to wonder what Futurologists might have had to say about them, had Futurologists—in their present quasi-scientistical form—been among us, which they surely should have predicted being.

The Great Depression, which happened when I was nine. We are told that some savants saw it coming, and that others—not savants, but smart—made their money out of it; nevertheless, it may fairly be allowed to have been a surprise to many, including my parents.

World War II was, or should have been, fairly predictable, not only from the Depression and the German inflation, not only from the establishment of Fascism in Italy in 1922 and in Germany in 1933, but from coming attractions shown all over the world from China, Ethopia and Spain in the middle to late thirties; yet it was not predictable to Neville Chamberlain and his government in 1938, and although it was foreseen by many in our country it was also unforeseen by many in our country, and the mode of our entry into it two years after it started was totally a surprise.

The Drug Culture. All during our youth, the most noticeable sign on any Main Street after dark was, after the movie marquee, one saying DRUGS. Written in letters of light a foot high, and stating its import as plainly as possible, this might have been, and ought to have been, a pillar of fire by night to our soothsayers. But as far as I am aware, no one ever took it in its prophetic sense.

So also with Korea, Vietnam, the rebellion of the youth (probably not over, only sleeping), Watergate, and the derivative Koreagate (which doesn't seem to have the same box-office appeal, maybe too comic).

Atomic fission and fusion inspired so many prophets of what had happened that by now it is hard to remember what they said, save that things was bad all over. We are so delightedly appalled and thrilled with announcements of The End by our sages that we—and they—fail to notice how many great things *have* ended, with cities destroyed, nations going down, torture reinstituted as a matter of course, great empires collapsing in war or revolution or both; as if these things were not sufficiently universal to suit our apocalypticians, who went right on wrongly predicting the next nonevent.

Some time ago I found two simple rules to cover all this sort of thing, and I offer them for the edification of whoever will be edified by them. One was the statement of a general from the Pentagon addressing the Congress: The period of greatest danger, he told the legislators, lies ahead. One imagines everyone nodding solemnly. The other is a fine remark

attributed to President Eisenhower: Things are more like they are now
than they ever were before.

Armed with those two laws we can't go wrong, can we? But I've just
remembered a third, that a friend quoted in our youth as a family proverb:
The future is in the lap of the gods, and they're standing up to see what's
going to happen.

O yes, and while I was writing this I happened to see a headline on
the sports page: MERCY ENDS LOSING STREAK. I surely do hope so. And
you never know what sort of statement is going to be prophecy.

Lewis Thomas, Montaigne,
and Human Happiness

NONE of you is likely to mistake what follows for the Third Annual Thomas Hall Lecture in Biology; nor, unhappily, is the title "On Nature's Mistakes" any longer applicable, unless one of them is being exhibited before you at this very moment. Nevertheless, my thanks to Tom Hall and the Department of Biology for letting me fill in by saying a few things about Lewis Thomas, who has been prevented by illness from addressing us this morning. By the way, I am delighted by the poster publicizing the event. Note its visual wit. [The poster ingeniously showed the process of cell division turning into a flower and I said to my hearers that if I ever found out who made it I would shake his hand or kiss her; turned out to be the latter.]

Every so seldom, the reading public leaves off enriching the authors of those large, loose baggy monsters of novels usually advertised as "blockbusters"—though "insomnia-stoppers" would be more appropriate—and puts its money on good sense, great learning, cheerfulness, and charm. This happened several years ago to Dr. Thomas's first book, and seems to be happening again to his second; we might pause a moment to applaud our own taste and judgment, while wondering a little why we don't exhibit these qualities a touch more often. Indeed, I came pretty close to not reading *The Lives of a Cell* in the first place, just because, being a snob, I thought it might be a touch too popular. But curiosity won out, and I started reading, and was hooked. After the first, the title essay, I warned myself to take the book easy: one essay a night, I told myself, would be the only way to do fairly by such a work; so of course during the first night I read through the whole damn thing, about thirty brief essays; and the second night I did the same, and the third night the same again.

By that time even I knew I was beginning to be interested in Dr. Thomas, and as soon as *The Lives of a Cell* appeared in paperback I ordered it for my class, as I expect to do with *The Medusa and the Snail* as well, when that gets into paperback. What the class was doing playing hookey from Great Literature and reading a work described as "Notes of a Biology Watcher" is an interesting question chiefly because I can't answer it. But many years ago a student did a tutorial with me in which we read not whole books but a few sentences; our thoughts about the few sentences made up the tutorial hour; whereupon the student gave me this enlightened definition of reading, "I see what reading is," she said. "It's putting together what you've got with what it says." So I put it to the class that we would read aloud from *The Lives of a Cell* for a few minutes at the start of the hour, the governing rule being that students could stop the reader at any point at which they (a) didn't understand, (b) wanted further elaboration, (c) disagreed, (d) had something pertinent to add of their own. I hoped that perhaps something of Dr. Thomas's style might rub off on us, along with his marvelous complex-yet-integrated mode of composition— composition in its literal sense of putting things together, or as Kenneth Burke calls it, What Goes With What? And if an English class happened to learn something about biology—not learn biology, of course, but learn about it—well, that was probably forgivable.

I don't know whether our results from this exercise show failure or success. For I remember that at our first attempt, instead of the few minutes' reading we had planned, the hour and a half went by and we hadn't got quite through the second page. Dr. Thomas not only thinks, he is also the cause that thoughts are in others.

Of course, many of our initial difficulties came from our not knowing the language; the first two pages bring up, quite without explanation except what is supplied by context, such items as mitochondria, prokaryocytes, rhizobial bacteria, and others that had to be explained by one of our few biology students or else looked up. All the same, we already had the sense of being talked to as grown-ups by a grown-up and not by a textbook; and we found it bracing.

Besides, Dr. Thomas's method of instruction is itself instructive, organized on a sort of musical contrapuntal model, something like a passacaglia with melodic variations played over a more or less constant progression in the ground, so that if something eluded or baffled us on its first appearance, we had but to wait a bit for it to turn up in several new forms, or be introduced from several new angles and in new applications. For instance, when we predictably broke down at the phrase "opaque to probability" on the very first page, my having run the book through several times was a help, as I could direct the class's attention ahead some twenty pages to where the phrase was elaborated, and again two dozen essays further on, where an entire piece was given over to the discussion of how improbable we are. Perhaps this very point, our opacity in the face of "opaque to probability," offers a good opening illustration of Thomas's combinatorial style:

If, as I believe, the urge to make a kind of music is as much a characteristic of biology as our other fundamental functions, there ought to be an explanation for it. Having none at hand, I am free to make one up. The rhythmic sounds might be the recapitulation of something else—an earliest memory, a score for the transformation of inanimate, random matter in chaos into the improbable, ordered dance of living forms. Morowitz has presented the case, in thermodynamic terms, for the hypothesis that a steady flow of energy from the inexhaustible source of the sun to the unfillable sink of outer space by way of the earth is mathematically destined to cause the organization of matter into an increasingly ordered state. The resulting balance act involves a ceaseless clustering of bonded atoms into molecules of higher and higher complexity, and the emergence of cycles for the storage and release of energy. In a nonequilibrium steady state, which is postulated, the solar energy would not just flow to the earth and radiate away; it is thermodynamically inevitable that it must rearrange matter into symmetry, away from probability, against entropy, lifting it, so to speak, into a constantly changing condition of rearrangement and molecular ornamentation. In such a system, the outcome is a chancy kind of order, always on the verge of descending into chaos, held taut against probability by the unremitting constant surge of energy from the sun.

If there were to be sounds to represent this process, they would have the arrangement of the Brandenburg Concertos for my ear, but I am open to wonder whether the same events are recalled by the rhythms of insects, the long, pulsing runs of birdsong, the descants of whales, the modulated vibrations of a million locusts in migration, the tympani of gorilla breasts, termite heads, drumfish bladders. A "grand canonical ensemble" is, oddly enough, the proper term for a quantitative model system in thermodynamics, borrowed from music by way of mathematics. Borrowed back again, provided with notation, it would do for what I have in mind.

What a splendid bargain we get in a passage like that! Before reading it, we had just one thing we didn't understand, and now we have ten more. But that is the way we learn, really; by listening to the great conversation, parroting the big words, making the truly interesting mistakes that may turn into discoveries; understanding comes along later. In this way we imitate, however feebly, our first and greatest intellectual achievement, learning to talk, which we did in our first few years—beginning, indeed, when we couldn't say a word—and without even taking a course of lessons from Berlitz or going to a university. After that, we were schlepped off to school—shades of the prison house surround the growing boy and girl—and taught, with Miltonic labor and difficulty, the visual equivalents for the sounds we had been making so effortlessly all along. What a pair of triumphs! No wonder if after two such victories we slump our heads down on the desk and accomplish nothing further all our lives save sit around and listen to our hair grow. But that's another story.

Returning to the passage I read, there are several things to be remarked. One is the ease and authority of the style. Another is the learning, and above all the valency of the learning, that makes it possible. The whole paragraph is chockablock with information. It would be tempting to imitate, we may think; but if we tried to do it without learning we'd probably not get through a single paragraph before noticing that we were like little Disney animals who stand safely on a branch that's been sawn off, but only until they look down. Another thing to remark on is music, one of Thomas's big and constant analogies; the equation of music, but especially Bach's music, to thought occurs over and over again. That's why I have today asked the organist to supply a couple of examples for us. Dr. Thomas recommends the *St. Matthew Passion*, with the volume turned up all the way, if we want to hear thought thinking itself; but what does it for me is the *Mass in B-minor*, so because I am the one doing the show today I asked for the *Gloria*, with its wonderful fugue on *Et In Terra Pax*, and the *Domine Deus*. In the *Domine Deus*, the alto first sings to God the Father while the tenor sings in canon with her to God the Son; so that we happily infer without strain that the orchestra is singing to the Holy Ghost, completing the contrapuntal Trinity.

Here is another bit about music, about Bach. Thomas has been talking about communication with extraterrestrial civilizations, about an international program "to probe the reaches of deep space for electromagnetic signals making sense." And then he characteristically and, to my knowledge, uniquely, raises the dumbfounding question of what out of the world we're going to say to the other civilizations out there (assuming there are some; I think, myself, that never in the history of the world has anyone been alone the way we're alone; but that too is another story); and here is his recommendation:

Perhaps the safest thing to do at the outset, if technology permits, is to send music. This language may be the best we have for explaining what we are like to others in space, with least ambiguity. I would vote for Bach, all of Bach, streamed out into space, over and over again. We would be bragging, of course, but it is surely excusable for us to put the best possible face on at the beginning of such an acquaintance. We can tell the harder truths later. And, to do ourselves justice, music would give a fairer picture of what we are really like than some of the other things we might be sending, like *Time*, say, or a history of the U.N. or Presidential speeches. We could send out our science, of course, but just think of the wincing at this end when the polite comments arrive two hundred years from now. Whatever we offer as today's items of liveliest interest are bound to be out of date and irrelevant, maybe even ridiculous. I think we should stick to music.

Music is one of the big and constant analogies for our author. The other two are bugs and words.

Now I suppose that if I started out to give you a lecture on termites and suddenly began talking about language, you would charitably conclude that my senility was showing, or that I had merely confounded entomology with etymology. And you'd probably be right; it's one of the unforeseen disabilities of teaching as a profession that when senility sets in it happens in public. But when Dr. Thomas does it, somehow, he makes the resemblance work strikingly to illumination.

. . . but if you think about the construction of the Hill by a colony of a million ants, each one working ceaselessly and compulsively to add perfection to his region of the structure without having the faintest notion of what is being constructed elsewhere, living out his brief life in a social enterprise that extends back into what is for him the deepest antiquity (ants die at the rate of 3–4 percent per day; in a month or so an entire generation vanishes, while the Hill can go on for sixty years or, given good years, forever), performing his work with infallible, undistracted skill in the midst of a confusion of others, all tumbling over each other to get the twigs and bits of earth aligned in precisely the right configurations for the warmth and ventilation of the eggs and larvae, but totally incapacitated by isolation, there is only one human activity that is like this, and it is language.

We have been working at it for what seems eternity, generation after articulate generation, and still we have no notion how it is done, nor what it will be like when finished, if it is ever to be finished. It is the most compulsively collective, genetically programmed, species-specific, and autonomic of all the things we do, and we are infallible at it. It comes naturally. We have DNA for grammar, neurons for syntax. We can never let up; we scramble our way through one civilization after another, metamorphosing, sprouting tools and cities everywhere, and all the time new words keep tumbling out.

If one had to pick a single motto for the procedures of this kind of analogical, several-leveled and four-voiced kind of thought, it might be Dr. Thomas's saying—about every relation in the universe—"I suggest . . . we turn it around." Instead of trying to have thoughts about music, start with music as the model for thought. Ants and termites are not miniaturized human beings, but human societies have remarkable resemblances to insect societies. We make language in rather the way termites build their mounds. And so on.

Counterpoint is but one aspect of the process of combination, separation, recall, and recombination. Dance is only one aspect of the movement. The darting forward to meet new pairs of notions, built into new aggregates, the orbiting and occasional soaring of massive aggregates out of orbit and off into other spaces, most of all the continual switching of solitary particles of thought from one orbit into the next, like electrons, up and down depending on the charges around and the masses involved, accomplished as though by accident but always adhering to laws—all these have the look of music. There is no other human experience they can remind one of.

I suggest, then, that we turn it around. Instead of using what we can guess at about the nature of thought to explain the nature of music, start over again. Begin with music and see what this can tell us about the sensation of thinking. Music is the effort we make to explain to ourselves how our brains work. We listen to Bach transfixed because this is listening to a human mind. *The Art of the Fugue* is not a special pattern of thinking, it is not thinking about any particular thing. The spelling out of Bach's name in the great, unfinished layers of fugue at the end is no more than a transient notion, something flashed across the mind. The whole piece is not about thinking about something, it is about thinking. If you want, as an experiment, to hear the whole mind working, all at once, put on *The St. Matthew*

Passion and turn the volume up all the way. That is the sound of the whole central nervous system of human beings, all at once.

To me, this sort of thing represents the revitalized return of the polyvalent, polysemous kind of thinking you can hear in *The Paradiso*, even perhaps, attenuated, in *The Tempest*, and which tended so to go under during the scientific revolution before the new linear logic—sponsored by, among others, Blake's favorite villains: Bacon & Newton & Locke. But as Blake forgave that demonic trinity at the end of *Jerusalem*, so the old contrapuntal and deeply physical style of thinking now comes back redeemed by the addition of so much that has been learned during the intervening centuries. What a fascinating theme! But I must get on to the second and third items of my title.

Edward O. Wilson, on the dust jacket of *The Medusa and the Snail*, says that if Montaigne had possessed a deep knowledge of twentieth-century biology, he would have been Lewis Thomas. Something about this comparison, or the way it is put, strikes me as strained, perhaps because the earlier man ought always to be given the advantage of being the compared to, not the comparative. But perhaps bug-scholars, because they study such small things, are given to grandiose comparisons; one of Professor Wilson's precursors in entomology, William Morton Wheeler, was described by one of his colleagues as the only living human capable of conversing on equal terms with Aristotle. I take "only living human" to be Cambridge shorthand for "only living human on the Harvard faculty"; but never mind.

There's something to the comparison all the same. When I couldn't get *The Medusa and the Snail* for my class last term, I—as if naturally—got a selection of Montaigne's essays instead. And Dr. Thomas's affection to Montaigne comes up in a friendly essay called "Why Montaigne Is Not a Bore." The idea is that as Montaigne wrote always and only about himself he ought to have been a bore merely by definition; but he isn't, and the reason is that he was the scientist of himself; as Dr. Thomas says of him:

He is, as he says everywhere, an ordinary man. He persuades you of his ordinariness on every page. You cannot help but believe him in this; he is, above all else, an honest and candid man. And here is the marvel of his book: if Montaigne is an ordinary man, then what an encouragement, what a piece of work is, after all, an ordinary man! You cannot help but hope.

I think the appropriate basis of comparison here is happiness: "For my part," says Montaigne in age and pain, "I love life and cultivate it." And again, in age and pain, "I speak ignorance opulently and pompously, and speak knowledge meagerly and piteously ... there is nothing I treat specifically except nothing, and no knowledge except that of the lack of knowledge." Again, "Wonder is the foundation of all philosophy, inquiry its progress, ignorance its end."

Happiness is a difficult and dangerous subject, especially before an audience of youngs, the brightest of whom are probably just discovering the tremendous literary and erotic mileage to be got out of such ultraviolet words as *despair* and *angst* and *suffering* and *the human condition*, just discovering Kierkegaard, meaning *churchyard* and Kafka, meaning *jackdaw*.

And yet happiness is what it's about. I don't mean unitive experience, ecstasy, visionary rapture, a high however brought about, transcendental muddletation—though Thomas has a piece "On Transcendental Meta-worry (TMW)," from which one last illustration, the mantra:

The word "worry," repeated quite rapidly ... the recollection that it derives from the Indo-European root *wer*, meaning to turn or bend in the sense of evading, which became *wyrgan* in Old English, meaning to kill by strangling, with close relatives "weird," "writhe," "wriggle," "wrestle," and "wrong."

It's nice to catch him out for once. He missed *war*, which belongs to the same cluster.

The happiness meant is rather the steady sort of delight that comes from doing something well, knowing you are doing it well, and being modestly pleased at doing it well; the sort of feeling you might have on setting forth in fair weather for your work, heart, lungs, bowels, and brain doing what they're supposed to so you don't have to think about them— indeed, happiness is not thinking about yourself, as health is not having to think about your body, and to what effect? As Thomas says,

If I were informed tomorrow that I was in direct communication with my liver, and could now take over, I would become deeply depressed. I'd sooner be told, forty thousand feet over Denver, that the 747 jet in which I had a coach seat was now mine to operate as I pleased. . . .

That is the sort of happiness I find, in so different yet resembling ways, in Lewis Thomas and Montaigne. Had Montaigne never written as he did, no one in the late sixteenth century could have found expressed what it sounds like to be a human being in the midst of his days and preoccupations—an ordinary human being, instead of a factory for chewing up books and excreting smart-ass notions. Lewis Thomas relates in somewhat similar fashion to the present time, when to watch the morning news is like starting the day with a nice rousing Black Mass, when newspapers never carry such items as that Joe Soap of 1492 Locust Avenue was nice to his mother yesterday . . . and so on and so on.

You will have observed that the curriculum contains no course labeled Felicity 297, and maybe it's just as well, even if the Founding Fathers assert our right to pursue the stuff. Maybe it's significant that the U.S. Air Force designation P for Pursuit aircraft faded out about 1945 or so, to be replaced by F for Fighter.

But happiness, like philosophy—if indeed it isn't just what Socrates meant by philosophy—begins in wonder, in simple amazement (which means being lost in a maze) or astonishment (which means being hit by lightning and the all-dreaded thunder stone) that things are exactly as they are.

And now this piece about Lewis Thomas's essays has gone on so much longer than one of his essays as to be a disgrace. I conclude, for no good reason at all, with my one homemade Jewish joke:

> Why did God permit evil in the world?
> God permitted evil in the world so we could
>   all have jobs.
> Aha! then what about unemployment?
> So evil he didn't make perfect either.

And we may hope that next year Dr. Thomas will be here to give us the word "On Nature's Mistakes."

With what measure ye mete, it shall be measured to you again.

—Matthew 7:2

For it is not meters, but a meter-making argument that makes a poem.

— Emerson, "The Poet"

Lively boys write to their ear and eye, and the cool reader finds nothing but sweet jingles in it. When they grow older, they respect the argument.

—Emerson, "Nominalist and Realist"

On the Measure of Poetry

I BEGIN with my first assertion: poetry is a way of getting something right in language. I call that either a point of faith or an axiom because that is what it has come to be for myself. I do not mean that it is beyond discussion or that I refuse to discuss it, only perhaps that if you do not agree there is no logical proof of the assertion. So I ask you to consider it as a hypothesis and of possible interest not so much for a precedent and supporting reason it does not in any case have but for the somewhat radical consequences that flow from it.

I am fairly certain that some of you have already raised a couple of related objections in your own minds. "What he is saying is, after all, only subjective," is one; and the other: "His rightness will not always or even very often be mine; how do we decide between them?" Whereupon we find ourselves back in the criticism and aesthetics business once again, condemned to the enunciation of a good many eternal principles of art which, as a matter of experience, fail to outlive the works they pretend to judge.

There are many ideas of rightness, both at the same time and at different times. To admit this is not in the least to make the idea of rightness disappear. If you glance over very rapidly the successive periods of poetry in English you see that one or more ideas of how to do things govern the poets of an age. We ourselves, coming so much later, seem prepared to put up with, and even appreciate, all these different views of being right, until we come down to our own time. The poetry of our own time is my subject, but I shall take my own time, too, about getting to it.

Here is a convenient example. In Donne's time the way of doing things that later become the heroic couplet did not have, either among poets generally or in Donne's own idiosyncratic way of going, the qualities of balance and snap and decisiveness that marked it in the hands first of Dryden and finally of Pope. It may have been Donne's satires, which show him at his roughest, that in equal parts provoked and inspired Coleridge to write his epigram:

> With Donne, whose muse on dromedary trots,
> Wreathe iron pokers into true-love knots;
> Rhyme's sturdy cripple, fancy's maze and clue,
> Wit's forge and fire-blast, meaning's press and screw.

Donne is acknowledged to be a god, but the god is Hephaestus. Now Pope seems to have had similarly mixed feelings about Donne's satires, that Donne was a true poet, that the satires were remarkably good stuff . . . only they just weren't right. So Pope rewrote some of them. Perhaps, though I do not know for certain, his reason was the same as that so often given by the revisers of Shakespeare: that both poets were possessed of genius but wrote in a still barbarous state of the language that a century of innovation had refined. Anyhow, the comparison is instructive. I suppose that what Pope chiefly meant to do was to regularize the measure, close the couplets, prevent run-ons, and suchlike; but of course like any translator he ran into trouble both with Donne's and with his own gifts so that he wrote in essence very different poems, smoother and more harmonious, but less complex, less rapid, and with less immediacy following the motions of the mind. Donne seems in these poems always urgent, always hurried, in the quick forge and working-house of thought; Pope's versions are more reflective and at a greater distance from their subject matter.

The Age of Pope makes the most convenient example for the discussion of rightness at a particular period because it is the simplest idea, at least in the sense that the poets of that age simply did heroic couplets as though there were nothing else; once or twice in a lifetime, as J. V. Cunningham has observed, such a poet might commit a song, hymn, or ode; otherwise, heroic couplets were identical with poetry. In consequence of that very simple notion of what was right to do, poets—and most visibly

Pope himself—developed the keenest power of hearing wrongness as
well; the principle this power illustrates is most tersely put by Wallace
Stevens in two propositions and a conclusion:

> A. A violent order is disorder; and
> B. A great disorder is an order. These
> Two things are one.

Only someone persuaded he knows what is right is capable of being definite about what is wrong. Saint Paul said it: by the law I came to know sin.

One can see from the examples Pope collected, from his own early
verses as well as from his enemies', in the essay called "Peri Bathous; or,
The Art of Sinking in Poetry," that his strictures, especially when they bear
on the musical part of poetry, have become almost unintelligible to us
with our more permissive views of the art. He himself had a lofty, austere,
and narrow view of what was canonical, and though the principles of it
were largely musical, physiological, and hence tacit, he could condemn by
ear whatever did not live up to them. His favorite among his own verses
is said to have been one from "The Dunciad"—

> Lo where Maeotis sleeps, and hardly flows
> The freezing Tanais thro' a waste of Snows.
>   [3.79–80]

The point here seems to be not wit (though wit is the point of the passage
from which it is drawn) but beauty, a very complex harmony drawn from
the infinite possibility of arranging and relating sounds. It reminds me of
having heard a composer say that a theme of Mozart's extending over only
four measures contained more parameters than a computer could digest
at once. (Leon Kirchner, in conversation.)

Concluding this part of the discussion, I recommend to you, for further
study of this aspect of rightness which I have called musical, physiological,
and hence tacit, a beautiful essay by Kenneth Burke, "On Musicality in
Verse," in *The Philosophy of Literary Form*.

If, in your rapid survey of the periods of poetry, you can acknowledge
the existence, more visible at some times than at others, of a kind of period sense of how to do it, what Owen Barfield calls, with reference to the
Elizabethans, "joint stock company poetry," I believe you will also see the
idea, as you approach our own century and our own time, becoming more
various and, what is almost the same thing, more dubious. This is partly

owing to the accumulation of history and partly perhaps to a growing self-consciousness. To each successive age the forms of one more past age become available, if only to be rejected. And sometimes, probably very often in fact, it is the outward and visible part of the form that is copied, and not its inward spirit: so that English poets in the nineteenth century who turned to drama wrote fake Shakespearean drama; and so, as Coleridge tartly said of Prior, piling two quatrains on top of a hexameter does not really make a Spenserian stanza. Considerations of this kind bring me to the next subject, the relation of the idea of rightness to verse forms.

The misunderstanding of this relation has produced, and continues to produce, a good deal of abuse by critics and self-abuse by poets. "Get rid of the idiocy of the iambic!" cries a contemporary critic, somewhat iambically or at any rate more so than in the verses he sometimes writes. And much might be said of the successive revolutionettes in the art of poetry that begin their brief lives of manifesto and example on the slogan "Look, ma, no feet." But I shall resist the temptation in favor of holding to the subject, on the motto I have adopted from a hero of Henry James's, who "didn't aspire to be thought profound, but only decently continuous." And yet it is puzzling to reflect how very much of the attack on tradition in the name of "the modern" and even "the postmodern" has borne hard upon the liberation from rime and regular measure, as though somehow these two negatives would add up to the positive freedom everyone desires, and as though this same freedom were always to be won again; though it is quite well known that liberty from "the troublesom and modern bondage of Rimeing" had been successfully asserted by Milton, and only a little less well known that Blake in *Jerusalem* did the same for regular measure, or what he called "a Monotonous Cadence." Both poets, it is true, considered these liberties peculiarly appropriate to heroic, or epical, poetry, and we do not at present visibly have any of that.

In the recurrent outcry against "iambic pentameter" I do not remember anyone's having addressed himself to the following problem, that when we speak, we just *do* hover about an iambic norm. Between two accents our language in the main admits of either one or two unaccented syllables, three being a rare exception and four, I suppose, almost impossible. Any four- or five- or six-beat phrase in those two sentences will illustrate their claim.

English verse, in other words, does not consist in the introduction of a regularity instead of chaos; rather it brings out, by relatively slight insistences, a regularity already there in prose. Writers in prose must surely notice very often that part of their job is the suppression of this regularity and tendency to lollop along iambically, which, being intrinsic to the language, is not always easy to resist, and especially hard to resist as one rises in the direction of eloquence, solemnity, the sublime, etc. And the prose writer must do this without failing into the trap on the other side, where anapest and dactyl lie waiting to destroy his sense with their jingling. It is as though verse were the primal way of going about by mouth, with prose the late, sophisticated, and difficult derivative.

2

Now it is very obvious that regular measure and rime, and stanza or sonnet or whatever, may be used to give a perfectly fraudulent impression of rightness; it is in fact this glib and empty neatness that distinguishes greeting card verses and the poems of lady poets (of both sexes) with three names, such as Emma Woodbine Weed. One would have thought it equally obvious, if only by the continued employment of these mechanisms by masters right down to the present time, that there must be something more to the matter. Maybe the stanza is not the mere box, the room to which its name alludes, most likely an attic to be filled with whatever is of least use somehow-anyhow, but rather more like—there must be many better comparisons—a labyrinth through which the sentence dances, a slalom to be run exactly and with elegantly appropriate variations of the pace:

> Blasted with sighs, and surrounded with teares,
>   Hither I come to seeke the spring.
>   And at mine eyes, and at mine eares,
> Receive such balmes, as else cure every thing;
>   But O, selfe traytor, I do bring
> The spider love, which transubstantiates all,
>   And can convert Manna to gall,
> And that this place may thoroughly be thought
> True Paradise, I have the serpent brought.
>   Donne, "Twicknam Garden"

This is not a manifesto, and I am not exhorting young poets to return to the triolet, or the sonnet, or whatever; in fact, I've an obscure sense that they would disgrace themselves if they did. A good many things may definitely be over, and with good reason beyond reviving. "Certain ideas gestures rhymes," said cummings, "like Gillette Razor Blades / having been used and reused / to the mystical moment of dullness emphatically are / Not To Be Resharpened." But it might not be amiss to think for a moment about what these regularities signified.

They are mechanisms, that is quite clear, though it is also true that they are very flexible ones; English heroic line is already about as close to freedom as many of us dare go, for freedom is as dangerous as it is attractive. They are mechanisms, the patterns of feet, the patterns of rime, the patterned stanzas and closed forms such as the sonnet, but they are not mere mechanisms. In an odd way they seem to represent the world itself in its either pious or stupid comings and goings, its regular recurrences and rhythmical repetitions, cosmic in the heavens, terrene in the tides, physiological in the beating of the heart. They represent the outside, the constancy in what is constantly there, and what they represent may be somewhat cold and not altogether lovable—but it doesn't go away on that account. They existed in poetry, I think, as a continuing reminder to the poet that he didn't do it all on his own; they were there to be worked with and against simultaneously, and they beat perceptibly beneath the most extravagant and beautiful variation—

And with old woes new wail my deare times waste

—which is why we apprehend it as a variation and not as something else entirely.

The patterns, I say, *represent* the outside, the unalterable conditions of things; they are not themselves those conditions, so they are dispensable. But the conditions are not so dispensable, so that it comes to this: when you get rid of the regularities of verse, what regularities will you find to replace them? This is not the occasion for a lecture on versification. Doubtless many poets abandoned the regularities because they thought it easy and contemptible to secure an impression of rightness by mechanical means. And many poets abandoned the regularities because they wanted life to be easier than it is. Neither party, whether shunning ease or seeking it, found any continuously effective replacement for what had been thrown out, but enough remained over to keep things going with sufficient, or almost sufficient, appearance of order. What remained? Grammar remained, rhythm remained (though measure didn't), and the sentence especially, that stern though possibly corrupt guarantor that anyone who opens his mouth makes sense, the sentence especially remained, though its rather complex relations with line and stanza were gone or occurred at the best adventitiously. It is pertinent to ask, in these revolutionary times, how does it happen that the sentence has not been banished from poetry? Possibly because the sentence is received by us so early as the principle of order in language and indeed in the universe that we find it unthinkable to be without it. When people make the attempt, as some now and then do, in Dada and in Concrete Poetry, they seem to find it necessary to fall back on more primitive principles of patterning such as repetition of nonsense syllables, acrostic variations, or typographical rearrangements of single words, and so on ... which of course bring back in the regularities that have been thrown out. It is possible in this way to have order without meaning, just as it is possible for a society to have order without justice.

With the sentence, too, there remained, if only because it was as near as not language itself and could not be suppressed by any speaker, the quasi-accidental patterning of relations among a relatively small number of like sounds, which makes it inevitable that four lines, say, of a poem in free verse will yield about the same number of cross-relations among their vowels and consonants as a line or so of a Shakespeare sonnet.

To sum up on forms and rightness. No one wants poetry to be like filling out a form, though plenty of poems look dismally like it. The forms were there to be wrestled with mightily, because they silently and emptily, till one filled them up with the thing said, stood for the recalcitrant outside and other that knows nothing of the human will. The mindless rigidity in principle of the verse patterns suggestively compounded with the sinewy nature of the speaking voice that flowed in continuous energy through the marked-off graph of foot and line and strophe. Together they might be taken to stand for two powers of the mind that ought to work with and against one another to the same effect: the streamy nature of association, said Coleridge, that thinking curbs and rudders. Ezra Pound's commandment to the poet, to compose in the sequence of the musical phrase, not in the sequence of the metronome, is a good warning against monotonous cadences; but taken literally it invites the reply that Beethoven did both. For art is a place where you make choices, sometimes difficult ones that require you to decide not between good and bad but between this good and that: very often it is between the beauty of a line and the sense of the whole thing. A proverb says that you can't do two things at once, but it is conspicuous that in art you must always be doing two things at once, knowing that that is only the minimum requirement:

And twofold Always. May God us keep
From Single vision & Newton's sleep!

Of course, it will be objected, all that is changing, we're bored with it, we want something else. I quite agree, and have no interest at all in telling people what they must do or ought to do in the practice of an art. But I want to be as clear as I can be about what is changing, what is being abandoned, and what remains. For I do believe that one's stylistic choices in art are moral ones and that the set of the spirit at a given time toward the apparently trivial question of whether to write in quatrains has probably a more telling effect upon the life of the world outside of poetry than does the content or meaning or moral of any poet's poems. Style is the ultimate morality of mind, said Whitehead, and bless him for not explaining what he meant.

The sense of the foregoing discussion is twofold. I have tried to show that there has visibly existed at various times a way of doing things in poetry that seem right; that idea of rightness, in effect, is what enables us to distinguish various periods, and a more elaborate inspection of the idea would have included comment on poetic diction. Then, in dwelling upon forms and what they meant, I came close to suggesting that the present age might be abandoning not merely the external trappings by which one comes to the idea of rightness in poetry but also the thing itself. I must now deal with the thing itself more directly.

3

When you look at a poem you see that it goes down the page and goes across the page; not quite as prose does, for in prose going across the page is only a way of going down the page. Prose is a way of getting on, poetry a way of lingering. Going across the page, that is, becomes something like an independent dimension, one having to do with sense, sound, breath. Poetry shares with prose the phrase, the sentence, and even something which the strophe has to do with the paragraph; only the line, the idea of the line, is distinctive. I suppose that is as true of free verse as of bound. Maybe more conspicuously true in free verse, or cadanced verse, for when you subtract the notion of a steady measure you are left with only the set of the voice, the set of the phrase in a sentence, to tell you what is a line. If you wanted to describe the difference between prose and poetry, you might go at it in that manner, remembering however that all

border areas are disputed areas; the line that defines something is equivocally in that something or outside it.

Does it mean anything that poetry should emphasize going across the
page as well as down the page? Maybe something like this, that being
somewhere matters as much as going somewhere; the unit is to be looked
at for itself *and* as a part of something larger than itself. Observe that often
one quotes from a poem not a sentence, but a line—

> the viol, the violet, and the vine. . . .

> the apple tree, the singing, and the gold. . . .

> when the bronze annals of the oak tree close. . . .

—and that these things have a singular existence, a peculiar beauty as
themselves apart from their other, not negligible, contributions to the whole.

I have observed further that some poets seem to think of the line as
the unit of brilliance, the unit of the image, even perhaps to the extent of
creating beautiful lines at the expense of the poems to which they belong:
Hopkins, for example, or Dylan Thomas; while others prefer a plain con-
secution of argument to which they may sacrifice—at least I suspect so—
lines splendid in themselves, which by an effect of lingering slow the pace
and moil the clear waters of the thought.

In poems, then, you have to consider lines by themselves, and lines as
moving beyond themselves.

What is a line of poetry? Probably a hopeless inquiry, if you want absolute definition. For it is in the nature of syntax that numerous lines have
to exist largely for the purpose of getting on and will be of little interest,
and no very decisive character, alone. Yet something may be said.

> O carue not with thy howers my loues faire brow.

This line of Shakespeare's is distinguished by no great individuality of
sentiment or figure. Recognizably a line, it may be scanned in five or four,
it completes itself syntactically, and so has a cadence inseparably related
to our sense of its meaning. Saying it over, you notice some other small
factors enforcing the idea of its being one thing: the relation of sound
whereby "brow" echoes "howers," "loues" a little more glancingly echoes
"carue," the rv of "carue" is audibly turned round in the br of "brow," and
so forth. It might be tempting to say that there are certain relationships.

But if you say so, you are forced to allow that they are most uncertain relationships, unsystematic and unpredictable, not the same in (probably) any two lines. Nor is it likely that the poet gave a great deal of conscious attention to the matter or began by putting the problem thus: rv... br. Not likely, but not impossible either. The point seems to be that *some* relationship of like sounds was thought appropriate, or inversely that one characteristic of a person who writes poetry is an odd affinity for echoes and consonances.

In the archaic economy of poetry, a relation in sound is a relation in sense, though often enough a magical and unprovable relation in sense:

> For ruin hath taught me thus to ruminate ...

where one might wish to say that ruminate comes up "because of" ruin, where the prose word might have been "think" or "meditate." Attic shape, shape, fair *atti*tude. Yeats has supplied an apt descriptive name for this not wholly conscious activity of the mind poetizing: he calls it "stitching":

> A line will take us hours maybe;
> Yet if it does not seem a moment's thought,
> Our stitching and unstitching has been naught.

Now the same thing, of course, happens in prose, though we tend not to think as much of it while reading prose; yet I think the difference observably a difference having to do with the nature of the line, even if it is probable that the secret of all good style, in prose or in verse, has to do with the more or less subtle disposition of related consonants which mark the rhythm and give as it were a bite to the attack even of the inward voice that reads in silence.

From a book lying open on my desk the first sentence I hit on tells me that "The historical process of human society exhibits a rhythmical tendency." This breaks into two lines of verse, even into a rude sort of couplet:

> The historical process of human society
> Exhibits a rhythmical tendency.

When it is so broken, one reads it with the sort of attention that fetches up relations of the sort we found in the Shakespeare line. Perhaps it is a characteristic of poetry, both writing it and reading it, that this attention seems to be limited so that the phrasings of poetry, and even its larger syntactical units, will likely be shorter than the phrasings of prose; this too has something to do with the nature of a line.

This stitching of like sounds takes place within rather narrow limits between the extremes of absolute likeness and absolute difference; even the nearest one could rationally come to absolute likeness—"Never, never, never, never, never" (*King Lear*)—remains a very special effect; while to absolute difference the approach may be no closer. Even where a poet seems to have set himself against "music" in every obvious sense, the relatively small number of sounds at his disposal insures that some sort of "music" shall be produced. For this reason, the common habit of praising poets for their "ear" (as if, what occasionally seems true, they had but one) does not usually produce significant statements; the poet can't help it altogether, and a shopping list may be capable of as eloquent a recital as a song. For instance, an English train whose departure is announced from Paddington:

> Reading Didcot Swindon
> Bath Bristol Taunton Exeter
> Newton Abbot
> Plymouth
> And Principal Stations to Penzance.

It weakens, as things will, in the middle. But what a last line!

It

(Commencement Address at Bennington College)

WHAT I want to describe is somewhat mysterious, and has so many names that in effect it becomes nameless; for the moment I shall leave it as nearly in that condition as possible and refer to it only as It.

We are all in it, even or especially when we feel we are not of it, or are outside it.

It is so constituted that everything any of us says about it is simultaneously true, false, meaningless, and irrelevant; moreover, what we say about it is said within it and so expresses as much it as what we think about it: as though the needle of a speedometer should believe its movement constituted thoughts about speed.

We believe that no proper description can be part of what it describes; yet it happens over and over that our descriptive attempts reveal themselves to be symptoms. I notice already, for a trivial example, how many times I am compelled to say "it" in the casual course of a sentence, when I don't mean It at all but only one of the many its within It, some of them having only a grammatical existence.

Our all being in It strikes each of us in a different way, in many different ways, yet nothing about It seems more constant than our wish that It may exist in one way, preferably specifiable, preferably determinate . . . but failing that we think we would settle for one way unspecifiable and indeterminate—which we realize, however, that we could not stand. Our various ways of compromising with the situation have such names as art, science, religion, learning, all of them altars to the unknown It, wherein

are enshrined the sometimes heart-breakingly beautiful stories we tell of
It, or It insists on having told of Itself by our means.

To this dubious end it permits us miracles of apprehension wonderful
beyond the limits of belief: the mind can think such thoughts as make the
mind look stupid, even to itself.

At the same time It encourages us in the belief that any part of it,
anything so small as leaf or stone, might be all of It; a kind of external
soul, or the one brick whose removal brings down the cathedral.

Those legends are suggestive, but dangerous: do they mean our wish
is to understand It? destroy It? or are these things the same thing? Or is It
wishing in us to understand, to know, to destroy, Itself?

It seems at times to confer upon us a marvelous freedom, only by not
much minding what we say of It, what stories we tell of It, or whether we
call the stories metaphor, myth, history, faith, truth, hypothesis, theory,
law. Permitting much, It demands nothing. Admitting nothing, It allows
and even encourages and sometimes compels a great deal.

I shall try to list a few of the stories we tell of It, or It tells of Itself in
us; the things, perhaps, that It compels us to believe because they are
impossible, incredible, absurd, and contradictory to one another and even
within themselves.

We believe that we belong to It, that we do not belong to It—that's
why we feel so strange, so much of the time—that we are identical with
It, and absolutely separated from It.

We believe It has pattern and order, inferring from this that it must
mean something, though all the meanings we say we derive from it or
impose on it seem observably to be within it. Also, we believe that pattern
and order may be totally unconnected with meaning; may be an insane
regularity of a circular sort: that things go round and round, said one of
our theorists, has rather a classical sound. Further to this we also believe
that pattern and order in their turn rest upon abstraction derived from
meaningless and random motion of things—which are not in the ordinary
sense thngs at all—far too small ever to be seen.

We believe that, unlike the citizens of Nineveh, we know our right
hands from our left hands; but when we inquire, moving through the
successive stages of its either grandeur or minuteness, whether it is right-
handed or left-handed, echo answers; or perhaps it is ambidextrous.

We believe it has a direction, and is moving in a direction; but when
we inquire about the source of this belief we get a certain way—a roughly
circular, rather flat, revolving aggregate of pieces of It is moving out past
the star Vega in the Lyre, toward an emptiness we poetically call the Apex

of the Sun's Path—and then we stop: what we call direction, and movement in a direction, may refer only to the agreement among eyes, nose, mouth, genitals and toes as to which is front.

We believe that this compound of linear with circular motion constitutes one of Its most mysterious beings, Time, like a top gone spinning down a road; or like the needle of a phonograph, which goes in a shallow arc by following a spiral path. Time, too, is believed to have a direction and to be moving inexorably in that direction, even if we cannot tell whether it is moving through us or we are moving through it; this direction and motion we commonly agree is irreversible in practically everything—reserving some doubt, again, as to the motion of those extremely small things already alluded to, possibly too insignificant, each one by itself, to come under the notice of Time except as statistical aggregates, so that in their not quite chaotic dance it is only the democratic agreement of the vast majority that constitutes the direction of Time, while the square root of the majority vote may actually be going backwards in time and maybe even sideways, much good may it do 'em.

We believe that it is continuous with itself, and that it is discrete; that it is composed of lines, but that the lines in their turn are composed of points; moreover the points are dimensionless, so that a long line contains the same number of them as a short line—which, however, we do not believe is the thing numbers were invented to tell us, it being not at all canny.

Finally—or not at all finally, but to break off short of exhaustion—we believe that it does Itself (and us), that we are doing It, that It loves us, hates us, and is indifferent to us, all at the same time; that Its purposes are ours (that's very ambiguous even so), that Its purposes are not ours but can be discovered by us, that It has no purposes. Sometimes we think of It as a machine, these days; It has also been thought of in somewhat humbler and somehow more lovable ways, as a tree, a river, a fountain rising from and falling back into a still-reflecting pool, as a dream, as a ship, possibly the ship of fools, sailing a limitless deep ocean from where to where? but all these things, besides seeming to express It, are in It . . . and when we think of the ship, perhaps we should be thinking of the sea?

I know of one place conspicuous in our stories where It is discussed with an impeccable smiling decorum that seems for an instant to achieve liberation: the occasion is a drunken party and the liberation certainly trivial enough in appearance; still, it will do to sum up:

Lepidus: What manner o' thing is your crocodile?

Antony: It is shap'd, sir, like itself, and it is as broad as it hath breadth. It is just so
  high as it is, and moves with it own organs. It lives by that which nourish-
  eth it, and the elements once out of it, it transmigrates.
Lepidus: What colour is it of?
Antony: Of it own colour too.
Lepidus: 'Tis a strange serpent.
Antony: 'Tis so. And the tears of it are wet.

The foregoing contradictory, confused and confusing propositions and
predications concerning It are, I think, abstract and general enough to
apply to many of the names under which It is thought about, discussed, or
acted on: God, the universe, the world, mankind, society, history, nature,
the mind, language ... together with the many institutions, church, state,
army, college, business, industry, in which those terms more and less formally embody themselves. The vast range of such terms from divine to
demonic, from ideal to excremental, has been splendidly catalogued in
sequence by Kenneth Burke, toward the end of his *Rhetoric of Motives*, to
which I refer you for a more orderly consideration of this matter than I
am able to give.

I hope you will not believe that my descriptions intend to be applied
only in the world of ideation, knowledge, and timeless philosophy. On the
contrary, they have their applications equal in intensity but greater in pathos to the world of action, in which the virtues we most rely on, faith,
honesty, courage, intelligence, require us to act all our lives upon fictions
concerning their absolute sanction—somewhere—and upon knowledges
which are provisional, partial, incomplete, and, pursued to any distance at
all, would wind up as metaphysical speculations fading back even further
into a strange mythology filled with gods, demons, monsters, pursuing
wildly independent careers in a Black Forest which might be somewhere
on earth but whose vegetation somehow resembles that of the brain. It is
especially that world I mean to point helplessly to, the world into which
we are born, out of which we die, while in between whiles we suffer from
law and suffer from accident, from justice and injustice, from love and
hate, from beauty and ugliness, suffer the body, the mind, the spirit, suffer
our own sufferings and those of others that we are helpless to remedy ...
suffer from knowledge and from ignorance, desire and fear, and from the
last reflexive suffering in which we see ourselves compelled to love our
very sufferings if thereby we can only live.

I hope most of all that you will not think I am speaking cynically of
knowledge or thought, or, deeper than knowledge or thought, wiser and

more silent, of that prolonged aesthetic meditation belonging everywhere and only to discovery and vision, whether in arts, sciences, or other disciplines, wherein it seems as though both thought and knowledge, which nevertheless have to be present in quantity, fall silent and pass over into something as immediate and mysterious as perception itself: the wordless mysterious recognition that, after all our words, *is* understanding, *is* creation, *is* metamorphosis; what Plato called "unspeakable" and Aristotle "without word." On the contrary, I think that no one can look without wonder—though in the wonder there be both pity and terror—at the immense power of the human dream, individual and collective at once and by turns, that has raised up out of the ground, as by a succession of stunning magical blows, the human world into which we were born and of which, before we leave, we can know so very little. Imagine yourself as the eponymous ancestor of the tribe, dropped into a field between the forest and the sea while a divine voice said, not even very loud, "Why not derive the universe?" Where would you begin? By inventing the paper clip? identifying Polaris? writing The Book of Genesis?

We begin, as children, in a world of sensations soon penetrated by the first manifestation of a strange principle of order called language. We don't learn this order at all in the way we later learn things at school, by the separation of theory and material, grammar and vocabulary, followed by the slow laborious putting of these together again to check their fit; we learn, and this is sort of paradoxical, little by little yet the whole thing at once: not grammar and words, but language itself, complete and compresent at every instant. At first it must be language that we learn, not thought: we say it is, and it is, as it were immediately; and I remember now it was before the Fall that Adam named the creatures. But, if we are guided by that old story, by all those old stories in the first eleven chapters of that first book that seems to have given something of shape to any stories we can possibly tell later on, the Fall happens soon afterward.

I shan't attempt interpretation, but ask only that we should look at the nexus of elements in that strange and arbitrary-looking tale, and look at it in as naïve a way as possible, as though in a child's drawing: a talking snake, a round ripe fruit, eating followed by knowledge of nakedness and shame followed in turn by guilty fear . . . and then the being driven out—by that voice which I imagine from what is quoted as courteous and imperturbable, not even very loud—to a declared destiny of loneliness, separation, labor, sorrow and death.

In my phantastic game of let's pretend that our ontogeny repeats even so unscientific a phylogeny, the story might be identified with the mo-

ment—only hypothetically a moment, the realization might take years—
at which we see that in learning language we were also learning to lie;
and not only to lie wilfully, which might have been enough, but to lie
helplessly and by accident because the language itself had this power of
lying, a magnificent and terrifying power in itself, and strange indeed in
its effects on us, the chief of these being a double separation, once between words and things, once between words and thoughts, which thence
and since has compelled us simultaneously or in succession to formu-
late—and to doubt the fit of our formulations; and then to doubt even the
doubt, and so to spend much time in puzzlement and mystification. But
this strange power of lying had further effects than that. Swift was quite
right to call it "saying the thing that is not," but it is necessary to add
another clause to the definition, that very often saying the thing that was
not was the first step in a process that brought that very thing into being.
Language, by this power of decisively standing off from the world as it
was, began to dream its many transformations of the world as it was into
the world that might be ... and then that standing off, that separation,
produced other separations, in particular that between Cain and Abel, the
first murder, and the enterprise of The Tower of Babel, or the separation
of languages. That enterprise, like murder, is still progressing among us
nowadays; and it comes to me to think that the story of the Flood and the
story of the first drunkenness—the inundation from without and from
within—are interpolated between the other two in a tragic tryptich, the
two side panels telling the disasters of division, the central one the disasters of merger: the tragedies of Apollo, and the double tragedy of Dio-
nysos.

The poets tell this better; and sometimes with a difference. I would
not wish anyone to feel bound by my rhapsody on these old themes. And
because I spoke a moment ago of merger and division, Burkean terms,
here is Mr. Burke's *Creation Myth*:

In the beginning, there was universal Nothing.
Then Nothing said No to itself and thereby begat Something,
Which called itself Yes.
Then No and Yes, cohabiting, begat Maybe.
Next all three, in a ménage à trois, begat
    Guilt.
And Guilt was of many names:
Mine, Thine, Yours, Ours, His, Hers, Its,
    Theirs—and Order.

In time things so came to pass
That two of its names, Guilt and Order,
Honoring their great progenitors, Yes, No,
    and Maybe,
Begat History.
Finally, History fell a-dreaming
And dreamed about Language—
(And that brings us to critics-who-write-critiques-of-critical-criticism).

In the following version, a magnificent passage from T. S. Eliot's *Gerontion*, the tone of voice is different, and the point of concentration is not on the fusion of myth and logic, rather on its terrifying consequences for life and thought; but the tragic story is again the same:

After such knowledge, what forgiveness? Think now
History has many cunning passages, contrived corridors
And issues, deceives with whispering ambitions,
Guides us by vanities. Think now
She gives when our attention is distracted
And what she gives, gives with such supple confusions
That the giving famishes the craving. Gives too late
What's not believed in, or if still believed,
In memory only, reconsidered passion. Gives too soon
Into weak hands what's thought can be dispensed with
Till the refusal propagates a fear. Think
Neither fear nor courage saves us. Unnatural vices
Are fathered by our heroism. Virtues
Are forced upon us by our impudent crimes.
These tears are shaken from the wrath-bearing tree.

And so, still children, we were put to school, beginning a long and still continuing process wherein we learned to take the world apart in order to put it back together, to the end, it was claimed by our grown-ups, of understanding whether practical or speculative. (The word understanding really does mean to stand under, just as Shakespeare says it does in a charming parable that seems to say it is the body that understands the soul as the servant understands the master; but that I leave you to interpret on your own, it happens in *Two Gentlemen of Verona*.) We went to school, and began learning the ins and outs, the corridors and drafty dark chambers, of the lower levels of the Tower of Babel, where the masonry still

looks pretty solid and one can hardly hear the occasional falling beam in
the adjacent apartment, or the continuous sound of jack-hammer and bull-
dozer upstairs. We went on to College, higher up in the building, and
there, though the noise was confusing so that often one could hardly think,
and though even with our great and growing powers of discrimination it
was hard to tell by the sound alone whether the stories above were being
built or falling down or both at the same time, we were occasionally given
a tour through the soundproofed rooms where the physicists thought about
stress and the ultimate constituents of matter, where the architects and
city-planners designed stories so high up and far in the future that even
their children's children might never see them, and where occasionally
one came across a dusty-looking old man who muttered as one passed
something about the very idea of building a tower, something one hardly
heard and didn't at all want to understand ... and then we arrived, as
tomorrow you will have arrived, at what? Not the end, no, scarcely the
end; but at a stage, nonetheless, that marks a kind of completion and has
an identity of its own, just as a wave does although it is but one wave in
an ocean ... and now? and here?

Well, the languages up here are a good deal more confused than they
are downstairs. And the construction work, which down below used to be
done with honest brick and stone, has for its material at this stage only
some rather airy bits and pieces of stuff, or possibly not stuff at all but
something else, energy maybe, or words maybe, or thoughts maybe, each
one of them so tightly packed with nothing at all, absolute emptiness, that
it's hard to see what can be built of them at all, in the old sense in which
one built, say, a house; and indeed everything is so attenuated, and time
goes so fast, up here, that not even the master builders are able to tell
falling down from going up, though some of them look to be having rather
a jolly time and some even whistle while they work ... and to some extent,
some indefinite extent, you are given a choice.

It is not what we call a free choice; choices are rarely that. For in some
sense you will be working at the Tower even if you reject it with all your
heart, even if you elect to live in the sub-basement; because it is only by
metaphor that we speak of bricks and stones: the material of the Tower,
first and last, is human lives, its stuff is blood, bone, brain, and the rest,
including time, human time.

But you do have some choice, though when you look back many years
later it will seem to you that you scarcely made it yourselves. You can go
back down: the nineteenth century, for example, from up here, looks to
be a comfortable sort of old place (though it wasn't then). Or you can stay

up here, making youself useful—within the limited meaning of that term—chiefly by doing something you very much want to do and care about doing.

The life here is problematic indeed, and disaster an everyday occurrence. You are exposed to the weather, too. But when the night is clear the stars burn very brightly, and appear to be closer than before, though you realize that is an illusion—the same illusion, it may be, that began this strange adventure. For what did light want when it first went forth, if not the eye?

Rainer Maria Rilke

RILKE happened to me early on, when I was still an undergraduate and just beginning at my own verses. Memory shows me on a Cape Cod beach that summer, a copy of *The Duino Elegies* in my hands, the just-published translation by J. B. Leishman and Stephen Spender, reading to a girl. Memory insists, indeed, on the book's being *in my hands*, for it had a blue dust-jacket, turquoise or aquamarine, of low brilliance but great pathos, and the blue came off on my fingers, where it stayed indelibly for many days. So much for memory, also indelible for many days. I have forgotten the girl's name. And the summer ended and the war began.

The impression made by *The Elegies* on a young man innocent of German except for an ambition to sing Wagner, is easier described—angels, great glamor, a certain emptiness as to content and sense—than accounted for: the young man was innocent of vastly more than the German language, and when told this was the book of a Great Poet he accepted that for fact and read with reverence, if not with judgment.

Rilke was not entirely absent from his thoughts in the forty-five years following, during which he read, among other things, Leishman's translations of *New Poems*, M. D. Herter Norton's translations of *The Sonnets to Orpheus* and *Translations from the Poetry of Rainer Maria Rilke*, as well as her English version of *The Notebooks of Malte Laurids Brigge*, and took account, especially in the past few years, of a fair number of new renderings of *The Elegies* and other things. He even got a little, a very little, homemade and bookish German in an attempt to see what was really going on, what a Great Poet was, and why Rilke was one, if he was. The attempt has not been altogether successful, for the ideas of a Great Poet, and of Modernism, and what its canon came to be, and how and by whom established, remain largely hidden, sometimes in mystery and sometimes in mere confusion, obscurantism, and special pleading. But what he is able to say is as follows.

A Great Poet does not become one, it appears, solely in virtue of his verses, for above a fairly low level of competence one lot of poems is about as good as another. There must also be the Life, followed by The Letters, followed by a vast accumulation of scholarship, criticism, biography, analysis, and legend.

Like the other masters who made the modern canon between 1910 and 1930 or so, Rilke was born to the old world of the nineteenth century and lived—just half his life—into the new world of the twentieth. Like those others, too, his productive life had to cross the Great Divide of 1914, of which Valéry wrote five years later the somber, brooding sentence that begins one of his essays: "We know now, we other civilizations, that we too are mortal."

Rilke's life was exemplary almost to the point of parody for the myth of the modern poet, or the romantic and symbolist poet born late into a strange new age in which Byronic loneliness and destiny came costumed à la Charlie Chaplin. If Hollywood were given to epics of The Life of the Poet, Rilke's life would be the ideal subject, as offering the maximum concentration of characteristics together with what, seen unsympathetically from outside, would look like low comedy tending to farce in its perfecting, taking to the end of the line, traits that other lives show only in solution and complexity.

Even from his birth, in Prague but of German-speaking parents, he was the prototypical displaced or stateless person. His mother raised him as a girl, and if that were not a good enough start, his father then gave over his further upbringing to a couple of military schools in which he was, expectably, miserable. He lived his life in a series of self-imposed exiles, had no homeland nor, it seems, cared to have one, and restlessly peregrinated Europe from Russia to Spain, from Paris to Switzerland and Italy, learning as well as Dante did, though voluntarily, about other people's stairs and other people's bread. His inner life was dominated by an introspection so intense and so unsatisfied that it sometimes seems objectless and empty of content, introspection for its own sake; while at the same time, and without contradiction, his eye for the outside world was shrewd and his observation of it precise. Indeed, it was the putting together of inward and outward that gave him, poetically, his greatest troubles and his greatest triumphs in equal measure. His artistic life was marked by prolonged periods of aridity and depression, punctuated in legendary romantic manner by such breakthroughs and furious spurts of inspiration as gave him and us the first of the Elegies in 1912 and their completion, with the unexpected gift of *The Sonnets to Orpheus*, in 1922. To complete the account, he was generally miserable in love and about love, and when he died of leukemia at only age fifty the legend put about of his being poisoned by the thorn of a rose got some credibility from the legend he made to be inscribed on his tomb:

> O rose, reiner Widerspruch, Lust,
> Niemandes Schlaf zu sein unter so viel Lindern.

> Rose
> o you
> paradox
> pure and simple
> pleasing yourself
> to be
> under all those eyelids
> the sleep of
> no one
> —tr. Elizabeth Sewell in her book *Acquist*,
>   Durham, N. C., 1983

Leishman (with Spender for the Elegies) and Herter Norton, remain my favorite translators not only because I came upon them first. They seem to me superior also in giving the literal sense without adding things of their own invention to eke out the measure; even so, Leishman's courageous willingness to undertake the rimes of the original leads him quite often into serious awkwardnesses of diction and lapses from English idiom;

> Praising, that's it! As a praiser and blesser
> he came like the ore from the transient mine.
> Came with his heart, oh, transient presser
> for men, of a never-exhaustible wine.
> —*Sonnets to Orpheus*, I, 7, first stanza

The opening sounds like a cheerleader exhorting, or an ad for a product named Praising, and while the meaning of "presser" is quite clear the overtone from dry cleaning rather gets in the way. The passage illustrates also two out of three trivial but nevertheless real difficulties for the reader of English: Rilke says "O" a great deal, which the translator's rendering as "oh" makes just slightly more embarrassing; Rilke is also ever so fond of the exclamation point, which must have an entirely different tonality in German than it does in English, where it usually means that something has gone frightfully wrong with the writing. The third such difficulty is italicizing as a means to providing intensity where it would not otherwise exist:

> And he himself as he lay there in such relief,
> dissolving, under his drowsy eyelids, the sweetness
> of your light shaping into the sleep he had tasted,
> *seemed* to be under protection. . . . *Within*, though: who could avert,
> divert, the floods of origin flowing within him?
> Alas, there *was* no caution within that sleeper,
>
> &c.
>
> The Third Elegy

That passage will illustrate also a major difficulty. Checking it against the original as far as I am able, I can see that the translators have followed the syntax of the German faithfully, and I sympathize with what I imagine must often have been their thought: "That's what it says, isn't it?" as they grit their teeth and plough on through, italics and all, but still must record my impression that English just doesn't sound that way. It is perhaps reassuring, but not a present help, to be told that

The *Duino Elegies*, Rilke's greatest work, are exceedingly difficult. . . . Even the German reader must struggle with their uncommon use of common words, with their sentences that tear open to let displaced parts of speech press into the gap, with their obscure allusions and mystifying or wildly farfetched metaphors (when fully understood, they will appear wonderfully apt and illuminating).—Gregor Sebba, in *The Poem Itself*, ed. Stanley Burnshaw, NY, 1981

To my complaints about idiom the translators might reasonably reply that they are trying to represent not merely a foreign tongue but also a style and manner in that tongue that is in the highest degree idiosyncratic and personal to its author: no wonder it sounds odd. And it is one of our cherished tenets about modern work that the really new (and hence the truly valuable?) will not sound like the poetry of the past at all. Against this, though, we should put the opinion of M. D. Herter Norton: "one is easily trapped, in one's absorption with the German, into certain inversions that accord neither with English idiom nor with the natural prose sequence of modern poetry, whereas Rilke's style being straightforward and simple, the translator is liable to misrepresent it if he departs from the simple and straightforward idiom of his own language."—Foreword to *Translations from the Poetry of Rainer Maria Rilke*. New York, 1938.

If the poets are full of contradiction, and they are—between the life and the work, between this work and that—, it is the essence of their vocation to represent to us that we are full of contradiction too, contradiction which our ordinary lives with their ordinary language will neither account for nor take account of. The disagreement of translators as to whether Rilke is exceedingly difficult or simple and straightforward in such things as diction and syntax may be duplicated among his critics: his admirers have their doubts of him, his detractors doubt themselves.

For instance. An American scholar, Walter Kaufmann, begins an essay called "Rilke: Nirvana or Creation" with the plain statement that "Rilke was one of the greatest poets of all time," which one would have thought enough. But he follows on at once with some half-dozen generous concessions to the other side, e.g., he wrote bad poems (who doesn't?), he does not come across as an exemplary human being, the person depicted (in the Letters) is weak, precious, lacking in humor, many poems are marred by affectations, and even some of the best narrowly miss self-parody ("But they do miss it"), and, maybe most telling of all, the Elegies are uneven "and might be accounted a noble failure" but that the poet replaced the Fifth with a new one at the last moment; even so, fully half the ten are inferior. And then the essayist bases his claim for "one of the greatest poets of all time" on *theme*: "the choice between . . . intensity and peace," adding that Moses himself had offered the same choice some time before: Choose life or death this day.

That Moses had recommended the choice first is no obstacle, save that Moses was unequivocal about it, which Kaufman does not claim for his poet: "It cannot be proved which choice is better, and a poet's business is not with proofs or arguments. He can try to explore experiences and show us what they are like. This is what Rilke does superbly."—In *Rilke: The Alchemy of Alienation*, ed. Frank Baron, Ernst S. Dick, and Warren R. Maurer. Lawrence, Kansas, 1980.

"Superbly" appears to substitute the arbitrary for the argument; or, as Freud said, "we must not be misled by the evidence." I bring up the instance not to criticize Kaufman, but to suggest briefly the problems raised by the assertion, as by the denial, of "greatness" in poetry.

For my own part, and to conclude, I should locate the essential tension for Rilke not in theme but in method, in the tension between inside and outside. There are at the one extreme the Ding-Gedichte, or Object-poems, in which, as E. M. Butler and J. B. Leishman handsomely say, Rilke spoke not merely of things but for them; and, at the other, the quasi-religious assertions of the Elegies and the sometimes empty praise of the Orpheus poems, from which things and their thingness have largely departed.

Bringing together the inwardness of mind and the outwardness of world has always been implicit in the poetic attempt, though it seems to have become more of a critical question for the poets of this century than it was for their precursors. I like Rilke best—indeed love him best—when he appears to accomplish this with the least possible forcing of thoughts on things. For example, in "The Courtesan" of *New Poems*, where the courtesan and Venice, bridge, canal, and sea, are brought together by subtle yet probable bonds of high civilization, culture, preciosity, the city founded in the sea, leading to the conclusion, so striking and at the same time just,

> And many a hopeful youth of high extraction
> will not survive my mouth's envenoming.

But at the same time, right in the course of this triumphal progression, there comes in that silly dog, whom people envy for her resting her hand on him; where the tone goes to pieces, Groucho Marx replaces Charlie Chaplin for an instant, and one can see the point of Hans Egon Holthusen's remark on Rilke's humorlessness and want of irony as "a highly gifted tastelessness."

What Rilke is best at, superb at to revert to Kaufman's word, is farewell, and especially to childhood. From the poet's life one might conclude that the escape from childhood was matter for congratulation; but in the fictive projection of Malte, and in the poetry, losing childhood is worse, losing "that land that long remains in sight/ before it ultimately disappears," and towards which we are always looking back:

> Just as he,
> on the last hill, that shows him all his valley
> for the last time, will turn and stop and linger,

> we live our lives, for ever taking leave.
> —The Eighth Elegy

And it is, because poetry is full of contradictions, the poet's and our own, when he puts together the elements that dominate his thought, or obsess it—childhood, aristocracy, the figure of the poet, and death—that Rilke seems most to triumph over, or be reconciled with, his narcissism, snobbery, and vanity. For poetry removes the poison and the curse from these traits, and allows the poet to undertake in verse, as he was so little able to do in life, the burden of the reality of others and the outside, his inwardness not lost but reenforced by all those famous "things." So it is in my last instance, "The Singer Sings before a Child of Princes," an elegy for Paula Becker-Modersohn, which ends so appealingly in image, inheritance, aesthetic, and lament scarce to be distinguished from praise:

> You pale child, you make the singer rich
> with your destiny that can so well be sung;
> so a great garden festival is mirrored
> with many lights in the astonished pool.
> In the dark poet silently each thing
> repeats itself: a star, a house, a wood.
> And many things that he would celebrate
> are standing round about your moving form.
> —tr. M. D. Herter Norton

This, and some others like it, continue to move me, after so many years, as they did at first when I was nearer childhood. In it, Rilke is neither "the Santa Claus of loneliness" (W. H. Auden) nor "the Saint Francis of the Will to Power" (Erich Heller), but the legend of himself, free of all doctrine, even his own.

The Other Vision:
On the *American Scholar*'s Issue Called
Vision 65

THE architects, engineers, town planners, and so on, had just designed and built New York City: a beautiful job, there it stood, in sunshine, in rain, that mighty heart . . . then someone said, "What do you think it'd be like if now we introduced people into this here set-up?"

Something like that, I guess, is my simple and maybe simpleminded thought about Vision 65 and related matters, so simple that I spent a few days trying to make it sound rather scholarly and abstruse, which it did at several times the length of what I have to say. The following is probably unfair, then, because I shall be criticizing the symposium for something not included in its intentions. Nor may I apologize for this bad behavior, because the exclusion is a mighty one, and necessary at least to mention.

First, then, something so obvious it is easy to overlook. The attitude in the word *vision* has changed right around from what it used to be, and this, like many another change we are concerned with in the world—like, in fact, the electronic revolution itself—is not a thing any particular person or persons decided on, although many persons must have cooperated in bringing it to pass; like any large-scale change in the nature of social assumptions, it looks as though it came about on its own. Visions of the Last Judgment, Visions of the World's Vanity, the visions of Ezekiel, Isaiah, John on Patmos writing Revelations, The Vision of William Concerning Piers Plowman—thoughts of the durable sorrow of the world's condition, dire predictions of local doom, lurid paintings of the everliving End . . .

these qualities have disappeared, being replaced, in Vision 65, by a shrewd and genial speculative intelligence, basing on fact, orienting to action, optimistic in expectation while scrupulously cautious against claiming too much.

The change is so imposingly there that an opinion as to its being simply good or simply bad could not be more than trivial. What I mean to stress is that it took place, not by decree, not by planning, scarcely by the direction of consciousness at all, so completely that the presence in the *Scholar*'s Spring issue of a contributor with the other vision would rightly have been felt to be an impropriety; William Blake on the assumptions and consequences of an imperially successful technology would not, to my mind, be obsolete at all, but in this company he would appear to be talking unhelpfully far out in left field. For the burden of the technological symphony is not "Shall we do this or not do it?" but "Here it is, let's get on with the job." The predominating optimism begins well past the point of choice. *Ducunt fata volentem, nolentem trahunt.*

There are significant exceptions, and I mention a few of them. Joseph Wood Krutch and Gerald W. Johnson recite eloquently a list of perils no less real for being by now familiar. J. Bronowski describes a probably intrinsic limitation upon the mind's power of viewing itself as a machine, and the part of his essay dealing with self-reference in science and in literature is splendidly complemented by Richard Hoggart's discussion of the sort of knowledge of itself a society may hope to gain by the study of its literature. Robert McClintock argues convincingly against certain cybernetic pretensions to philosophy, and Walter A. Rosenblith tells us that the immense usefulness of computers does not proceed from "gross and overall analogizing" with the brain. But in the papers presented at Vision 65, I find a rational and progressive optimism to be the rule, and one looks a long time for the kind of thought to which Lynn White, Jr.'s, essay "On Intellectual Gloom" seems designed as the antidote. Here are a few sample conclusions.

"The move toward the center; the recognition that science and technology are integral to mankind's adventure; the building of a democratic culture: these are clearly only three aspects of one thing that is occurring—the achievement of a unity of human knowledge and experience such as no earlier age has imagined." White, p. 226.

"Perhaps the most exciting prospect of change resulting from our new technology of information processing is the likelihood that it will halt and reverse [the] progressive isolation of idea from idea and man from man.

Mankind, in its professional as well as its nonprofessional aspects, will
again become the proper study of man." Simon, p. 264.

"Perhaps for the first time in man's history, he can afford to think truly
long thoughts." Hertz, p. 271.

I think it is not the optimism I am arguing against—we need all of it
we can have—but its exclusively professional and engineering and planning and intellectualizing nature. Not that those voices ought not to be
heard, but might not the symposium have cast its nets somewhere more
widely? The opinions of women, for instance, of union officers, of persons
at various levels of work who had been displaced by technology—the
inclusion of these, and others, either not "expert" at all or else qualified
in some seemingly remoter area (medicine, psychology, government, law),
would have given a somewhat less tidy appearance to the general result,
while adding, in counterpoint to the theme of What We are going to do
with It, the theme of What is It likely to do to Us?

What I have said of the change in the word *vision*, then, probably ap-
plies in the realm of technology more than elsewhere (George Orwell
being a fair example of elsewhere). In that realm it seems as if optimism
is itself an assumption, a convention of literary style, a piety belonging to
some tacitly specified form of public address. That's fair enough in itself;
the Old Testament bit is all too easy these days, and very few modern
prophets, imprecating their various dooms upon Nineveh, will have Jonah's luck to be altogether wrong. And if you mean to talk about the near
and temporal future, rather than the eternal one that is ever-present, it is
also fair enough to exclude more than a pious passing mention of nuclear
annihilation in favor of getting on to happier alternatives that at least leave
more to talk about. And yet, something about the writers' procedures—
the generalized plot that emerges when I put together a number of their
scenarios for the future—is dissatisfying.

In Proust's novel there is a place at which the Narrator, dawdling and
fiddling through today, keeps deciding that he will be a writer tomorrow;
in one form or another a familiar experience for most of us, which the
intelligence of Proust, however, enables us to understand better. For when
the Narrator examines his unthinking belief that tomorrow will be more
auspicious for his purpose than today, he comes upon a tragically illuminating answer: the sole relevant factor that makes tomorrow better than
today is that he has not yet corrupted it by being in it.

Applying the lesson, I see that what dissatisfies me about some of the
papers is the writers' scholarly enthusiasm for the future that leads them

to overleap this point. I am sure none of them believes that electronic means alone will make the future better than the past and present, yet when they come to the point of transition—after having discussed the present in a tone of the most grimly realistic awareness—they get past it rather rapidly, so that it is almost invisible.

In H. F. William Perk's scenario, "The Great Transformation," written by a historian in 1985, it happens this way, in the years 1968–69: "For reasons that are still a subject of dispute among historians, the established order in almost every region of the world was replaced—by one means or another—with a new leadership dedicated to the proposition that peace and abundance shall become the common condition of all mankind" (p. 360). The project of the new leadership bears for its title a familiar but still sinister metaphor: "World War on Want."

In Buckminster Fuller's essay the same transition is accomplished conditionally rather than declaratively. After surveying, with great brilliance and brevity, the evidences of a real improvement of the human condition during his own lifetime, and linking this improvement to the history of energy and its transforming use of materials, he sets up his program from the near future extension of the benefits of technology to all humanity— and then declares in effect that the only thing holding us out of the Garden is the combined dishonesty and incompetence of "the politician." Utopia will come, he says, through "a design science revolution of spontaneously coordinate university-aged youth. This revolution is trying to articulate itself everywhere. It gets bogged down by political exploiters of all varieties."

I sympathize with his impatience, but as to the truth of that diagnosis— that politics is an arbitrary, capricious and unnecessary injection of dishonest stupidity in an otherwise happily engineered human condition, I guess I find myself of the other persuasion.

And I've gone on too long already. Only one more point. Buckminster Fuller's own analysis of our immense technological advance during this century specifically relates it to the two world wars; a further step in the analysis specifically relates warfare and technological progress to commerce; but he will not acknowledge the possibility, if not the likelihood, that these relations are as necessary as they are intimate, and that they work in both directions, human sacrifice on an immense scale being the price paid for longevity and other benefits.

I suppose I mean that the triumph of techne, like any other sweet fruition of an earthly crown, is as cruel as it is splendid. Not, as some writers have said, a reflection of man's inability to choose himself, but a reflection of the tragic circumstance that whatever of himself man chooses to actualize, he is compelled to choose something else along with it, as to whose spectral nature I might better keep quiet than speak.

An Interview with Howard Nemerov

Neal Bowers and Charles L. P. Silet

NEMEROV. Do you want me to provide answers first?

INTERVIEWER. That might be a better way.

N. I've got a good answer.

I. Okay.

N. Yes, theoretically, but in practice it comes up so seldom as to be negligible.

I. Can you tell us a little bit about how you go about composing poetry? For example, do you write every day? How much do you depend upon inspiration? Do you have a form in mind before you start writing or does that develop as you write the poem?

N. There are several questions in there. I do not write every day. In fact, except for correspondence, which is fairly extensive, I may not write for a couple of years. And, of course, you worry about that, and worrying about it is part of the process itself. I've got a notion you have to get depressed before something happens. On the other hand, after twenty books it is harder to get depressed than after two. You know, so if you didn't write anything . . . so what? I would like to do it but the world is full enough of literature; probably my little mite would not be missed if I didn't do any more. When it is there it's wonderful and it's easy, and when it's not there it's impossible. And I don't know what makes it be there. Unlike many friends who write, I do my best, such as it is, very fast. Ninety-five percent of the *Western Approaches* was written in four months—again, after two years of . . . "I can't write." You would think that if you wanted to be a professional and make a business out of it that with, you know, what even my nastiest reviewers allow to be virtuoso technique, I could turn the poetry crank seven lines every morning and come out with far too much at the end of the year, but it doesn't work that way at all. When it's not there I tend to whistle on my walks. Horrible little tunes I can't get rid of go through my head—things I wouldn't want to listen to. When it's there things start saying themselves in my head, usually in blank verse, but that's my fault, sometimes in rhyme. And the little things in two and four lines make themselves up and I can remember long enough to get to the desk and put them down. The other things, you get the beginning of something, a notion, a line, a line-and-a-half, and it's always—not always, I never thought about it in earlier years—but latterly, it's always remarkable to me that one thing should follow another. It's the most remarkable feature of thought, and nobody seems to study it; perhaps people do and I just don't know about it. As to the form things take, well, those little epigrams, gnomes, they tell you "I'm not going to be the *Iliad*." I sent one to Kenneth Burke who said, "You know, if you do something this short, you have to rhyme it." I said, "Kenneth, you're right." I up and ripped the whole thing apart and rhymed it, six lines; I thought that was a great achievement. That little couplet of Pope's on the collar of the dog he gave to the Prince of Wales: "I am his highness' dog at Kew./Pray tell me, sir, whose dog are you?" That wouldn't be anything without the rhyme, would it? In the longer things there is a slight tendency for my laziness to turn them into blank verse, but sometimes things clearly say, "I'm a sestina" or "I want to be rhymed and quatrained." If I know it's going to go like maybe two pages, I tend to write it in blank verse. I'm always worried I might not find a rhyme for the last two lines or something. But rhyme is a marvelous thing all the same. It makes you think of things you would not be forced to think of—wouldn't have had a chance to think of—otherwise.

I. What do you see as the relationship between your fiction and your poetry? Is there an overlap? Are they part of the same process?

N. I would have said earlier, when I did more fiction, that I tried to make them as different as possible. No poetic prose when you're writing a novel, or at least try to stay away from it.

I. Do you write novels in the same sort of burst of energy as you write your poetry?

N. Well, I didn't write enough to be able to generalize about it. For a story or a chapter I think I tried to get it all done in one day because you can never be certain that the idea will still be there the next morning. In novels, the first one I wrote took me three years during the summers, and the second one I wrote in 58 days, and the third one in 28 days. Then I said to my wife, "The next one I will write on Labor Day." It didn't work.

I. Some critics speak of a progression in your work from a somewhat more academic style reminiscent of Eliot or Pound to a much more conversational, relaxed style. Do you see such a progression in your poetry?

N. It may be true. You know, writing poetry is just one of the specialized forms of what happens when you grow up or grow older. Of course, you live life forward and think about it backward. You might spend a lot of time in embarrassment about the silly, trivial things you did when young, that you didn't know you were doing silly trivial things when you were old too. You know, there is a beautiful place in Proust where the painter Elstir talks to Marcel about this. Marcel has just discovered that this great master must have been the silly young man who was referred to at parties, and Elstir, instead of turning away and refusing ever to see him again, sets him down and gives him a little talk about growing up and about how it's only nonentities who have nothing to be ashamed of in their past, how you have to overcome what you were before, and it's only, he says, in this way that something a little above the common life of the atelier is achieved.

I. Do you consider yourself to be a poet of reflection—in the Wordsworthian sense? And, if so, do you feel this necessarily implies an absence of emotion?

N. Yea, I might be a pretty cold fellow in some ways, except I know I'm a weepy slob. But I don't see that the two are incompatible. We mostly have both capacities at once. In younger days, my colleagues and friends from *Furioso* magazine used to tell me solemnly that I was a meditative poet, and in those days meditative poetry was a very dirty word in that you were not dramatic like John Donne—"Busy old fool, unruly Sunne," he says just before he starts meditating on the subject. Those terms all collapse as soon as you look at them, like a world full of traffic lights with no cars. Yes, I've got a touch of the Wordsworthian or what Keats called the egotistical sublime, but only a touch, I think. And some of my poems are obviously dramatic in the sense that somebody not myself is talking in a particular situation. That's about as dramatic as I get. I never did quite feel at home in that idea that the dramatic is always conveyed to me as some opera singer making huge gestures and stamping his foot petulantly on the stage.

I. You have been a teacher for a long time.

N. Yes, longer than Jesus lived.

I. Does being a teacher influence your poetry?

N. I'm quite sure it must. As a very nice review in the *Times Literary*

Supplement said about a poem of mine called "The Pond," "it is like Frost but it's more sophisticated than Frost, and also it's a teacher's poem." The reviewer didn't go on to explain, but I could sort of see. You know, if you're brought up under the New Criticism of Eliot and Empson there are certain things you probably do as a matter of course without realizing that they are matters of convention. There is one particular convention that I'm sure I don't do as much as I did when I began, cute little puns and stuff, but I'm sure I still do it some.

I. What do you think about the position of someone like Robert Bly, for example, who deliberately keeps himself away from a position in a university because he thinks a poet should not earn his living by teaching but should, somehow, divorce himself from that kind of a pursuit?

N. As John Ransom said about a similar question, "It's a free country isn't it?" I mean, you know, is it for me to criticize how Robert Bly runs his life?

I. Several critics have pointed out, for lack of a better word, the pessimistic side of your poetry. Do you consider yourself basically pessimistic?

N. That's a hard one, isn't it? The optimist thinking the glass is half full and the pessimist thinking it's half empty. You see, pessimism has gone out of fashion. I notice that in reviews they treat me much nicer than they ever used to. But there is this notion that he's too bitter to be a really great American poet. Whereas, I was brought up under this great tradition of things like *The Waste Land* and *Ash Wednesday*, where you'd better be bitter because that's what poetry was. And even if Dante ends up in paradise with the sight of God himself, he doesn't sound exactly what you would call happy about the situation on earth.

I. Can you elaborate on a comment that you've made in several different places (and I think this is a direct quote), "The serious and the funny are one"?

N. How about *King Lear*, which I would rate (as I tell my students, this is enthusiasm, not theory) as one of the few great human achievements. What about when Gloucester thinks he is jumping off the cliff and falls flat on his face on the stage? That may be my only example, but it's quite an example to get by. That is, many people have recorded the feeling that they want to laugh at a funeral and that they mustn't, you know. Because whether something is serious or funny, solemn or unsinging,* is but an expression of our predicament, where for every soulful sacred notion we have there is some wonderful bodily analogy to it. So if you are seated

---

*I have no idea what I said that made the tape recorder invent "unsinging." hn

among the angels it is still on your butt. I know I do have a tendency to
be funny in what people say are serious places. I remember Randall Jarrell
saying I spoiled a perfectly good poem by saying something cute right in
the middle of it. I only just say I don't think so. These things are matters
of opinion.

I. Do you see this bonding of the funny and the serious as producing
a fundamental tension in your poetry?

N. I suppose so. There have to be always at least two voices. You wouldn't
want to be all one nervous system or you'd fly to pieces, or be all the other
nervous systems or you'd shrivel up. Nietzsche was very strong on all this
business that everything that is ironic, joyous and evasive belongs to life.
Everything absolute belongs to death. I have more and more come to take
the view that little Howard Nemerov is not the fellow who is responsible
for deciding these mighty matters. People are so inclined, especially in
writing, to behave apocalyptically—"Depart from me. Thou my elect." Five
minutes later the situation has changed. Like one of those pictures of Bruegel's, it's hard to decide which lot is headed for heaven and which lot is
headed for hell.

I. Is humor a way of handling that darker side?

N. Humor is a remedy against lust. It's very often been said to be a way
of dealing with that. It's like dirty jokes, which provide some kind of release to something. Many subversive tendencies are probably not directly
connected with sex as such but connected with our wonder about whether
we live in the body or whether we are the body. So, something Innocent
III said, only a little piece, *"De Miseria Humanae Conditionis."* Wit is essentially ascetic against the flesh.

I. What about the relationship between your criticism and your poetry,
and then the criticism of others of your poetry?

N. That's two questions, isn't it? As to the first, I think I quoted in there
something Leonardo said about "He is a bad master whose work outruns
his criticism." Well, there's some sense to that. I've learned that the real
criterion, in which I have learned to trust somewhat, is not verification but
falsification. That is, you can never prove of a theory that there is no fact
in the known or unknown universe that contradicts. Or what you do once
you've got your theory is to try to disprove it as hard as you can. As for
people's criticism of my poems, you do get inured to that. Also, you're
never going to like public contumely followed by private apologies, but
you damn well get used to it—guys writing sneaky little letters saying, "I
didn't really mean to destroy your book." Well, they didn't destroy my
book. I think I've come not to worry about it. I had a beautifully salutary

experience—some chap who said he was writing a bibliography of me. I thought he meant 12 pages of titles, but no, he'd collected reviews and swatches of reviews for 30 years called *The Critical Reception of HN*. It's very funny to look back on those things, the lady writing on a book, a novel of mine, I forget which one, who said, "It's good, but finally, is it good enough?" That's the kind of a sentence you might have heard at a Harvard cocktail party in 1940. And I thought, "Well, that's criticism in the highest and unanswerablest degree." Then I had the answer; I said, "Well, lady, it depends on what you're gonna use it for."

I. Do you learn from critics? Are there critics, which you have respect for and who are judicious in their treatment of your work, that you'd pick up something from?

N. Yes. I think that's true. These are serious people. They are not reviewers as a rule, like Mary Kinzie, in *Parnassus*, 57 pages, by God, about me! I thought some of that was pretty illuminating, and some of that I even didn't know. And there's another critic, Julia Randall, who is a splendid poet herself; well, she wrote in *Hollins Critic* a dozen pages on what I was about. Stanley Hyman told me one day he was going to take a few months off and write a piece about my poetry that would show me so much I would never write again, but maybe I was lucky. He never got around to it.

I. Do you ever change anything? Do you ever question what you've done as a result of somebody else's criticism?

N. I don't think so. After all, those things are by definition written about things that are published already. I tell you, Mary Kinzie wrote me a letter about some 20 new poems I sent to her, which caused me to agree that I should simply suppress 4 or 5 of them—that they're just not up to it. I think perhaps one reckonable result of receiving prizes, getting to be a slight bump on the horizon, is that you do think about next time. Maybe you ought not to put in every little remark you make; maybe you'd better wait. I hope to wait another five years before the next book. It may come earlier than that.

I. Is criticism easier to take when you're younger?

N. Well, I think when you're younger you get most use out of criticism by your fellows, not your teachers. They will say things to you that the teacher would gentle down a bit. Then you get to a point; I remember Stanley Hyman saying to me, "Howard, I couldn't tell you about your poetry. I might not like something in it but I figure he's grown-up; it's his business; he knows what he's doing and he wants to do it that way."

I. Do you enjoy talking shop with your fellow poets?

N. I don't think we do, mostly, talk shop. Lowell told me once that he circulated his poems to fellow poets for advice and criticism, and I was shocked. Yesterday afternoon was the only time I've ever done it and it was partly because I didn't know what else to do—give a lecture. That's why I told the audience yesterday, "I'm not going to take any of your advice; I'm just trying to pass the time."

I. Some critics seem to think that you're getting mellower as you get older, becoming more accepting of the limitations of life and being less angry. Do you feel that's correct, and if so why?

N. Well, you're looking at the complacent, smug old slob instead of the nasty, mean young slob. It's true, when I was reading the proofs of my *Collected Poems*, I kept thinking about the first two books, "What did that young fellow think he was doing?" And I say, of course, he was trying to be bitter like Eliot and Pound and the other fellows. A lot depends on what time you come into the world, like the early Yeats, looking around. People spend volumes and hours of class time worrying what those early poems mean. But he's an 18-year-old fellow come from Ireland. He's trying to find a way of doing something that isn't either Browning or Swinburne. He avoided Browning pretty well, but he doesn't avoid Swinburne too well. That's too bad; we don't come into the world fully formed, but there it is, back to that lecture that Elstir gives to Marcel. That's the way it is. What Keats said, this is "the vale of Soul-making," with the stress on making.

I. Is that just a gradual realization, you think, that most people come to?

N. Well, there's a gradual realization, in plain, literal terms, of what the world is. You may continue to have high ideals, but you know they are high ideals. A favorite exercise of mine is trying to imagine that you were born, say, in the time of Pope. For one thing, the first imagination is that you would have been Pope. How do you know you wouldn't have been one of the dunces? And second, if you were born in any time, it would be a time of usual apocalyptic expectations. John Donne, Thomas Browne after him, believed that there wasn't much point in doing much because the world had pretty much run its course. Pessimism of the darkest sort informed their thoughts about everything but the resurrection. But nobody recognizes it as that now because we read them with eyes conditioned to the idea that the universe has a very considerable future and that discovery is proceeding at such an incredible exponential rate of acceleration that, who knows, the place will be transformed tomorrow with results both wonderful and terrible. We're supposed to be learning not to expect that the future will be some kind of steady prolongation of the past. You know the fashionable example of the very respectable physicists around 1890–1900, who said, "Well, we really do know the universe pretty well;

there are some details to fill in but we know pretty much how it works in large." They didn't know relativity and quantum theory were coming in the future. You know, not just little finagles but absolute change in the way people thought.

I. Are you disturbed by science and technology?

N. I'm fascinated by it. Talking with Stanley Elkin about it—he said, "Science is marvelous; I wish I'd gotten more of it." And I said, "Me too, it's such fascinating stuff." And he said, "It's not fascinating, it's true." And there is a point there.

I. So you don't see that traditional division between science and art?

N. No, the two cultures, I agreed with a physicist once, the two cultures are really the monsters who do the work and the nice guys who talk about it.

I. The monsters being . . . ?

N. People like Einstein, Freud. Geez, if I knew enough I'd want to write a book about the rise and decline of that Freudian business, which transformed the world about as much as Edison did. People were worrying about the Marxist revolution when the Freudian one was going on inside them the whole time, making the world again incalculably different from what it had been. I'd like, if I could write one more book, to write about the nature of theory and fashions in theory. I shall never know enough because I can't read in a scholarly manner consecutively, and I rarely take enough notes or keep them in order if I do. But what a wonderful subject for somebody, to write about fashion in thought, about the rise and fall of the most powerful and influential theories. Much more interesting than the rise and fall of even the British Empire. How people can be taught to teach and think this way for a generation, to make enormous conquests and it all looks like knowledge, finally we've got it, now it's solid, and if some small voice speaks up and says Plato said only geometry was solid, only mathematics because it's entirely self-contained and has no relation to the world, he would be snowed under and told, "You don't know; we've got it, kid. All this before was just theory, but now this is structuralism," or whatever it's being called this decade. You know, I am reminded of what an awful lot of garbage we all talk. Sometimes it is conspicuous because it pretends to affect the real world, to be a scheme of government, of methodizing knowledge, and so forth, but what we talk in our classrooms, I would say, is probably not fundamentally so different.

I. Don't you think we grasp sometimes, though, with a certainty, the theory that ties all the loose ends together?

N. Well, remember that when you're young, if you get into this stuff at all, you're an intellectual. I think that's the only way people do get into teaching, writing, and so forth; they want to know. My favorite book, from 18 on, probably still is, is *The Magic Mountain*, because while it is a fiction it also teaches much which, incidentally, is probably no longer true. But you are compelled to learn as you get older. Again, this exercise of thinking of yourself as having been born in an earlier time and having long since died without having seen the end of the world after all. But, you know that you're going to be as ignorant on your death-bed as you were in the crib. Well, it may or may not be a happy thought, but it's one I think is a salutary thing once in a while. It needn't stop you from making all the effort to do what you can. But you see, the most enormous effect of literature upon the world is to make people believe, including ourselves, that the world is a story. But so far it's a bedtime story where all the children fall asleep before the end. And probably it will be the same for us, even supposing a shattering series of nuclear explosions in Russia and our country; the rest of the world would say oof and go on about its business. Our apocalypticians are so fond of proclaiming that the end is coming that they scarcely seem to notice how many great things have ended, cities destroyed, great regimes gone down in dust and rubble, the end of ways of thinking. This world is always weaving itself over the ruins. It's sort of like a fountain that flowers in its fall; it's always going on. That doesn't mean that it will always go on, only that we have no reason to suppose otherwise.

I. So then the whole world is a series of construction/destruction.

N. Well, now that we've put it so bluntly it seems to be one of the oldest ideas in the world. Hindu mythology is full of it. Most other mythologies appear to have some derivation from it.

I. Was it Freud who said that the only certain thing is uncertainty?

N. How could it have taken Freud to think of that? It sounds like something the PTA might have got up. I'm sure he said something like it. But it is remarkable, when you read the greatest sayings of the great philosophers, how ordinary they come to seem sometimes. There is so much a matter of glamor and fashion, and of course style, in the way of putting things. "Style is the ultimate morality of mind." Makes you feel about ten foot tall to say it, but it doesn't mean anything identifiable.

I. Somewhere you have said that style is that fire which consumes what it illuminates.

N. Well, something very like that.

I. Would you say that's one of those ornate witticisms?

N. Well, yes, but I'm not pretending to be an informative philosopher.

I think I've always admired statements which were in the last degree un-informative and tautological. The greatest saying in the world is found in Edwin Arlington Robinson's Arthurian poems, in *Merlin*: "And that was as it was." Ah, absolute! Well, when they say things like that, that's what snows you about poetry. Imagine inventing a cliché, inventing your own plati-tude. Now that's what it's about. You've got to have a bit of natural knowl-edge first, but that's what it comes to. That's the way it is. It's over, kid. Wonderful sayings, we don't use them for information, we use them for some nonsense we call wisdom.

I. Do you think your poetry is getting simpler; I don't mean to say simpleminded.

N. I would accept simpleminded. The object, now that I'm nearing my 60th year I can say this, the object is to get dumber not smarter. That's another thing *King Lear* has to say. Eyes are made for weeping, not seeing. The Chinese Taoists have a similar saying, "The student of knowledge learning more every day, the student of Tao forgetting more every day." That's not so much a recommendation as a statement of fact. I certainly forget more all the time.

I. Have you been consciously working the poetry to touch a broader audience?

N. Oh, no. I've never thought about that. I'm not a salesman, not a preacher (I hope I'm not a preacher). If people want to read what I write, it's there; it's offered for sale in the usual manner. But about poetry and its turning into truth, you know I was saying to Howard Moss that lines you admired when you were 20, that sounded like beautiful poesy, turned into the most commonplace statements of fact without losing any of their beauty at all. And I saw also the literal truth of that supposedly feeble-minded Platonic doctrine of archetypes, that the idea comes first. And it's easy enough to jeer at it if you use his example, the idea of a chair or table or the good. But it is absolutely the indestructible basis of everything hu-man that we've done with the world. You don't throw a lot of stuff in the corner and expect it to turn into a television set. No, you've got to have the idea of a television set first. You've got to dream about flying for 500 years before anything comes of it: five different kinds of aftershave in the forward cabin of an American Airlines jet. Of course, you lose something when the dream turns into fact, but it's all done on this Platonic basis. The only place where you might question is to ask whether God did in fact found the world on the same basis by having the idea of it first. But for everything that has made the human world rise up out of the natural one, the theory of archetypes, which is still, I believe, believed by most people on the earth, is absolutely sound. There is a logos and it's up here. Well, end of sermon.

I. Well, we could draw you toward a conclusion here by asking you what you're currently working on. You say you don't plan to publish another book for five years.

N. Well, it's not a plan. I do, as I've said, write in bursts. It comes in a great rush, and I attend to business with considerable constancy while it's happening. And when it's not there, just no voice speaks, then there's not much good sitting at the desk, so you might as well study, learn a little something, read. I'm afraid most of my access to the world is from reading. At my age, I'm not expected to have radically new experiences except of the disastrous kind. Stanley Elkin said to me, "Howard, do you expect any pleasant surprises?" It's a good question. Well, yes I do. There are still lots of pleasant surprises. So, it's not a plan not to publish for another five years.

I. Well, what do you see yourself doing in the future?

N. I hope to win more battles in the losing war.

Robert Burns:
An Address to the Burns Society
on the Poet's Birthday

WHEN your Chairman first honored me with the invitation to address you, I was able to turn him down on the reasonable ground that three weeks was too short a time; when he next asked me, I hadn't that excuse, for there was just under a year. So I accepted, forgetting that we were on that circular religious calendar whose first law is that the further you are from something like Burns's birthday the nearer you are getting to it again. That, and procrastination, are why it's always too late to do anything properly.

Looking through, among other things, the proceedings of the St. Louis Burns Society—some of 'em called reprehensibly "St. Louis Nights Wi' Burns"—I discovered a number of things I hadn't known. One was that the address in 1911 was given by John Livingston Lowes, later one of my teachers. So that we have here the beginning of a tradition dictating that sixty-eight years hence one of my students, by then also, as Lowes was, and I am, professor of English at Washington University, will be addressing you on the equivalent of this occasion and misremembering his teacher as I misremember mine.

Another of my discoveries was that almost everyone giving the Burns Night talk believes it appropriate to begin with an account of his disqualification for doing anything of the kind. Mine are spectacular, but the account may be brief.

I am a New York City boy, of Russian, German and Polish Jewish ancestry, with accent overlaid by Harvard, the RAF, the BBC, and thirty-five years of marriage to an Englishwoman from Gloucestershire; there is no likelihood of my being able to sound like Sir Harry Lauder in Roamin' through the Gloamin' Wi' my Lassie by my Side; indeed, even when I try to do Chaucer by the rules of pronunciation I wind up after only a few lines in a kind of stage Irish. I do not like to read dialect poetry anyhow, because having to look up words in the glossary at the back reminds me of doing Latin in high school, and learning, e.g., that *houghmagandy* means *fornication* just doesn't seem to matter enough; some glossaries seem to think that its appearance at the end of The Holy Fair means pregnancy, but I suppose one meaning might imply the other. Burns's girls could certainly have used The Pill, or failing that the prayer to the Virgin popular in parochial schools: O Thou who conceived without sin, help us to sin without conceiving.

My acquaintance with Scotland consists of having been stationed for a few dreadful winter months at RAF Silloth and looking out at that country across the Solway Firth; it was thereabouts that Burns had his greatest triumph as an exciseman, bringing in some troops from Dumfries to capture the smuggling vessel Rosamond. He and his party were under fire, but because of the ebb tide the ship was canted over so that her guns could not bear; but on that account also the smugglers escaped on foot across the flats to the English side. Burns later bought four carronades off the vessel and sent them to the French revolutionary government.

There was also a day's visit to a destroyer at Greenock, implementing Coastal Command's fond hope that its pilots would be able at least to recognize a destroyer when met in the wild state, though whether we could tell a German from a British example remained (thank God) moot. But my chief knowledge of Scotland, and a pleasant one, has been of its best bottled product. Indeed, I learned only just in time for this evening that for an *Ausländer* to say things like Scots and Scottish is a solecism comparable to saying Paree for Paris or München for Munich when you don't belong to those towns.

Burns's character and career are no less full of oddities, contradictions, paradoxes even, than another's.

To be all but starvation poor—to be raised to fame in Edinburgh by a first book and by the favor of men he was unable to know and women he was forbidden to love—to go boozing among publicans and sinners—to

be a publican himself not to mention a sinner—to be always in ill health—
to be a merry ploughman type with a roving eye who rimed for fun—to
have for his favorite bible verse that from Revelations: "They shall hunger
no more, neither thirst any more; The sun shall not strike them, nor any
scorching heat. . ." down to "and God will wipe away every tear from their
eyes"—to describe five and forty years as the extreme limit of old age—
and then to fall short of even that by a good deal—to mock at hypocrisy
and be the unwitting occasion of so much of it—to leave poems and songs
whose fame goes forth from Scotland all over the world—to rise to a
posthumous reputation evoking comparisons with, e.g., The French Revolution, Democracy, Jesus Christ . . .

Well, the point to end this catalogue is that there's something about
Burns that transcends the category of poetry, of literature, and gets to be
more like a natural, if not a supernatural, force. To try to say something
both new and true about him would be like trying to commit an original sin.

Of course, to transcend "mere literature," even if you don't mean to,
even if you continue to rime for fun—excluding his occasional attempts
to write periwig English Literature stuff under the influence (more heady
than booze) of Pope, Shenstone, Thompson, full of standard sentiments,
clichés, rimes—is not without dangers, specifically the danger of becoming a cult figure and the god of a sentimental religionette whose worshippers go about priding themselves on their ordinariness. To have your
verses and airs spread about the world by Scotch emigrants whose only
other reading was the Psalms of David is a wonderful thing; but maybe
having allowed for the wonder we may ask why the same did not happen,
in the same way, to the same extent, to other poets, many of whom also
died young after lives of similar sufferings and miseries: e.g., George Herbert, Keats, Shelley.

Well, much of this is an embarrassment, not always admitted or faced
up to, for Burns's scholars and critics. None of the ones I've looked into
has a good word for Burns Nights or the Burns Societies that sponsor
them. For example, David Daiches comments, ". . . in spite of advances in
scholarship and criticism, the same sentimental rubbish about Burns tends
to be spouted forth each year by hundreds of Burns Night Orators" (*Robert Burns* [London: Andre Deutsch Limited, 1966], p. 7). In a different context, a Vice President of the Burns Federation could find no higher praise
than that "No one can pretend that all those who congregate there (at
Burns Suppers) are models of wisdom and decorum," adding that Burns
himself might have written a satire on his admirers. "Still, all allowances

made, Burns Suppers have a worthy element in them. Those who frequent them might be much worse employed," and so on. In other words, it keeps us off the streets.

The attempt to keep Burns on the pedestal, or to wedge a bit more plinth in under it when it seems likely to collapse, engenders some very self-conscious critical writing of a moralizing nature. Catherine Carswell's remark that "to lack sympathy with Burns is to lack sympathy with man-kind" (*The Life of Robert Burns* [London: Chatto & Windus, 1930], p. ix), quoted with approval by at least one other biographer/critic, is just the sort of moral blackmail that turns me stubborn; I take my poets on my own terms. *Scottish Poetry of the Eighteenth Century* ("Robert Burns," ed-ited by George Eyre-Todd [London and Edinburgh: Sands & Company], Vol. II, p. 172), asserts that "what the Revolution of that time did for France at a cost of untold horror and streams of blood, the poetry of Burns did for Scotland."

I thought that merely a peculiar nineteenth-century hysterical exagger-ation.

But in our own time I find Hugh MacDiarmid using the poet as a stick to beat Scotland with, being awful to and about Burns suppers, and mak-ing the smooth transition over several stanzas from "Rabbie" to "Rabbi" to the punch lines one can by then see coming—"Christ wa'd been Chief Rabbi gin he liked," and even "A greater Christ, a greater Burns, may come" (*A Drunk Man Looks at the Thistle*, lines 89 and 117).

The difficulty here is the common one to criticism: that no one knows what is good, what is great, or what identifiable factors make anything either; while at the same time everyone now and then suspects that some opinions are better than others, if only for a time and under the fashion governing in that time; which may be why literary criticism, dry as it may seem, is such a desperate adventure, full of snobbery gnawed by ill-hid doubt. Robert T. Fitzhugh (*Robert Burns: The Man and the Poet, A Round Unvarnished Account* [Boston: Houghton Mifflin Company, 1970]), the poet's latest and maybe best scholar, puts this way the difficulty I had been ex-periencing: "Burns' admirers have long trumpeted his broad humanity, his championship of Freedom and Equality, his challenge to the Establish-ment and Kirk tyranny. They celebrate his patriotism and his success de-spite a lowly origin. They lament his failure to win patronage, and his early death. And they argue about whether he is a 'national' voice. But his lasting fame arises from something else entirely—his distinction as a poet" (pp. 83–84).

But to talk at any length about anyone's "distinction as a poet" ain't easy either, and may be particularly hard with respect to Burns. As Christina Keith observes, "You might miss a point of Dunbar's for the aureate gods and goddesses nearly smothering it. Nobody in this world ever missed a point of Burns's."

Which one would have thought might settle the critical question then and there. But Keith, like the others, goes on to write a long book quoting from this poem and that poem and explaining to us why we are liking it, or how incompetent we are if we are not liking it: "if you cannot jump to what is to come, from all these clues, you had best leave 'Tam o' Shanter' alone, for the fault is not Robin's"* (*The Russet Coat: A Critical Study of Burns' Poetry and of Its Background* [London: Robert Hale, Limited, 1956] pp. 21 and 95). And so it goes.

What I've come to care for most in Burns is the marvelous freshness and friendliness of his voice. Much as he may have admired—to the point of emulation—Milton's figure of Satan,† he doesn't sound that way at all, though he has his own dignity there is not much that's awesome about it. He sounds like a friend if you want him to be, a trait he shares with such great writers as Socrates, Montaigne, and Freud.

Also his musicality—in the songs, yes, but not there alone, the musicality of the verse itself is fine, especially in his handling of measure and the rime of that favorite traditional stanza—the triple rime cut off by a bob and then an added fourth and a bob again—for instance:

> Ah Nick! Ah Nick! it is na fair,
> First showing us the tempting ware,
> Bright wines and bonnie lasses rare,
> To put us daft;
> Syne weave, unseen, thy spider snare
> O' Hell's damned waft.

Making that sound easy, colloquial, conversational and idiomatic as it does is something that demands the greatest skill, a virtuoso's mastery of the instrument of speech—the line, the rime, the weaving of the sentence so as to fit just right with the stanza . . . our impression of its simplicity comes from his hardest work.

Of the songs I am not one to give a proper impression. One of my

---

*Cf. Jane for Jane Austen

† For the poet's admiration for Satan in *Paradise Lost*, see Thomas Crawford (*Burns, A Study of the Poems and Songs* [Edinburgh and London, 1960], p. 218).

graduate students has loaned me a record of a dozen or so sung by Ewan MacColl, and they are indeed marvelous to hear: a strange, lilting, yet irregular sort of music unlike anything I know from elsewhere in Europe. I wish he had included one of my favorites, "I'm o'er young to marry yet," with the girl's beautifully teasing yet innocent conclusion: "But if ye come this gate again, / I'll aulder be gin simmer, Sir."

One last and decisive distinction belongs to Burns. He may sometimes seem a touch simplistic in his idea that the solution to the better half of our earthly woes is a stiff prick wi' a tear in its e'e. Yet to the extent that the eternal dilemma for man has been how to look down a girl's shirt while looking up her skirt, why you can survey most of the poetry in English without getting more than a hint of the fact, while Burns, bless him, keeps it steadily in mind—our mind, and his.

Against that, or with it, though, you should put this of John Keats in a letter to John Hamilton Reynolds from Scotland, 13 July, 1818 (*The Letters of John Keats*, edited by Maurice Buxton Forman [London: Oxford University Press, 1935], p. 178): "One song of Burns's is of more worth to you than all I could think for a whole year in his native country.—His misery is a dead weight upon the nimbleness of one's quill—I tried to forget it—to drink Toddy without any Care—to write a merry sonnet—it won't do—he talked with Bitches—he drank with blackguards, he was miserable—We can see horribly clear in the works of such a Man his whole life, as if we were God's spies."